SOCIAL MOVEMENTS
BETWEEN THE BALCONY AND THE BARRICADE

D1552259

DATE DUE

AUG 3 0 1985		
NOV 3 2000		

DEMCO NO. 38-298

SOCIAL MOVEMENTS

BETWEEN THE BALCONY AND THE BARRICADE

RON E. ROBERTS
UNIVERSITY OF NORTHERN IOWA, CEDAR FALLS

ROBERT MARSH KLOSS
CALIFORNIA STATE UNIVERSITY, SACRAMENTO

THE C. V. MOSBY COMPANY
SAINT LOUIS / 1974

This book is dedicated to Nic Roberts and Alan Roberts with
the hope that they will be able to devote their lives in part
to the demystification of oppression wherever they find it,
in themselves, in those around them, and in the institutions
that shape their lives.

Library of Congress Cataloging in Publication Data

Roberts, Ron E
    Social movements.

    Bibliography: p. 182.
    1. Social movements.   I. Kloss, Robert Marsh,
1939-   joint author.   II. Title.
HN8.R6   301.24′2   73-12577
ISBN 0-8016-4134-9

Cover photograph: Reproduction of Delacroix's *Liberty
Leading the People*. Courtesy the National Museums
of France.

GW/S/B   9   8   7   6   5   4   3   2   1

FOREWORD

MICHAEL HARRINGTON

Here is an important book by two young social theorists that is crucial to students of social science because Roberts and Kloss discuss the liberative possibilities as well as the negations of human social forms. Theirs is not an optimism born of naïveté, but a hope, perhaps vision, born of a despair with the world as it has become. They look over the graveyards of aristocracies and social movements from the standpoint of the democratic left, and have derived the humane possibilities as well as the oppressive tendencies in the history of world institutions.

They are not detached—when detachment in sociology has been in vogue for a number of years. They have attempted to produce a "sociology with a human face." Roberts and Kloss have a commitment to human equality and substantive rationality—not an easy task when inequality and functional rationality (expedient efficiency) are growing. Mysticism and empiricism, cynicism, and blind faith, as well as a concern for status dominate the political as well as the intellectual community. Despite the ostensible commitment of government to fight-

ing poverty, making peace, and harnessing technology, the outcome and effects are increasing bureaucracy, inequality, and an awesome increase in political scale. Despite the professed detachment of many sociologists, sociology has often been the "handmaiden" or "house nigger" of the ruling elites in a given society.

In their selective discussion, Roberts and Kloss deal with a number of crucial worldwide trends (underlying movements) that cut across regime, national boundary, and these modern times of ours. Axial to their discussion is the industrialization of the world and the related political tendencies and movements. Perhaps the most recent change in this industrial process is the creation of the multinational corporation. Multinational corporations proliferate while lesser groups squabble over defense dividends at the expense of peace possibilities. I say this because the increase in scale of the economic power and political potency of the multinational corporations is inextricably bound to the prospects for a *peace* movement in the next several decades.

There was no peace movement in the 1960's and early 1970's. There was an antiwar movement, and that is something quite different. The distinction between an antiwar and a peace movement should be obvious from the terms themselves, but let me nevertheless make it more explicit. The antiwar movement developed in response to an American commitment that a peace movement should have kept the nation from making in the first place. The antiwar movement could, and did in its last stages, involve disgruntled hawks as well as doves, and it tapped a deep trend of exhaustion and disillusionment as well as more generous and idealistic emotions. It was therefore wrong to say, as some activists did, that the people were "with us."

A peace movement, as I use the phrase here, would not be a reaction to an existing tragedy, an episodic mobilization of opposition to bloody policies already in effect. It would be an ongoing effort to influence American politics so that Vietnams would not happen in the first place. It would therefore have to develop alternatives to the official line in a rather undramatic, peace-time context.

It is obvious that the United States needs such a movement. Is there any possibility that it can be built? And if so, what would be its political basis?

First of all, it is necessary to understand that the "radical," neo-Leninist critique of American foreign policy is not only inaccurate but an argument for a militant-sounding passivity. In that version of our troubles, the internal contradictions of American capitalism—specifically, its tendency to generate surpluses that cannot profitably be invested within this society but that must nevertheless be disposed of if a depression is to be avoided—drive it to expand in the Third World. This brings it into conflict with other capitalist powers, which have the same drive, and with the communist and national liberation movements, which oppose imperialism. Thus conflict is structured into the very nature of the world market.

Two brief comments are in order about this theory. To begin with, since World War II, American investment has been less and less in the Third World and more and more in Europe and Canada. In 1950, the U. S. Tariff Commission reported last February, there was more direct American investment in Latin America (4.4 billion dollars) than in Europe (1.7 billion dollars) or in Canada (3.6 billion dollars). In 1970, the American stake in Canada, Europe, and other developed areas was more than 53 billion dollars, compared to 14.7 billion dollars in Latin America or a total of 24.9 billion dollars in all of the developing nations. During the last twenty or so years, in short, the Leninist theory has been contradicted by the massive growth of intracapitalist investment and the relative decline in economic importance of the poor nations on the world market.

Second, and more to the point of this analysis, the neo-Leninist approach leads to a quietism. For if America is inevitably fated to act imperialistically as long as it is capitalist, and if there is no imminent prospect of America ceasing to be capitalist, then a "radical" analysis proves that there is not much point to doing anything. One can turn to terrorism as a fifth column of the Third World revolution (which is what the Weathermen people tragically did) or be content with proving political machismo by incanting the Leninist formulas and doing nothing.

If, however, one thinks that it is not only necessary but possible to build a peace movement in America, then a critique of Leninist fatalism is essential. Specifically, such a movement must assert that it is possible for the United States to act democratically and peacefully within the world, under the auspices of a principled liberal administration that would make serious inroads upon, but not radically transform, the corporate power structure at the heart of the American system. I think that such a proposition is true. And I am certain that it is the only possible basis for a realistic peace movement in the foreseeable future. In all of this I assume that it is understood that my predicting that a socialist reordering of American society is not imminent does not mean that I am happy with the trend. I want to push for basic anticapitalist change as fast as possible; but I do not want to delude myself, or help a potential peace movement delude itself, about the immediate prospects for a transformation that I most devoutly wish.

But even if there is a realistic, objective possibility for a peace movement within the framework of American society as it is likely to remain during the next period, it is still no easy matter to make that potential real. One difficulty that we face—and I analyze it carefully since it bears on strategy—is that domestic issues are normally the main determinants of political behavior.

In "normal" times, employment, wages, prices, and similar issues are primary for the voters. And since we are talking about the possibility of a peace movement in just such a period—a movement that would prevent war rather than oppose it once it had begun—we must work to find a way to relate those basic concerns of the mass of people to the question of peace. That means that domestic policies are critical to the peace movement. For only a movement that has won public confidence on breadand-butter problems will be able to reach a mass audience with regard to such infinitely more complex, distant, and seemingly mysterious areas as disarmament, the economic development of the Third World, and the creation of a new global system.

This obviously does not mean that the peace movement should completely submerge itself in domestic politics, that it should abandon its distinctive role of exploring and educating about nonviolent solutions to international conflicts. It does mean that in carrying out the special mission the movement should always be looking for links between the problems of individual economic and social survival and the whole sphere of foreign policy. An anecdote might illuminate my point. In the late 1950's, when SANE emerged as the center of the great campaign against nuclear testing, an untried recruit went out on a leafletting expedition. A friend of mine,

who was worried that this novice would not be sophisticated enough to cope with public hostility, stuck close to him. Someone took a leaflet and launched into an attack on the Communists who were pushing such ideas. The newcomer asked, "Do you like tuna?" His critic admitted that he did. "Well these nuclear tests are poisoning the tuna and that's one reason we're against them."

What is the political equivalent of "poisoned tuna" today—the issue that will dramatically relate the immediate concerns of working people to the issue of war and peace? In part, the answer is that there is none, and that suggests the magnitude of our task. Nuclear testing was a single issue, one that lent itself to agitational statement in terms of strontium-90 in children's milk or radioactive fish on a Japanese boat. There is no transparent, easily understood symbol for an alternative to Nixon's policy (or, for that matter, to the Kennedy-Johnson axioms that dominate the discussion of defense in a work of liberal scholarship like the Brookings Institution analysis of the 1973 budget). But there may be a question, considerably more complicated than poisoned tuna, that does unite domestic and international politics. I mean the multinational corporation.

The country is clearly becoming aware that the absolute American hegemony over the capitalist world market, which was the rule from 1945 to 1960 (and which we continued to assume was the case until at least 1967), is over. The Common Market and Japan have become more than competitive in a number of areas, and that has had important domestic repercussions. As foreign companies—and American companies that invest abroad in order to tap cheap labor and then sell in the domestic market—have made major inroads upon the American share of automobiles, clothes, hi-fi sets, and the like, working men and women and their unions have, perforce, become concerned about the international economy.

For most unions, the initial response has been protectionist. The Hartke-Burke bill, which would fix a certain percentage of the American market for American firms producing in this country, has its passionate advocates in the labor movement. There is not, to be sure, unanimity; the United Auto Workers, a union that has been affected by foreign competition, is still trying to develop a positive nonprotectionist policy. And the AFL-CIO representative to the International Labor Organization has made some significant moves against the multinationals. Still, in the absence of a viable alternative, it is hard to see what the Ladies' Garment Workers, the Amalgamated Clothing Workers, and the Electrical Workers (IEU) can do except demand a protected quota for the goods produced by their members.

Therefore, I argue, the peace movement should be particularly concerned about creating that viable alternative. It links domestic and international politics, for the struggle is joined against corporations based in the United States but operating on a global scale (two-thirds of the multinationals are American owned). Moreover, if the American unions are forced by an unresponsive nation into protectionism, that has the effect of pitting the living standard of the American worker against that of the worker in the Common Market, in Japan, and perhaps most important of all, in the Third World. That, in turn, means that the struggle against an impoverishing backwardness in Asia, Africa, and Latin America will become all the more desperate, a situation guaranteed to intensify the kind of instabilities so dangerous to world peace.

The UAW and, to a lesser but still encouraging extent, the AFL-CIO, propose an international corporations law. They want to have some minimum standards imposed, worldwide, which would stop the planetary companies from speculating on poverty (some of England's most prestigious and righteous firms have recently been charged with profiteering from South African apartheid) and would curb some of the practices that allow them to evade taxes and social responsibility, and to ally with rightists and dictators. In addition, the UAW has argued

that the United States should emulate a Swedish law requiring any investor who is going to get government guarantees of his overseas outlays to prove, first, that his action will not hurt Swedish workers and, second, that his money will not be spent in a racist, antiunion, or gouging fashion abroad.

The core idea behind all of these proposals is to tie in, rather than counterpose, the interests of American, European, Japanese, and Third World workers. In this perspective, it is in the interest of factory hands in this country to strive to raise wages in South Korea, Taiwan, and Latin America. Developing this strategy will encourage international labor contacts through the various trade secretariats of the International Confederation of Free Trade Unions (ICFTU). This winter in Brussels, the European Trade Union Confederation (ETUC) was established at a meeting attended by the ICFTU's affiliates in the Common Market. Vic Feather, of the British Trade Union Congress (which, unlike the Labor Party, is not boycotting European institutions), made it clear that membership in the ETUC will eventually be open to both Catholic and Communist unions, that latter point being a major development in the cold war détente within the labor movement.

There is, in short, reason to be hopeful about a new kind of working-class internationalism, born out of the necessities of struggle against the multinationals. After more than a century of failure in this area, it would be foolish to read these portents as sure signs that the workers of the world are uniting. They do, however, indicate that there is more of a practical need for labor concern with international issues than at any time in recent decades. That could result in protectionism; it might also provide the basis for a new internationalism. This last possibility should obviously be of central concern to the peace movement.

However, let me immediately throw some cold water on what I have just said. Suppose that the peace movement succeeds beyond its dreams and that the internationalist tendencies within the world labor movement triumph beyond anyone's present expectations. Then there would be a harmonious relationship between the workers of the rich and poor nations, because they would have defined a common interest. Even if all of that were to come to pass—and I am being audaciously optimistic in speculating that it might—there would be no guarantee of peace. The old illusion, shared by some corporate free-trade advocates and some sections of the Left, that equity in trade on the world market would guarantee peace is just that: an illusion. The causes of war are more complex than a simple economic determinism suggests, and therefore even my most hopeful scenario does not assure peace.

But even so, this area of work opens up the possibility of an important first step for the peace movement. The United States is going to lower its profile in the world and yet work to construct a five-power balance. The United States, the Common Market, Japan, the Soviet Union, and China will agree to disagree amicably and to settle conflicts through arbitration. This means that the non-Chinese Third World will be excluded from the decision-making process and that a Metternichian concert of great nations will conspire out of self-interest to create an international order.

If the peace movement is serious—if it is a peace movement as I defined it earlier, and not just an antiwar movement—it must offer some alternative to this proposal. But if it is relatively easy to expose the weakness of this conspiracy of self-interests, it is quite difficult to formulate an alternative. But one reason already for that, paradoxically, is that the present situation is so caught up in radical possibilities. There are some tentative moves toward labor internationalism, but there are already established and profound tendencies toward capitalist internationalism. Technology has literally burst the bounds of the nation-state, as the members of the Common Market or the denizens of the international money market (which is only about twenty years old) can testify. Therefore, what is required

ultimately for the solution of these antagonisms is structural change in the very organization of world power: not only the growth of international institutions but of socialist, or at least social, international institutions.

That is not going to happen tomorrow. Therefore, even in defining this necessity one has to search for intermediate solutions that promote the final goal but are also attainable within the rather miserable constraints of the present. And at least one strand of a solution can be stipulated. If America had a genuine full-employment policy —one that guaranteed every worker a decent job—then the greatest single incitement toward labor protectionism would be removed in the best possible way. There are many reasons to struggle for that full-employment policy: for example, it is good in and of itself; it provides the only context in which economic racism and sexism can be combated. But the peace movement has the opportunity to stress its own special reasons for championing full employment: that it opens up the possibility of American union policies that coordinate with the labor movement of the globe and that unite, rather than divide, the workers of the various countries.

I suspect that I have mainly demonstrated how incredibly difficult it is going to be to build a peace movement. Yet I see no alternative to accepting the challenge. And I think that the crucial step forward is for peace activists to define and develop those domestic issues that are also international, to elucidate the immediate economic stake that American working men and women have in a more just earth. That is frightfully hard and utterly imperative.

This book by Roberts and Kloss is perhaps a small step toward that difficult end. For it is true that a consciousness of worldwide trends and social movements is a necessary prelude to action by the "peace makers." May their tribe increase!

NEW YORK CITY
Summer, 1973

PREFACE

Thus one arrives at the equality or equation between philosophy and politics, between thought and action. . . .

Antonio Gramaci

The intention of this book is to continue the sociological tradition of analyzing social change in terms of social movements and social trends. The central objective, detailed in the introduction, is to present a conceptual scheme of movements and trends that fits, we hope, into a general sociological theory of social change, but does not get bogged down in grand theory. Assuming that social processes and social actions, as well as social movements and developmental trends, generate conflict, discontinuity, and social insecurity between groups and institutions, we adopt a dialectical analysis.

Although the topic is comparatively broad and historically complicated, the existing knowledge seems to be bifurcated along a continuum into two general positions. The first position is on the descriptive side. It is the journalistic, the reportorial chronicle with all the pitfalls of observations without theory—and in those instances where theory is invoked, there is more ideology in the description than theory. The

second position, in the extreme, is historiographical. In the attempt to become explanatory rather than descriptive, concepts get in the way of the facts. The first is the man-in-the-street view, which can be said to have the barricade bias; the second is the man-in-the-tower view, which has the balcony bias.

To be between the barricade and the balcony is no easy task, because one might wind up straddling the barricade. This is especially true when one deals with elementary collective behavior as it relates to movements, tendencies, and change. To be there, we have had to be selective in content and method. Because this is a text, we must justify why we choose one circle of theorists as opposed to other circles; we must justify our view of causation as dialectical in terms of other approaches. As sociologists, we tend to see many things in these terms; therefore, our view of this phenomena is limited. So experts—be they praxeologists keeping order on the street or engaging in action, or theoreticians,

PREFACE

or smug elites in the tower—may have a field day with our selective perception and conception. So be it. There is still a need for a text with a mediated view of social movements which makes humanitarian as well as sociological sense. The reader may decide whether we begin to fulfill this need.

Finally a note about the title of the book. Book titles are selected for stylistic or scholarly purposes, or both. Ideally, they should provide the most parsimonious key to the book for the reader. Unfortunately these days, there is much pop writing in the field of the social sciences— and this is most characterized by the hundreds of pop titles on books that disappoint discriminate students, intellectuals, and scholars. We hope our title avoids this disappointment.

We are looking forward to a whole host of "prestigious devastators" to tell us how we have failed to be *Freischreibende Intelligenz* (free-floating intellectuals). Much of this is to be expected when one deals with the term "social movement"—an area which once had more dignity than it does now.[1] Add to this our attempt to analyze those movements in terms of egalitarian liberative or repressive hierarchical possibilities, and the probabilities for intellectual conflict grow.

We present to the student a volume that lays claim to the idea that the dialectical method[2] can enlighten us about social processes, namely those creating social movements. We do this in a period of time when sociology is undergoing great vexations. Norman Birnbaum in his *Toward a Critical Sociology* presents the dilemma in this way:

At the moment, it is true, sociology presents the appearance of Chaos, an intellectual tower of Babel. It is noteworthy in this connection that at Berkeley, Berlin, Beograd, Nanterre and Warsaw the students of sociology have been in the vanguard of the student revolt. The refusal by the students of a technicized discipline which puts its technique only at the service of the bureaucratic forces directing their lives is an expression of a valid criticism of the discipline.[3]

Birnbaum's comment on the fermentation within sociology is critical in two ways. First, it outlines the dilemma of the social scientist in his relationship to the outside political world. Second, it speaks of the great refusal of certain students of sociology to conform to what C. Wright Mills termed the "bureaucratic ethos."

This "ethos" has developed in western sociology generally. A current French sociologist surveys the state of the discipline in his homeland:

A study of contemporary sociology that would identify the various currents of these works would show, we think, the extent to which they share a common ahumanistic, ahistorical and aphilosophical attitude; which is to say that all of them favour, implicitly or explicitly, the current technocratic society.[4]

This unconscious acceptance of the status quo is a temptation to all social scientists. It is sometimes expressed as a fetishism for methodology (with a concomitant unconcern for the lives and activities of humans) or as a kind of "functionalism," which somehow reveals the conservative basis of institutional relationships but cannot account for meaningful social change. Both the "abstracted empiricism" of many methodologists and the functionalism of many current theorists lack a concern for history. This static view of man fits nicely with an uncritical perception of human institutions, yet it is an anathema to the craft of sociology. Moreover, we will take the philosophical position that

---

[1] Albion W. Small, "The Meaning of the Social Movement," American Journal of Sociology, 3 (November, 1897), pp. 34-54, as quoted by John Eric Nordskog, *Contemporary Social Reform Movements: Principles and Readings* (New York: Charles Scribner's Sons, 1954), p. 4.
[2] See Louis Schneider, "Dialectic Sociology," *American Sociological Review,* 36 (August, 1971). Raymond Aron, *Progress and Disillusion: The Dialectics of Modern Society* (New York: New American Library, 1968).

[3] Norman Birnbaum, *Toward A Critical Sociology* (New York: Oxford University Press, 1971), p. 230.
[4] Lucein Goldmann, *The Human Sciences and Philosophy* (London: Jonathan Cape, 1969), p. 13.

man is defined by his possibilities and that many of those possibilities are not met in current institutions. This may be viewed as a utopian position and it is that. The other possibility which we reject is to seek theoretical explanation (and justification) for the current status of man. We could invoke many demons here, "aggression," "territorality," "future shock," "the killer instinct," the "rage for order," or the like. We will not do so. Apologists for the status quo are welcome to use these terms for some time to come.

It is clear at this point that this text is not value free in the traditional sense of the term. Philosophically, we would argue that it is impossible to present any theoretical model of human affairs that is truly value free. Alvin Gouldner in his *The Coming Crisis of Western Sociology* argues for what he calls a "reflexive sociology."

> Yet while I believe that a reflexive sociology must have an empirical dimension I do not conceive of this as providing a factual basis that determines the character of its guiding theory. . . . I do not conceive of these researches or their factual output as "value free," for I would hope that their originating motives and terminating consequences would embody and advance specific values. A reflexive sociology would be a moral sociology.[5]

The sociology presented in this book does have an underlying value and that value is equality. We view equality as a process rather than a status and as an ideal rather than a concrete reality. We believe that equality is perhaps the most profound ideal in western political thought and that human misery can be lessened only by massive and chronic egalitarian change.

> A reflexive sociology . . . implies that sociologists must surrender the assumption, as wrongheaded as it is human, that others believe out of need while we believe—only or primarily—because of the dictates of logic and evidence. A systematic and dogged insistence upon seeing ourselves as we see others would, I have suggested, trans-

form not only our view of ourselves but also the view of others. We would increasingly recognize the depth of our kinship with whom we study.[6]

If this is the case, we, the authors of the text, bear a clear responsibility to confess, as it were, the social sources of our egalitarian bias. At the time of the writing of this book both of us were, alas, over thirty (but ever so slightly). Both of us completed our doctoral training at Louisiana State University, where empiricists and theorists have jousted for years. More importantly in terms of our egalitarian values, both of us have working class backgrounds, coming from families of coal miners and factory workers. It is not strange then that we would derive leftist or social democratic politics from this background. It was not unusual either for individuals with this biography to become involved in antiracist, antiwar activities, as well as the union movement.

The student forewarned is forearmed. We do not set forth a doctrine in this book, but an orientation. Our text is basically just that, a text and not a guidebook for social action. Yet we feel the activist can derive useful concepts from our work. We do not assume a godlike superiority to those involved in social action simply because we can make educated guesses concerning their motivation and class status. Neither do we apologize for the intellectual craft in its relationship to current activism. Theory and praxis do go together, and it is not simply a quaint truth that those ignorant of the past are doomed to repeat its errors.

The academic community to which we belong is noted for its genteel cynicism. If we have erred in this book it will have been on the side of hope rather than despair, and possibility rather than containment of the human spirit.

We are illustrating this book on social movements with cartoons. They summarize a great deal more than pictures by capturing the spirit of the times—*Zeitgeist*. In the words of W. G. Rogers:

---

[5] Alvin Gouldner, *The Coming Crisis of Western Sociology* (New York: Avon Books, 1970), p. 491.

[6] *Ibid.*, p. 490.

It is not an arbitrary extension of the definitions of cartoon to apply them to pictures that do not ridicule, that do not exaggerate, but that do passionately attack social ills, that cry out for peace, that excoriate war, injustices, oppression, and bigotry. They are works of art; they are exposés. The French have a more general word for this kind of picture: *charge,* meaning attack.[7]

We have gone through dozens of books, hundreds of newspapers, magazines, pamphlets, and the like to make the right point at the right time. Yet we feel that we have not done enough because tens of thousands of cartoons and caricatures are available. Oftentimes we will leave it up to the readers to draw their own conclusions from the cartoons and caricatures much as they do about the writing. This is as it should be.

Another reason for illustrating some of our points with cartoons and caricatures is because it makes our point of the intellectuals' position between the barricade and the balcony. Again in the words of Rogers:

> In one sense the cartoonist or caricaturist is half-man, half-artist. His head is up in the clouds where creative people live; his feet are down on the ground where you and I walk around. He brings a message from up there down here to us. Since he addresses you and me rather than museum-goers or historians or scholars, he employs the terms we would employ.[8]

We are deeply indebted to many individuals, students, friends, and colleagues who facilitated our efforts in this work. They include the following unruly mob and we send our thanks to them: the Faculty Research Committee at the University of Northern Iowa, for their financial assistance in the preparation of this study; the students and faculty of Kivokoni College, Dar Es Salaam, for their information on the Ujamaa villages of Tanzania; Sherry and Richard Kaplan, for their aid on our whimsical annotated bibliography; graduate student B. B. King, for her help in the indexing and preparation of the manuscript; dear friend and feminist, Patti Roberts, and wife and feminist, Marie Kloss, for their comments on the chapter on the oppression of women; colleagues Worth Summers and Robi Chackravorti, for critical comments on the book's organizing principles; Elaine Whittlesy, colleague and union partner, for struggling through errors in the manuscript; Connie Brecht, for her hours of typing on the manuscript; and many others, including graduate assistant Norm Holsinger and students of Social Change and Social Movements at CSUS; Angelo Buttoni, Doug Fisher, Gail Ann Mabbutt, Scott Chadd, Gary Long, Bobbie Dovinney, and countless others, who constructively reacted over the last several years to ideas presented in this book. Thanks also to Rudolf Heberle, for critical comments, cajoling, and encouragements, as well as Herbert Blumer and Richard Braungart, for critical reading. We must acknowledge all of our colleagues at LSU, CSUS, and UNI who supported us with good humor and the right questions at the right time as we proceeded with the tragedy of errors and the comedy of successes with a book of this type.

RON E. ROBERTS
ROBERT MARSH KLOSS

---

[7] W. G. Rogers, *Mightier Than the Sword: Cartoon, Caricature, Social Comment* (New York: Harcourt, Brace & World, Inc., 1969), pp. 16-17.
[8] *Ibid.,* pp. 18-19.

CONTENTS

PART THREE

MOVEMENT OUTCOMES: REALITY AND POSSIBILITY FOR OUR TIME

APPENDIX

PART ONE

TO BE BETWEEN THE BALCONY AND THE BARRICADE

It is now the social scientist's foremost political and intellectual task—for here the two coincide—to make clear the elements of contemporary uneasiness and indifference.

C. Wright Mills

In the title of this book we say that the social theorist of social movements must be somewhere between the barricade of change and the balcony of the status quo. The barricade is the symbol of revolution and dramatic change rather than reform or reaction. It is the symbol of involvement, dissent, and conflict, be it in the form of a picket line or a pile of rubble in the streets of Paris, 1968 or Belfast, 1972. The balcony is the symbol of reaction, conservatism, and the status quo. It may be the privileged position of the smug elites in the old regime who do not seem to understand what may be going on down on the streets or in the mountains. It may also symbolize the well-known ivory tower where detached scholars are supposed to reside— usually next to the balcony. But the social theorist is *Homo politicus* as well as social scientist. He looks both up to the balcony as well as across to the barricade. He may reside in the white tower of reflection and contemplation but is on the streets in his analysis. This is his dilemma. He is neither fish nor fowl. The philosophy of social science literature is full of debate about the intellectual's place in history.[1] It is in the discussion of social change, social movements, and trends where this dilemma is most acute.[2]

---

[1] Max Weber, "Politics as a Vocation" and "Science as a Vocation," in Hans Gerth and C. Wright Mills, *From Max Weber: Essays in Sociology* (New York: Oxford University Press, 1946), pp. 77-156. Florian Znaniecki, *Social Role of the Man of Knowledge* (New York: Columbia University Press, 1940). C. Wright Mills, *The Sociological Imagination* (New York: Oxford University Press, 1959). See Appendix A.

[2] Gary B. Rush and R. Serge Danisoff, *Social and Political Movements* (New York: Appleton-Century-Crofts, 1971) offers readings on this dilemma.

MOVEMENTS, TRENDS, AND THE SOCIOLOGY OF KNOWLEDGE

Within the philosophy of social science literature is a field called the sociology of knowledge. It provides a context for the student of movements and trends. It may be the best approach at this point toward the development of concepts and theory on social movements. Karl Marx, one of the founders of the sociology of knowledge, established the basic proposition that fact and values are inseparable, that ideology flows from the economic reality of history.[3] Emile Durkheim and Max Weber showed the way in which belief systems like religion are related to the socioeconomic world.[4] Karl Mannheim clarified the field by making the important distinction between ideology and utopia—the fact that differing groups in history see their place in history differently.[5] The place of the intellectual in ideology and utopia put Mannheim into a cul-de-sac. As social scientist, how was he to make any meaningful statements about what was going on in history? His way out of the dilemma was entertainment of the possibility of *freischwebende Intelligenz* (free-floating intellectuals) who could be objective and above involvement, something like Plato's philosopher-kings.[6] Since Germany of the 1920's, when

Explosive Academia, (From *The Nation,* June, 1970, by permission.)

Mannheim wrote, it is now known that he was too optimistic about this nice possibility. Except for a small school of methodologists (methodolatrists?), most social scientists accept the fact that there is no way to formulate concepts, conduct studies, and write sociologies without values and subjective intentions being inextricably linked with the "facts" they come up with.

Other sociologists have related ideas, ideologies, beliefs, and social reality in general to the social context in slightly different ways. Pitirim A. Sorokin profoundly shows the relationship of philosophic systems (sensate, idealistic, ideational) to social and cultural dynamics (wars, revolutions, and so forth) in an analysis that covers twenty five centuries.[7] C. Wright Mills in all his writings grounded in Marx and Mannheim is critical of philosophers, social scientists, and sociologists in

---

[3] Karl Marx and Frederick Engels, *The German Ideology* (Moscow: Progress Publishers, 1964). In this and other works they are reacting to Hegel and Hegelians who believed that ideas determine concrete reality. See also Walter G. Runciman, *Social Science and Political Theory* (London: Cambridge University Press, 1969), pp. 46-47.

[4] Emile Durkheim, *The Elementary Forms of Religious Life: A Study in Religious Sociology* (New York: The Macmillan Company, 1915). Max Weber, *The Protestant Ethic and the Spirit of Capitalism* (New York: Scribner, 1958). Both of these men mediate the materialistic position of Marx and Engels.

[5] Karl Mannheim, *Ideology and Utopia: An Introduction to the Sociology of Knowledge* (New York: Harcourt, Brace and Company, 1936).

[6] *Ibid.,* pp. 136-146.

[7] Pitirim A. Sorokin, *Social and Cultural Dynamics* (New York: American Book Company, 1937-1941). For a comparison with Karl Mannheim, see: J. J. Maquet, *The Sociology of Knowledge, Its Structure and Relation to the Philosophy of Knowledge, A Critical Analysis of the Systems of Karl Mannheim and Pitirim A. Sorokin* (Boston: Beacon Press, 1951).

their naiveté of values. Mannheim's *freischwebende Intelligenz* becomes Mills' "sociologically imaginative" social theorist, not free-floating but committed to the values of truth, reason, and freedom.[8] Most recently, Peter Berger and Thomas Luckmann have expanded the classic discussion of the sociology of knowledge into the social construction of reality; in other words, not just facts are related to the social context but all of reality.[9]

All discussions in the social sciences must be cognizant of these views. And, it is our contention that it is even more important when discussing social movements for three reasons: (1) because of the *criterion problem;* that is, how are the movements to be selected, and what concepts will be enlisted to deal with them? (2) because of the *value problem;* that is, what values are implicit and explicit and relevant when analyzing the movements and concepts selected? and (3) because of the *causal problem;* or how can the movement or series of movements be meaningfully explained in terms of the conducive conditions and motivations, given the state of affairs surrounding causal analysis in the social sciences today?

Some are still trying to debate a dead Marx over his contribution of the materialist interpretation of history and his sociology of knowledge, which flows from such a view of history. So far, he has not been refuted but only mediated on this point; theories, concepts, and

actions flow from the socioeconomic context in which they are born. The student, be he grand theorist or abstract empiricist, in the tower or on the barricade, attached or unattached intellectual, cannot escape the criterion problem, the value problem, and the causal problem. The social analyst must settle for stating his operating biases as best he can and proceed, because under the findings of the sociology of knowledge, there is no way out of his social (even spatial and temporal) context.

A NOTE ON THE LABELING PROBLEM IN SOCIAL MOVEMENT DISCUSSION

The concepts of social change, trends, social movements, revolution, reform, radicalism, disorder, violence, terror, and so forth, if viewed from the standpoint of the sociology of knowledge are either ethnocentric, temporocentric (time centered), or class-based. It is important to look at the historical and social context of such concepts. Nowadays, because of the awesome increase in the flow of information, it is hard to trace the sources of political and change labels. Insurgency, terrorism, revolutionaries, socialists, communists, un-Americans, resistance and liberation fronts, Zapatistas, antiwar activists, dissenters, protesters, guerilla warfarists, and similar labels are often attributed to the mass media, government functionaries, and only occasionally to the groups involved in the action. Labels of authorities who are the keepers of "law and order" range from the ruling class, ruling circles, power elite, and men of power, to the dehumanizing epithets of pigs, animals, brutes, hardhats, grunts, and fascists. *Most often such labels are applied and manipulated for tactical import by the labelers.* The individuals or groups who can label well and dominate the dissemination of information have a distinct advantage in the struggle between the politics of change and the politics of nonchange. In

---

[8] C. Wright Mills, *The Sociological Imagination* (New York: Oxford University Press, 1959), pp. 178-179. Mills' reactions to sociology of knowledge findings go back to his earlier writings: "Language, Logic, and Culture," *American Sociological Review* 4, no. 5 (1939), pp. 670-680; "The Language and Ideas of Ancient China: Marcel Granet's Contribution to the Sociology of Knowledge, in Irving Louis Horowitz, editor, *Power, Politics, and People* (New York: Oxford University Press, 1963); "Methodological Consequences of the Sociology of Knowledge," *American Journal of Sociology* 46, no. 3 (1940), pp. 316-330.
[9] Peter Berger and Thomas Luckmann, *The Social Construction of Reality: A Treatise in the Sociology of Knowledge* (Garden City, N. Y.: Doubleday, 1966).

sum, those who can manipulate the symbols—be they labels or flags—can have definite tactical advantage because the lines of conflict and consensus can be determined by the emotional appeal of labels and symbols. A recent example is the use of the terms peacenik and vietnik, connoting communist affiliation for antiwar dissenters in the U. S.

From these political labels, sociologists establish conceptual frameworks. The first step is to see what motivations and conditions surround the labels, and the second is to perceive their evolvement, use, misuse, and disuse in historical perspective. Gusfield says: " . . . our very concepts—protest, reform, and revolt—have meanings derived from experiences in the modern period and are limited in utility for other contexts."[10] To exemplify this, we can take two cases: first, radicalism and second, violence.

RADICALISM

Students of sociology should be among the best qualified to understand that radicalism is a fuzzy concept with ragged edges, like ideology or alienation, a term that might best be abandoned in serious discussion.[11] Nonetheless, it is a label used by almost everyone and, therefore, must come under our purview. As a sponge word, it can modify anything from in-

nocence to the extreme politics of the right and left—be they new or old.[12] There are at least two ways radicalism can be seen if we keep the social context of the label in mind. First, by those *who define themselves* as such; and, second, by those *who are defined as radicals by others*. Those who call themselves radicals may be in the beginning stages of radicalization or radicals for the hell of it. They may be rhetorical radicals or Groucho Marxists walking around calling for revolution because they are a part of the radical chic of the time. But if they get hit in the head by the forces of law and order, they might consider it unfair to their rights. In short, they are weekend radicals when it comes to political power transformations. Radicalism as determined by others, let us say elites and media manipulators, is a form of extremism different from their own point of view. In a sense, they are more to the point, since radicalism, coming from the Latin word *radix* or root, means to get down to the *root* of the matter. For example, Republicans were considered radicals by Southerners during the first reconstruction after the American Civil War; Louisiana's governor Huey P. Long was labeled radical by the New Dealers of the sobering 1930's. Also cited as radical are the university students of the East and West who protest, dissent, and call for changes in situations, universities, and fields of study. Their demands for changes are not only regarded as too global but also as too immediate—"Stop the war now," "End racism," "Redistribute the wealth."

The fact that we cannot burst out of the political labeling tradition of three and only three copresent ideologies, conservatism, liberalism, and radicalism, seems to exhaust logical possibilities when it comes to reconsidering

---

[10] Joseph R. Gusfield, editor, *Protest, Reform, and Revolt: A Reader in Social Movements* (New York: John Wiley & Sons, Inc., 1970), pp. 396-397. Consistent with this remark is Gusfield's statement that the definition of social reform fits into his definition of social movement. Perhaps his definition of movement best fits into the notion of *protest* rather than reform in that he says movements are socially shared activities and beliefs directed toward the *demand* for change. This definition is incomplete because social movements are not made up of demands—but rather actions based on them. This was related to us by Rudolf Heberle in private correspondence.

[11] Paul F. Lazarsfeld, William H. Sewell, and Harold Wilensky, editors, *The Uses of Sociology* (New York: Basic Books, 1967) in a statement made by Nathan Glaser, p. 63.

[12] Perusal of any good card catalog shows that the term radical can modify anything: Christianity, empiricism, the future, pietism, imagination, inertia, innocence, ions, literature, monotheism, nationalism, the novel, periodicals, policy, politicians, satire, sophistication, theology, tradition, philosophy, and sociology.

radicalism. What confuses us is that these three labels are used loosely by everyone; thus, they vary over time and place like the weather. So it goes; either radicalism is the opposite of conservatism with liberalism in the middle, or radicalism is the extreme of liberalism, taking the form of a disposition to accept innovations.[13] The second interpretation is that leftist and rightist extremism is radicalism, as in the "Radical Right."[14] Perhaps, the way out is to define it as Ash has recently: "a stand specifically opposed to prevailing ideology."[15]

VIOLENCE

Another example to show that our concepts are locked into the social context is the use of the term violence. The 1960's as a decade saw a re-emergence of ideology as well as action on the part of blacks and students in America. Much of this ideology and action led to violence. When American cities experienced urban unrest, riots, and violence, there came the Kerner Report (Report of the National Advisory Commission on Civil Disorders) which showed white racism as the cause of black rioting. Then came the Walker Report (to the National Commission on the Causes and Prevention of Violence) that concluded that violence was largely a function of the Chicago police. Last came *The History of Violence in America* (to the National Commission on the Causes and Prevention of Violence). The *History* quoted Rap Brown, the young black militant as saying, "Violence is as American as

War as official violence. (From *Cartoons Magazine,* vol. 7, no. 2, February, 1915. H. H. Windsor, editor and publisher, Chicago.)

cherry pie." The definition of violence the *History* writers conclude with is: "behavior designed to inflict injury to people or damage to property. Collectively, and individually, we may regard specific acts of violence as good, bad, or neutral, depending on who engages in it against whom."[16] Violence so defined is distinguished from force and protest as well as related to legality and legitimacy:

> In the perfect social order all acts judged legal would be regarded as legitimate by the community, all illegal acts would be illegitimate. No such clear-cut distinction holds in the United States as far as violence, force, and protest are concerned nor has it ever. Our nation was

[13] James Mark Baldwin, editor, *The Dictionary of Philosophy and Psychology,* Vol. 2 (New York: Peter Smith, 1940), p. 4. Also the perspective of Arnold S. Kaufman, *The Radical Liberal* (New York: Atherton Press, 1968). A dated discussion can be found in A. B. Wolfe, *Conservatism, Radicalism, and the Scientific Method* (New York: The Macmillan Company, 1923).

[14] Daniel Bell, editor, *The Radical Right: The New American Right Expanded and Updated* (Garden City, N. Y.: Doubleday & Company, 1964).

[15] Roberta Ash, *Social Movements in America* (Chicago: Markham Publishing Company, 1972), p. 229.

[16] Hugh Davis Graham and Ted Robert Gurr, *The History of Violence in America* (New York: Bantam Books, 1969), p. xiii.

founded in a revolutionary war that was illegal but widely regarded as legitimate. It survived a civil war whose competing causes most Northerners and Southerners thought both legal and legitimate.[17]

Tilly, from a European perspective, sees historical differences in primitive, reactionary, and modern collective violence. Primitive violence, he says, includes feuds, brawls, and mutual attacks of hostile religious groups. They are small-scale, have local scope, have communal members with inexplicit, unpolitical objectives. Reactionary violence is also small-scale but represents attacks by loosely organized groups against elites who in some way took away rights they once enjoyed, hence the label reactionary. On the other hand, modern violence by collectives, now involves specialized associations with well-defined objectives for political or economic action. This latest form of collective violence is forward-looking and includes the demonstration, the violent strike, the coup, and guerilla warfare.[18] The social trends that account for the changes in collective violence according to Tilly are urbanization and industrialization. Additionally, violent protests are related to two changes in political power:

> The first was the victory of the national state over rival powers in towns, provinces, and estates; politics was nationalized. The second was the proliferation and rise to political prominence of complex special-purpose associations like parties, firms, unions, clubs, and criminal syndicates.[19]

In short, Tilly sees violence in terms of the increase in the political scale of legitimate authority. Urbanization and industrialization necessitate this increase. This expansion will be developed in the chapter on cultural imperialism.

---

[17] *Ibid.,* p. xxxi.
[18] Charles Tilly, "Collective Violence in European Perspective," in Graham and Gurr, *ibid.,* pp. 13-24.
[19] *Ibid.,* pp. 10-13, 28-29.

Abu, The Tribune (London): Ben Roth

Official violence. (Reprinted with permission of The Ben Roth Agency Inc.)

In these two cases of violence and radicalism, we are mindful of being time and space bound; that is, what was radical or violent years ago may not be so now. Also, what is considered violent in one place may not be considered so in another, and what a given group considers violent or nonviolent may vary. These facts present difficulty, to say the least, for the student of social science. Relating violence to politics should convince us of the problem.

Skolnick relates politics and protest to *official* violence in his Report submitted to the National Commission on the Causes and Prevention of Violence. He concludes:

1. "Violence" is an ambiguous term whose meaning is established through political processes.
2. The concept of violence always refers to a disruption of some condition of order; but, order, like violence is politically defined.
3. "Violence" is not always forbidden or unequivocally condemned in American society.
4. The decision to use or not to use such vio-

lent tactics as "deadly force" in the control of protest is a political one.

5. Almost uniformly the participants in mass protest today see their grievances as rooted in the existing arrangements of power and authority in contemporary society, and they view their own activity as political action—on a direct or symbolic level—aimed at altering those arrangements.[20]

Thus, the preceding digression into the sociology of concept formation and use shows that it is the political context that largely determines not only concept definition but the consequences of word use as well. More will be said about officially sanctioned violence in Chapter 9 on the "Negation of the Negation."

We have divided the book into three parts. The first deals with some of the traditional approaches to the study of social movements and offers a scheme that is both social-psychological and sociological. The second relates the master trends of industrialization, bureaucratization, and cultural imperialism to the movements that have reacted to them. The third takes a look at the range of responses that society can make to social movements, from attempts to negate them to the possibilities of embellishing them and planning within the range of their humanistic possibilities.

In Chapter 1 we examine first "The Concept of Social Movement." Past views of movements like those of Von Stein and Marx, as well as more current views—Davis, Cantril, Laidler, Blumer, and Heberle—are reviewed. Then a scheme is presented relating movements to trends in a dialectical manner.

Chapter 2, "Conditions and Motivations Behind Social Movements" examines the social-psychological, psychological, and sociological approaches to the study of social movements. The social-psychological transformation centers around insecurity as produced by social trends and the quest for security as defined by the various collectivities in society. An argument against the psychological interpretations of rightist and leftist social movements by Hoffer and the neo-Freudians is then followed by our sociological perspective on movements and trends.

Chapter 3, "Collective Nonmovements as an Option," notes that while many individuals' lives have been drastically changed by bureaucratization, imperialism, or industrialization, many, if not most, individuals do not opt for the changes represented by social movements. For to participate in a movement means to struggle for political power, and this struggle may involve sacrifice, compromise, boredom, or profound commitment. The Jesus movement, counterculturalists, and Black cultural nationalism are examples of such collective nonmovements present today.

This book—as well as all books on the social world—is based on several simplifications to which people from both barricade and balcony will object: first, in its selection; second, in its causal analysis; and third, in its ideological inferences. Our selection, causal analysis, and ideological position should reveal to the reader that we tend to view the world in class terms and as conflictual rather than consensual. Moreover, we continually ask ourselves the humanistic questions: What are those on the barricade interested in? On the balcony? Inequality or equality? We frankly confess our egalitarian bias, yet we would add to this the skeptic's motto: Dubito ergo sum.

Hence, what follows is another in a long series of works dealing with social reality in terms of the sociology of knowledge. We must be aware that it is a product of our economic and political times. Finally, we tend to view the relationship between trends and movements to involve economic matters—that is, changes in power and control over property and income.

---

[20] Jerome Skolnick, *Politics of Protest* (New York: Ballantine Books, 1969), pp. 3-8. Other books on protest are being written. In addition to Gusfield's mentioned above, see: Walt Anderson, editor, *The Age of Protest* (Pacific Palisades, California: Goodyear Publishing Company, 1969). S. N. Eisenstadt, *Modernization: Protest and Change* (Englewood Cliffs, N. J.: Prentice-Hall, Inc., 1966).

CHAPTER 1 THE CONCEPT OF SOCIAL MOVEMENT

Revolt is first of all the acknowledgement of an impossible situation.

Albert Memmi

It has been stated that history is the graveyard of aristocracies. History is also the graveyard of social movements. History is of course much more than these; nevertheless, it is true that the passage of time does record the demise of seemingly all powerful groups of persons. The real question seems to be not so much whether a class of people will hold to power forever but rather what the cause of their decline from power will be. Many times decision makers in a given society are destroyed because of factors quite beyond their control. Plagues, earthquakes, droughts, or any number of natural catastrophes can scuttle a society along with its leadership. Yet it is far more likely that any group holding to power will be challenged, perhaps destroyed, by another group. Often the rich and powerful are subdued by the strength of arms of men of another nation, race, or religion. Just as frequently, the powerful find themselves challenged by those who represent the same nation, race, or religion, men and women who nevertheless despise the rich and the powerful.

It is easy to visualize the smugness en-demic to the ruling elites when a social system functions smoothly. The English aristocracy of the nineteenth century were only half jesting with their idea that "God is an English gentleman." In the American South the aristocracy cogitated on the benefits of slavery for civilization's progress. In India the Brahman classes continued to reassure each other that they were the "twice born," hence the only humans spiritually enlightened enough to rule. Smugness, it seems, is an occupational hazard endemic to those in firm possession of power. America in the 1950's was not immune to temptation toward smugness. It was believed by many prominent intellectuals that the nation had indeed become "the best of all possible worlds." With this conviction, Daniel Bell wrote in 1960 ". . . there is today a rough consensus among intellectuals on political issues: the acceptance of a Welfare State; the desirability of decentralized power; a system of mixed economy and political pluralism. In that sense, too, the ideological age has ended."[1]

[1] Daniel Bell, *End of Ideology* (Glencoe, Illinois: Free Press, 1960), p. 373.

9

America, it seemed, had arrived at a kind of near-perfect equilibrium that fulfilled the needs of all in a realistic and just way.

Just as it is easy to imagine the smugness of the powerful, it is not difficult to imagine the unhappiness of those who believe they have no control over their lives. Unhappiness is a vague word, though not a meaningless one. It could refer to the fact that in the developing nations parents can anticipate that half their children will die before the age of ten.[2] Unhappiness might refer to less tangible tragedies as well. What of the man who finds that he is no longer secure in his identity in the community of other men? This too relates quite clearly to the amorphous category of unhappiness. Other words have been used to describe the feeling of the loss of one's identity —insecurity, Angst, or the like. The fact is that the acute discomfort of physical hunger and the less acute but very real feeling of low self-esteem are both problems relating to man's social nature.

The social and behaviorial sciences consistently document the idea that man is more effective in solving his psychological as well as physical problems in groups. If men and women are hungry, they can band together to hunt, steal, or farm. If modern man or woman suffers from the opposite of hunger, over-indulgence, he or she can join a weight-watching club. Misery, it is said, loves company. Many of those who have endured the misery of alcoholism, drug addiction, or food addiction can testify to the fact that Alcoholics Anonymous, Synanon, or Take Off Pounds Sensibly (TOPS) has aided them in their personal struggle against destruction.

Many of the groups men and women form to solve their personal and collective problems are transient in nature. Some, however, survive over a period of several generations. These long standing problem-solving groups are frequently referred to as institutions. Institutions have, of course, been formed to solve every conceivable human problem. Those individuals who control the resources and decision-making apparatus of an institution are called elites, authorities, the ruling class, or the like.[3]

Nearly all institutional leaders who take their jobs seriously are given to the idea that their institution fulfills tremendously important human needs and that it fulfills those needs in a way excelled by no other. The problem with problem-solving institutions is that often the elites who control the resources and structure of the institution tend to confuse their own interests with those of the larger society. Is it possible that the American defense budget could be cut in half with no ill effect on the country? A resounding *no!* would echo from the corridors of the Pentagon. Is it possible that universities are not needed in the technetronic age? Few academicians would say yes. Should the institutional church dissolve itself to find "true" Christianity? This idea would be given little credence from older ministers only a few years away from a secure pension plan. What of the governmental elites in the U. S. S. R.? Should they not hasten to dismantle the state in consonance with the Marxism concept of stateless pure communism? Their response would not be unpredictable. Men seldom dismantle institutions that give them power, prestige, and a secure sense of identity.

Again, it is clear that large-scale institutions, be they economic, religious, or governmental, take on a self-serving mentality that may possibly be antithetical to the needs of the people it supposedly serves. H. Richard Niebuhr discusses this fact as he accounts for

---

[2] See William McCord, *The Springtime of Freedom: The Evolution of Developing Societies* (New York: Oxford University Press, 1965), p. 11.

[3] The coloration one gives to these terms depends in no small amount on one's political and aesthetic views. We, for example, tend to agree with C. Wright Mills' analysis of the term "power elite," although the phrase seems somewhat offensive to our sensibilities; it is horribly redundant.

the rise of left-wing radical churches of the disinherited in eighteenth century Europe. "There was present," Niebuhr argued, "the actual exclusion of the poor from churches grown emotionally too cold, ethically too neutral, intellectually too sober, socially too aristocratic to attract the men who suffered under the oppression of monotonous toil, of insufficient livelihood and the sense of social inferiority. There was present also the awakening of the disinherited to the consciousness of their human dignity and worth."[4]

When institutions such as the church, the corporation, or the government fail to meet the needs of the individual, a radical movement for change is not inevitable. Many men and women accommodate themselves to their alienation and unhappiness by simply developing a fatalism and detachment so characteristic of the aged who approach death with little remorse. Thus, we can see that the mere fact of having a mangled life is not the only requisite for radical social action. What remains is to translate one's personal problems into social issues which, for him, mean political issues. That, according to C. Wright Mills, is the purpose of political awareness. It may of course be true that not all personal problems can be translated into political issues. An extreme case in point is the fact that in New York City in 1971 both sadists and masochists organized themselves politically to fight the unfortunate stereotypes the public held of them.

Yet personal problems of a less esoteric nature may well be political at base. When an individual becomes unemployed in American society, he can attribute his problems to misfortune, an act of God, or personal incompetence. Yet, were he to come under the influence of a radical political ideology, he would begin to view his unemployment as symptomatic of institutional deficiencies in his society. By the

early 1970's many black intellectuals in America were speaking less of individual prejudice than of institutional racism—that is the failure of basic American institutions to give equal life chances to the black populace.

How then are men politicized into social consciousness of their deprivation? How do they become aware of the inadequacies of the institutions that supposedly serve them? Moreover, how do men mobilize for institutional change by revolution or by revitalization? The answer to these questions forms the basis for our study of the social movement. Systematic study of social movements is, like its parent discipline sociology, a relatively new concern.

Given these questions, what should be the focus of our concern? The work to follow will concentrate on three major trends of our time and the collective responses to them, namely: (1) industrialism and egalitarian movements, (2) bureaucratization and various antibureaucratic movements, and (3) cultural imperialism and nativistic-nationalistic movements.

There are, of course, other social trends such as secularization and urbanization that we will not deal with. Our reasoning here is that these latter trends (secularization or urbanization) are in a partial way subsumed under the headings of imperialism, industrialism, or bureaucratization.

VIEWS OF SOCIAL MOVEMENTS

What justification is there for choosing one set of theorists about social movements over another? Is it, as the cliché has it, "you pays your money and you takes your choice"?

Frankly, our view of social movements is dominated by the idea that they develop in class, racial, national, or sexual struggles. We see as important, then, those scholars who show this orientation in their work rather than psychological explanations for social movements. In our review of the pioneering scholars in the field of social movements, we have also tried to

---

[4] H. Richard Niebuhr, *The Social Sources of Denominationalism* (Cleveland: World Publishing Co., 1969).

acknowledge only those theorists who have a rather rigorous definition of what a social movement is. We do not accept the idea, for example, that a "flying saucer cult" is a social movement, or that religious fundamentalism is a social movement. Many excellent treatises have been written on those phenomena—yet they are outside the scope of our book.

We cite chiefly those scholars who have concentrated on social, economic, and political power and the way in which power relationships change through history. In 1842, Von Stein published his study of French socialists and other radical movements. Eight years later Von Stein published an expanded version of his *History of the Social Movement in France to the Present*. This version of his work contained valuable ideas for the social scientist. First, Von Stein anticipated Marx's idea of class conflict.

> Since labor without capital is necessarily dependent on capital, capital is able to dictate the conditions under which labor is hired. . . . The social position of each individual is now definite and unchangeable. It reflects a contradiction to the concept of labor by suspending the use of labor for acquisition and the gaining of property. It is a contradiction to the concept of the free personality in that it restrains the individual in the fulfillment of his aspirations. And it is contrary to the idea of liberty in that it fetters the development of human community . . . and in that it changes a society which in principle is committed to social freedom into one in which dependence prevails.[5]

Here Von Stein accounts for the French revolutionary movements by pointing out the inevitable conflict between the ruling classes and dominated workers. Like Marx, Von Stein saw the cause of revolutionary social movements within the fabric of the larger society. The economic institutions (capitalism) worked to further the dependency and alienation of workers while profiting economic elites.

Any society, Von Stein believed, existed in a state of inequality. Nevertheless, the state, man's institution for self-government, must be an influence to lessen society's inequality. The problem with this was that the state is controlled by those who have a vested interest in maintaining inequality. Was revolution, then, the answer? Here Von Stein diverged from the later theories of Karl Marx. Revolution by the proletariat could only result in tyranny since the poor had little experience or vision of self-government. The devious and the unscrupulous would soon control the state. To avoid revolution, reforms of the major institutions must occur. The poor, the working class, and the peasants must be given a stake in the existing society. From Von Stein, we learn then that the acquisition society develops a large number of "workers who, though free, have no capital; it is this contradiction which transforms the class of laborers into proletariat, and a social revolution will necessarily ensue unless the capital-owning class seriously supports social reform. . . ."[6]

Of significance, according to Heberle, is Von Stein's development of three points: (1) his conceptual distinction between the doctrine of the movement and the actual social movement, (2) his idea that social movements are central to sociology, and lastly, (3) his cogent description of the proletariat movement.[7]

Karl Marx, although not writing a specific sociology of movements, deals with class struggle in such a systematic way as to constitute a theory of social change that is all-encompassing. The student of movements can "rip off" from Marx a whole series of descriptions and explanations for movements, as the Marxist literature and action since Marx will demonstrate. Marx saw the final movement or class action as one generating out of the final clash between the forces of one class against another

[5] Lorenz Von Stein, *The History of the Social Movement in France 1789-1850*, Kaethe Mangeberg translator (Totawa, New Jersey: Bedminister Press, 1964), pp. 81-82.

[6] *Ibid.*, p. 315.
[7] Rudolf Heberle, *Social Movements: An Introduction to Political Sociology* (New York: Appleton-Century-Crofts, 1951), pp. 4-5.

—in his day the bourgeoisie and the proletariat. The conflict is over control of the substructure and superstructure of society. The movement is historically necessary, and the revolutionary life-style of the worker is inevitable as the ruling class tries to keep control over the production after its historical time is up.[8] Under this explanation, all other movements become subordinate; that is, if they seemingly relate to other issues, such as race, ecology, sex, and so forth, this is false consciousness or wrong theory and action.[9] This theory is so forceful as theory that we shall have to come back to it repeatedly as we proceed through the book.

Of significance is Marx's clear bias: (1) classes are the carriers of movements; (2) class action is above fundamental economic processes and the things that flow from those processes; (3) movements must be analyzed in historical materialist terms rather than idealist terms; and (4) the dialectical method is the correct method for looking at the socioeconomic processes of the world.[10]

Many commentators and scholars have come to write about tendencies and social movements besides Von Stein and Marx. Henri Saint-Simon dealt with socialism before Marx; Gustav LeBon made the classic statements on the nature of crowds in terms of collective behavior, Thorstein Veblen on labor movements, Georg Sorel on violence in politics, Robert Michels on democratic movements, Max Weber on religious movements, Alexis de Tocqueville on the French Revolution, and

V. I. Lenin on the necessity of organization in a movement.[11]

In 1930 Professor Jerome Davis of Yale University published his *Contemporary Social Movements,* which he claimed to be "the first textbook on modern social movements published in America. . . . These modern social movements are reactions on the part of individuals and groups to unsatisfactory conditions in the social life. There is a maladjustment which causes mental and social friction, and the movement develops as an effort to bring about harmony."[12] Davis, a progressive, saw many societal problems as economic at base. Movements to end war, he believed, would provide economic changes in the war-making society.

Eleven years after the publication of Davis' book, Hadley Cantril brought forth his *The Psychology of Social Movements.* Cantril oriented his book around the problem of individual susceptibility to social movements.[13]

In 1944, Harry W. Laidler presented *Social-Economic Movements,* which amounted to a handbook on social reconstruction as well as a sourcebook and textbook for students of economics, labor, sociology, political science, and

---

[8] Karl Marx, all works.

[9] This is the kind of analysis found in books and articles around the world in applying Marx to events and movements of the times. It is a "pat" analysis and readily discernible. Debates rage over the several revisions of Marxian analysis of theory and action. Literature is voluminous and growing. One bibliographical guide is: John Lachs, *Marxist Philosophy: A Bibliographical Guide* (Chapel Hill: The University of North Carolina Press, 1967).

[10] C. Wright Mills' offers an inventory of ideas from Marx, seventeen in all, as well as a criticism of these ideas. See his *The Marxists* (New York: Dell Publishing Company, 1962), pp. 81-131.

[11] A full list is beyond the scope of this book. Insight into the scope of the discussion here can be gained by looking at the various encyclopedic entries on collective behavior, social change, and social movements. Additionally, collections of readings on these subjects have come out recently, for example: John Eric Nordskog, *Contemporary Social Reform Movements* (New York: Charles Scribner's Sons, 1964). Ralph H. Turner and Lewis M. Killian, *Collective Behavior* (Englewood Cliffs, N. J.: Prentice-Hall, 1957). Robert R. Evans, editor, *Readings in Collective Behavior* (Chicago: Rand McNally, 1969). Barry McLaughlin, *Studies in Social Movements* (New York: The Free Press, 1969). Joseph R. Gusfield, *Protest, Reform and Revolt: A Reader in Social Movements* (New York: John Wiley and Sons, 1970). Gary B. Rush and R. Serge Denisoff, editors, *Social and Political Movements* (New York: Appleton-Century-Crofts, 1971). This last book has an up-to-date bibliography of political and radical social movements.
[12] Jerome Davis, *Contemporary Social Movements* (New York: The Century Co., 1930), p. 8.
[13] H. Cantril, *The Psychology of Social Movements* (New York: John Wiley and Sons, 1941).

ethics. Very much in the tradition of both Marx and Von Stein, he defined movements as evolutionary processes toward world socialism.[14]

Then in the late forties, two important American views were presented. Herbert Blumer's article (1946) seemingly set the broadest definition for a social movement: "collective enterprises to establish a new order of life." In addition, he presented a taxonomy of movements which has become most acceptable to American scholars, that is, his classification of general, specific, and expressive movements.[15]

Then, Rudolf Heberle, a German emigré to America, published his classic *Social Movements: an Introduction to Political Sociology* (1951). Heberle's book was remarkable both for the cogency of its content and for its pioneering effort in what Heberle calls "political ecology." Heberle's definition of a social movement ". . . is that it aims to bring about fundamental changes in the social order, especially in the basic institutions of property and labor relationships."[16] At this point, however, Heberle goes beyond Von Stein:

> But no longer can we identify the concept of social movement with the proletarian movement. The very existence of fascism and its derivations preclude it; and there are also the nativistic movements in the colonial possessions of European powers, the peasants' movements in eastern Europe and the farmers movement in this country to take into account.[17]

Here Heberle has expanded Von Stein's analysis to include all manner of groups seeking fundamental change in their societies. Note, however, that he does not include most religious movements. For if religious groups accept the basic social structure of a society as just, their influence on that society will be essentially conservative. For this reason the Billy Graham phenomena would not come under Heberle's definition of a social movement.

Heberle continues to surgically extract the essence of what a social movement is. First and most importantly, a social movement is not a trend. A social trend is a kind of social change that results from the "aggregate effect of many individual actions." In other words, social trends such as urbanization come about not through the concerted effort of an ideologically unified group. Trends are most frequently unplanned. Yet, as we shall see later, the relationship between trends and movements may be a dynamic and antithetical one.

Heberle then proceeds to distinguish political parties from social movements. A party, unlike a movement, has a formal structure. Moreover, "A genuine social movement . . . is always integrated by a set of constitutive ideas or an ideology,"[18] according to Heberle, while political parties may be held together not so much by a community of ideas as a simple network of individual patronage.

What Heberle has done with his concept of the social movement is to at once enlarge upon it while paring it of unnecessary vagueness. Social movements do represent individual and mass discontent. So, too, do nonmovements such as religious revivals or acts of individual terrorism. It is important to remember that social movements are political or at least prepolitical[19] in their concerns. This means that they are pointed toward shifting the power relation-

---

[14] Harry W. Laidler, *Social-Economic Movements* (New York: Thomas Y. Crowell, 1944). Updated and expanded as *History of Socialism*. See preface to Apollo edition, 1968, pp. v-vi.

[15] Herbert Blumer, "Collective Behavior," in Alfred M. Lee, editor, *New Outlines of the Principles of Sociology,* second ed. (1946), rev. (New York: Barnes and Noble, 1951), pp. 167-222.

[16] Heberle, *op. cit.,* p. 6. Heberle's earlier statement is "Observations on the Sociology of Social Movements," *American Sociological Review,* 14 (1949), pp. 346-357. A more recent statement is found in *International Encyclopedia of Social Sciences,* 1968.

[17] Heberle, *Social Movements, op. cit.,* p. 6.

[18] *Ibid.,* p. 11.

[19] The word "prepolitical" refers to the fact that some struggles for power take a religious or mystical set of symbols. A movement becomes "political" when the struggle for power involves secular rather than "sacred" symbols. Many nativistic movements are in this sense prepolitical.

ships in a society's basic institutions. Heberle reminds us of two very important aspects of all social movements when he discusses the constitutive ideas of a social movement and the fact that all social movements derive from a constituency—a social class, a nationality, or another group with common interests.

It comes as no surprise, then, that the major ideologies of social movements are often logically inconsistent but are almost always functionally consistent with the political and economic needs of a given group. Many conservatives, for example, might argue that the American government takes away far too many individual freedoms (such as the right to buy and sell without government regulation) while at the same time demanding that the young give up their freedoms in the military draft. Such inconsistencies can be found on the Left as well, when individuals perceive the courts as instruments of repression while seeking protection through the judicial system.

Many other views of movements have been advanced besides those of Blumer and Heberle.[20]

[20] Over 40 years ago, in two introductory sociology texts, classic statements were made. Park and Burgess (1924) dealt with collective behavior as "process"; Dawson and Gettys (1935) spelled out the stages of social movements. Then King (1956) stressed geography and time in movements. Turner and Killian (1957) distinguished movements and quasimovements. Lang and Lang (1961) discussed movements as "collective dynamics." Smelser (1963) gave a systematic theory of collective behavior encompassing movements. See the following works: Robert E. Park and Ernest W. Burgess, *Introduction to the Science of Sociology* (Chicago: University of Chicago Press, 1924). C. A. Dawson and W. E. Gettys, *Introduction to Sociology*, rev. ed. (New York: Ronald Press Co., 1935). C. Wendell King, *Social Movements in the United States* (New York: Random House, 1956). Ralph Turner and Lewis M. Killian, *Collective Behavior* (Englewood Cliffs, N. J.: Prentice-Hall, 1957). Kurt and Gladys Lang, *Collective Dynamics* (New York: Crowell, 1961). See also "Collective Dynamics: Process and Form," in Arnold M. Rose, editor, *Human Behavior and Social Processes* (Boston: Houghton Mifflin, 1962), pp. 340-359. Neil J. Smelser, *Theory of Collective Behavior* (New York: Free Press, 1963).

Hans Toch's *The Social Psychology of Social Movements* was launched in 1965. Toch's particular contribution to the study of social movements lies in his analysis of processes of affiliation to and disaffiliation from social movements. Toch's definition of social movements goes far beyond the idea proposed by Von Stein. For Von Stein, of course, social movements were political in the narrow sense of the word, while for Toch, "A social movement represents an effort by a large number of people to solve collectively a problem that they feel they have in common."[21] In a yet more recent work, Gusfield (1970) stresses "collective action," reemphasizing the relationship between collective behavior and social movements.[22]

Ash (1972) identifies the social movements in American history. She defines movements as attitudes and actions directed toward structural or ideological change.[23]

Some stress the role of collective behavior in movements; some tend to see movements as somewhat separate from collective behavior. Some stress political violence, while others play it down. Furthermore, some stress rapidity and scale of change, and others ignore it. All these views point to the disparity and truncation in the many views since the Von Stein and Marx statements in the nineteenth century. Thus, we see the need for a scheme to bring things together.

RELATIONSHIP OF MOVEMENTS TO TRENDS: A SCHEME

We shall define social movements after Heberle, as attempts at changing power and income (order) in reaction to social tendencies.

[21] Hans Toch, *The Social Psychology of Social Movements* (Indianapolis: Bobbs-Merrill, 1965), p. 5.
[22] Joseph R. Gusfield, *Protest, Reform and Revolt: A Reader in Social Movements* (New York: John Wiley, 1970), p. 2.
[23] Roberta Ash, *Social Movements in America* (Chicago: Markham, 1972), p. 1.

This is diagrammed below in the following figure.

Social change is made up of both social processes and social collectivities, that is, historical trends such as industrialization (including modernization, mechanization, and so forth); bureaucratization (including a politicization as increase in political scale, globalization, and so forth). Sometimes we see the terms industrialism, bureaucratism, and imperialism as the labels for social processes, trends, or tendencies. This suffix "ism" denotes the ideological aspects of these trends. Since according to Heberle,[24] a trend is "the aggregate effect of many individual actions," trends are most frequently unplanned. Movements are a special kind of social collectivity that is not organized, but may have members who belong to organized groups, and therefore a movement is a social collective that has some element of planning or goal orientation within it. Insofar as social movements that seek to change the power relationships of a society are political or prepolitical, there is political planning within the movement.

What about the relationship between trends and movements? We would argue that the relationship is a dynamic one. Trends are the stuff of history, the substructure that in turn sets the limits for the groups, both unorganized and organized. The industrial revolution is a basic process (or trend) that is seemingly irreversible. Along with it has come the democratic revolution with the many egalitarian movements, many of which are reacting to or attempting to negate hierarchical organization that has come with industrial revolution.

Now, movements may or may not be in harmony with trends. What do we mean by this? Again, referring to our dialectical framework, we will take the case of industrialization. As we have said, the industrial processes with their often inhumane practices disorganize, indeed destroy, human lives. Movements arise to protest this destruction of life, and they may take one of two tactics. First, they may oppose all further industrialization and the use of technology. If they were to do so, as some European conservatives or peasants did, their movement would be out of harmony with the trend. If, on the other hand, they were to oppose the oppression associated with industrialization and opt for more humane use of technology, we would say they were in a kind

---

[24] Heberle, *Social Movements, op. cit.* See also Robert M. Kloss, *Political Tendencies and Social Security: From the New Deal to the Great Society,* unpublished dissertation, Louisiana State University, August 1969, p. 5.

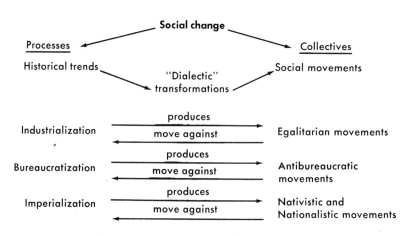

Social change, trends, and movements.

of harmony with the trend while attempting to negate its evil effects.

The same situation would hold true for those who rise up against the inhumane enlargement of political scale we call imperialism. European colonization of the third world was (as we shall later point out) a brutal and destructive mode of social control. Natives and other oppressed people have again two options in fighting their oppressors. The first goes counter to the trend of enlargement of scale by attempting to retribalize the native population. The other possibility is that the native will perceive the harm done by the forceful enlargement of scale called imperialism and decide to build a modern nation state, hopefully again, without the oppression associated with colonial domination.

As we look at the trend toward increasing bureaucratization, we can see that it involves the use of planning and rationality in human affairs; we can also see bureaucracy as a source of hierarchical control and irresponsible power. Some may react to bureaucratization by calling for a mystical alternative to rational planning. Another possibility would be to humanize bureaucracy by making more democratic and egalitarian its planning processes.

The egalitarian social movements described in this book all react negatively to the oppressive nature of the historical trends mentioned in this book (see outline). If, however, they do not react negatively to the liberating potential of the trend, we will state that they are in harmony with this aspect of the trend. *We also believe that social movements that choose to react negatively to planning as well as hierarchical control are doomed to failure. Likewise, a movement that rejects enlargement of scale as it works against racism will not survive. The social movements that attempt to end class conflict and the destruction of our environment will also be futile if they reject out of hand technological development.*

It is important then to understand the goals and aims of social movements and whether those goals are in harmony with the liberative

Master trends—their oppressive nature and liberating potential

I. Bureaucratization
   A. *Oppressive nature*
      Hierarchical control
         (alienation)
         (elitism)
   B. *Liberating potential*
      Planning
         (for the elimination of poverty)
         (to improve education and learning)
II. Cultural imperialization
   A. *Oppressive nature*
      Racism
      Colonialism
      Economic exploitation
   B. *Liberating potential*
      Enlargement of social scale
         (the creation of larger areas for trade, exchange of knowledge, solutions to ecological problems)
III. Industrialization
   A. *Oppressive nature*
      Class conflict
         (dynamic poverty)
      Destruction of environment
   B. *Liberating potential*
      Technological development
         (medical advances)
         (freedom from mindless labor)
         (abundance)

potentials of the master social trends. Heberle says the lack of harmony can lead to societal destruction:

> If the dominant minority in a society is unwilling to make the necessary adjustments, these will have to be achieved by concerted action of other groups—in other words, by a social movement. In this kind of situation, a social movement is the force which saves the society from destruction, although the dominant minority may not realize that at the time. This is probably one reason why it is so difficult to oppress permanently a movement whose aims are in harmony with *tendencies* of social change

which are imminent in a given society. If repression is at all successful, it may result in a high degree of conformity of overt behavior and in the illusion of preserved or restored social solidarity.[25]

These are processes at work, and in a sense they are *developmental;* growing, expanding in history. *Social movements arise in reaction to trends attempting to negate them.* So, in the case of the Luddites, the machine smashers of nineteenth century England, they may have wanted to return to a simpler world or have seen the machines as the reason for the lack of bread; in any case, the trend of mechanization was upon them and is seemingly irreversible. It would indeed seem futile today to attempt to blow up a computer center because we didn't want to become ciphers in a data archive, to be retrieved at a moment's notice by some bureaucrat. Yet computerization and automation are part of bureaucratization, and radical movements spring up to fight such tendencies. The idea that trends are developmental is one of the oldest ideas in Western history, says Nisbet.[26] *If industrialization, bureaucratization, and let us say urbanization are developing, then they are directional, cumulative, irreversible, have stages, and purpose.* In opposition to the dialectical, Kenneth Boulding most strongly argues for developmentalism as an explanation for social change, social trends, and social movements.

> On the one hand there are dialectical processes. These involve conflict and the victory of one group or system over another, and hence a succession of victors. On the other hand there are nondialectical (or developmental) processes in which conflict, even where it exists, is incidental, and in which the central pattern of the

process in cumulative, evolutionary, and continuous.[27]

Unlike Boulding, we do not see the growth of social movements as developmental. Rather our model will be conflictual and dialectical.

THE DIALECTIC AND SOCIAL MOVEMENTS

The notion of the dialectic conjures up images of sugar plums for some and terminological and political nightmares for others. The arguments continue over the use and misuse of the term, even its history.[28] Raymond Aron, in discussing the dialectics of modern society, says there are three themes: (1) modern industrial societies are both egalitarian in aspiration and hierarchical in organization, hence the *dialectic of equality;* (2) individuality is in conflict with the mechanism of production, thus the *contradiction of socialization;* and, (3) tendencies exist toward both unity and division (or primitive custom versus industrialization), therefore, the *dialectic of universality.*

> Each of these three themes is dialectical in the sense that it is defined by the contradiction between the reality and the ideal, or between various aspects of reality and various ideals. The use of the term dialectic in these titles is not a mere concession to fashion; society of the industrial type is intelligible solely in its becoming.[29]

So, the trends of hierarchy, mechanism of production, and imperialism are faced with egali-

[25] *Ibid.,* pp. 455-456. Also see Ash, *op. cit.,* who says "our proposition [is] that movements that resist substructural trends are doomed to failure," p. 84.
[26] Robert A. Nisbet, *Social Change and History: Aspects of the Western Theory of Development* (New York: Oxford University Press, 1969), p. 7.

[27] Kenneth E. Boulding, *A Primer on Social Dynamics: History as Dialectics and Development* (New York: The Free Press, 1970), p.v.
[28] Boulding, *op. cit.,* argues against the use of the dialectic as a philosophical tool, since it stresses the *victory* of one class, nation, or race over another. In short, Boulding sees the dialectic as conflict-oriented, whereas the concept of development and progress is problem-oriented. Conflicts generated by dialectical thinking pit man against man and work against a universalist morality in Boulding's view.
[29] Raymond Aron, *Progress and Disillusion: The Dialectics of Modern Society* (New York: The New America Library Mentor Book, 1968), pp. xvi-xvii.

tarian, individualistic, nativistic, and nationalistic movements.

Marcuse, in all of his works, stresses the role of the dialectic as opposition and negation to technical progress that extends to a whole system of domination and coordination. But this technical progress also created critical social theory:

> This ambiguous situation involves a still more fundamental ambiguity. *One Dimensional Man* will vacillate throughout between two contradictory hypotheses: (1) that advanced industrial society is capable of containing qualitative change for the forseeable future; (2) that forces and tendencies exist which may break this containment and explode the society. I do not think a clear answer can be given. Both tendencies are there, side by side—and even the one in the other. The first tendency is dominant, and whatever preconditions for a reversal may exist are being used to prevent it.[30]

These hypotheses, says Marcuse, lead to either repressive or liberative tolerance.[31] We will have more to say about this in later chapters.

The dialectic, so-called, is a way of saying that the world is in conflict over a whole range of things—logical, ideological, sociological, psychological—and that the struggle is open-ended. The historical trends are seemingly inevitable, but individuals and groups will see them differently. All is not consensus in society, just as all is not conflict. Sociologists, because they have studied how social order is possible, are only recently rediscovering the dialectic as a way of accounting for the changes in the range of social processes of structure and movements.[32] Despite the negative, even pejorative, connotations of the dialectic, it is useful to the student of social movements to characterize the relationship of trends to movements—as we have done on p. 16.

Viewing social movements as dialectical in their relationships to social trends can enable us to view the relationship between social movements and trends as a processal rather than a static one. Schneider explicates seven possible meanings for the term dialectic.[33] In this book we will combine several of Schneider's ideas to form this concept of the dialectic. *Dialectical process occurs when a social trend produces its own opposition by creating within a collectivity of individuals the psychological need for negation of the trend.* All of the significant trends described in this book do generate feelings of frustration and the desire for change in some individuals. When those individuals organize themselves to combat the trend, a dialectical pattern has been established. Men and women respond to contradiction in their lives with the desire for change. It is out of this potential that social movements are born.

SUMMATION

It may be good to bring together some of the basic points in this conceptual scheme. First, we would say that men and women build in-

---

[30] Herbert Marcuse, *One Dimensional Man: Studies in the Ideology of Advanced Industrial Society* (Boston: Beacon Press, 1964), p. xv. The basic book of Marcuse's thought is *Reason and Revolution: Hegel and the Rise of Social Theory* (Boston: Beacon Press, 1941). In the 1960 edition he adds a note on the dialectic that stresses the power of negative thinking. Dialectical analysis ultimately becomes historical analysis, and it is in this sense that we use the term after Marcuse.

[31] Robert Paul Wolff, Barrington Moore, Jr., Herbert Marcuse, "Repressive Tolerance," in *A Critique of Pure Tolerance* (Boston: Beacon Press, 1965), pp. 81-117.

[32] A recent summary of the re-emergence of the dialectic in sociology is to be found in Louis Schneider, "Dialectic Sociology," *American Sociological Review* 36 (August 1971), p. 667.

[33] The seven meaning clusters for the term are as follows:

1. A discrepancy between aim or intention and outcome
2. Goal shifts and displacements (heterogeny of ends or functional autonomy)
3. The idea that effective adaptations to a situation stand in the way of future progress, "success brings failure"
4. Development through conflict
5. Contradiction, opposition, or paradox
6. Contradictory emotions
7. Conflict dissolved in a coalescence of opposites

stitutions to fulfill their needs and to control the world. Those enduring institutions can be perceived as modes of control over other human beings; they can also be seen as trends throughout modern history. The trends or modes of control we confront in this book, bureaucracy, imperialism, and industrialization, have caused much human misery as we shall later document. This human misery is an excellent spawning ground for radical or egalitarian social movements. These movements are in dialectic opposition to the oppressive tendencies in the master trends just cited. While movements continue to rise up against all manner of oppression, they must choose ideologically whether they wish to go back to prebureaucratic, preindustrial, or preimperialist stages of development. The institutional elites who confront social movements must also make these conscious choices. We would maintain that it is not possible to go back in time and that any movement or elite that attempts to do so will find itself a quaint footnote to history.

We entertain the belief as well as the hope that modern social movements can humanize the results of social trends. Indeed, we perceive the history of the future as a constant dialectical battle between institutions and the humanizing potential, yet we are not unmindful of the fact that there is no intrinsic goodness residing in the poor or the oppressed. They are like other men, a mixture of altruism and self-interest, greed and kindness. We do accept the idea that the oppressed are more aware of the warts (or cancers) on the body politic because in any crisis, war, depression, or the like, they are the first to feel the contradictions of the large society in their own lives. Their analysis of why they are oppressed may not be correct, yet the view from the bottom gives one an understanding of the results of oppression unlike that proposed by any book such as this one.

This book will try to grapple with a number of questions, seen from somewhere between the balcony and the barricade. Some of the questions will be answered directly, others only hinted at. They include the following:

1. What motivates men and women to create, join, and maintain social movements?
2. What tactics and strategies are movements likely to use? Further, what are the social meanings of violence and nonviolence?
3. What social movements are likely to succeed in their struggle for power? What is success in a social movement?
4. A frankly utopian question—How are social movements related to the achievement of "the good life"?

CHAPTER 2   THE CONDITIONS AND MOTIVATIONS UNDERLYING SOCIAL MOVEMENTS

The motto, wrought on the gate of the Dachau concentration camp, "Labor means Liberty," dramatically highlights the condition of "moral man" who in malaise, drifts in "immoral society."

                                   Hans Gerth and C. Wright Mills

It will be recalled that when we looked at the concept of social movements in Chapter 1 we had two graveyards—one full of aristocracies and the other full of social movements. We also discussed smug elites and unhappy people in conflict. How is it that all this has come about? That is, what may constitute the conducive conditions for a movement, and secondly, what may motivate the many individual actions that make up any social movement? We have provided a tentative answer to the first part of the question by saying previously that it is social *trends* which are dramatically related to social *movements;* that is, trends are the basic stuff of the processes of social change since they are the aggregative effects of individual actions over time. Trends, as such, are not the result of ideologically unified groups and are most frequently unplanned. *And even though these trends are by definition constantly in motion, they represent institutionalized social order and control. They are substructural or at the base of*

collective actions and collective ideologies. When we say that these trends constitute the conducive conditions for social movements, we are attempting to assert that the explanation for the rise of movements is basically sociological and historical. But within the context of these conditions, we must, as students of social movements, account for the motivations, individually and collectively, of the thousands or millions of people involved in movements.

THE DIALECTICAL RELATIONSHIP BETWEEN CONDITIONS AND MOTIVATIONS

At the outset, it must be said that the distinction between the conducive conditions (trends) of movements and the social-psychological motivations of the members of the movements is an analytical one. In the reality of social action, they are extremely difficult to separate. But their separation has provided insight into the causes of social movements, and there is no reason for us to depart from this traditional way of analyzing movements. The disciplinary domain that has dealt with the type of analysis where social conditions and individual motivations come together is social psychology.

Our three dominant trends, industrialization, bureaucracy, and cultural imperialism, are worldwide trends and, as social orders in motion, naturally generate real or imagined insecurity and injustice in society. Heberle says: ". . . any social and political movement which rebels against existing social institutions will attract individuals who have been suffering real or imagined injustice under these institutions."[1] These insecurities and injustices lead to stirring, unrest and discontent, and finally to rebelliousness against the existing institutions.

Each of these worldwide trends produces its own negative because each social trend does tend to destroy old social institutions while creating many value conflicts and contradictions in the life of the individual. When individuals are uprooted by urbanization, for example, they may organize themselves into movements of protest. Likewise, individuals whose personality systems are threatened by increasing bureaucratization may form movements to combat what they feel are unfortunate changes in their lives. Strangely enough, as we shall see, politics does indeed make strange bedfellows as the ultrarightists of the George Wallace movements chastize bureaucrats in language remarkably similar to that of the New Left students in American universities.

This negation or opposition by individuals and collectivities to ongoing social institutions may be analytically called a dialectical transformation. This refers to the dynamic, some-

times antithetical, relationship between social trends as social conditions and social movements. This dynamic includes conflict, discontinuity, and contradiction between the existing social orders and the new collectivities in motion to change them.

Now we realize that the analytic use of the dialectic to characterize the relationship between trends and movements will receive a mixed reaction from the reader. We adopt the term because, as we stated at the close of Chapter 1, it facilitates an analysis that sees that the world is in conflict over a whole range of things. We refer here not to random conflict but rather conflict that evolves into certain patterns, patterns that ultimately pit groups holding tenaciously to sacred institutions against groups which, for reasons of insecurity, injustices, or both, want to transform them. Additionally, a dialectical characterization of the relationship between trends and movements is a radical portrayal of radical social processes, processes whereby society (social orders and oligarchies) is challenged and destroyed or destroys the rebellious challengers. The conflict is continuous and dramatic, and there are victors and victims.

The dialectic in this book does not refer to the objective idealism of Hegel.[2] Rather it refers to

---

[1] Rudolf Heberle, *Social Movements: An Introduction to Political Sociology* (New York: Appleton-Century-Crofts, 1951), p. 112.

[2] Herbert Marcuse, *Reason and Revolution: Hegel and the Rise of Social Theory* (Boston: Beacon Press, 1960). In this book Hegel's dialectical mode of reasoning is developed and compared to Marx. For Hegel, dialectical unfolding is the history of production and materiality; furthermore, Marcuse (p. 282) says both Hegel and Marx were originally motivated by the negative character of reality in its totality. Raymond Aron, *The Opium of the Intellectuals* (Garden City, N. Y.: Doubleday & Company, 1955) says: "The term dialectic is ambiguous, charged with mysterious overtones. Applied to historical development as a whole, it is susceptible of two interpretations—either a continuous interlacing of causes and effects ending up with a different system from the one existing before, or a succession of totalities, each in itself significant, the transition being one to another consistent with an intelligible necessity," pp. 182-183. Despite its ambiguity and mysterious overtones, we choose to use it because of its critical and radical import.

a specific social, psychological, and potentially political negation to a given social trend. If a given trend, such as bureaucratization, threatens an individual's sense of identity or self-esteem, he will be attracted to antibureaucratic movements. Likewise, if a trend such as cultural imperialism threatens an individual's "cognitive mazeways" (that is, his cultural world view), he is likely to feel a sense of solidarity with nativistic or nationalistic movements. Moreover, if a trend such as a change in the stratification system increases the relative and absolute deprivation of an individual, he is likely to feel an attraction to egalitarian movements.

THE SOCIAL PROBLEM CONTEXT OF CONCERN AND INSECURITY

The literature of scholarship is not always clear as to just exactly how and why certain groups and strata, individuals and collectives, define some part or whole of their social situation as problematic. Jessie Bernard, for a recent sociological example, says that the concept of social problem emerged at the end of the eighteenth and beginning of the nineteenth centuries as a result of four factors: (1) the stresses created by the new urban industrial order, (2) a growing humanitarianism, (3) scientific ideology, and (4) the middle-class reformist attitude.[3] Also, what is a problem for some groups is not for another, depending on which group is protecting its vested interest.[4] Recurrent social problems of recent times have been depressions, civil disorders, and wars. These problems produce *insecurity* in some or all of the population. How the insecurity of social trends is perceived politically, and what is done politically is our discussion to follow. Social problems must be defined here as a challenge to the polity and the economy as they are perceived.

Various types of change or transformation might be said to be related to the degree of insecurity felt by the individuals and groups that make up a society. In other terms, *social insecurity*, either individually or collectively, leads to social action, and such action leads to social movements. Karl Mannheim, for example, develops the idea of different forms of insecurity in terms of whether or not they are organized or unorganized. *The stage of unorganized insecurity (unemployment being the main symptom in the twentieth century) leads to psychological and emotional experimentation as well as sociological conditions in which ideologies are unmasked and the alidity of established principles and values comes to be doubted:*

> This is the moment of skepticism, hard for the individual yet productive for science, as it destroys the petrified habits of thought of the past. In this general experimentation, the individual who cannot reorganize himself may perish, but for the social body it means the possibility of a selection of new models of behavior and of new representative dominant types.[5]

Through stages, the collectivity goes from unorganized to organized insecurity—through gesture, utopia, and militarist pattern.[6] Social

---

[3] Jessie Bernard, *Social Problems at Mid-Century: Roles Status and Stress in a Context of Abundance* (New York: Holt, Rinehart and Winston, 1957), pp. 93-98. How the fourth factor, the middle-class reformer attitude, arose is not clear. We could say that these new definitions of the situation on the part of the middle class were due to its concern for "reason" and "rationality." See Marcuse, *op. cit.*, p. 253. For a historical treatment, see Howard Becker and Harry Elmer Barnes, "The Quest for Secular Salvation: Social Reform in Relation to the Sociological Impulse," in *Social Thought from Lore to Science* (New York: Dover Publications, Inc., 1961), Vol. 2, pp. 595-636.

[4] Elites in a population may consider something a social problem to them—but to nonelites there may not even be an awareness of the problem. For example, professional groups may consider government intervention into medicine as a problem, but nonprofessionals may think quite differently.

[5] Karl Mannheim, *Man and Society in an Age of Reconstruction* (New York: Harcourt, Brace and Company, 1940), pp. 125-130.

[6] *Ibid.*, pp. 135-143.

control comes about as the society tries to limit the variability of situations because, as Mannheim asserts, society cannot tolerate unpredictable situations in the long run. It uses every means in its power to ensure that its economic and political foundations are as firm as possible.[7] Thus, the impetus to change something to some extent occurs to individuals, groups, and, in general, the collectivities of society.

PSYCHOLOGY AND SOCIAL MOVEMENTS: AN ARGUMENT

One of the most facile theories for the explanation of personal commitment to a radical social movement revolves around the idea that radicals on the Right and Left are psychologically unbalanced, fanatical, or immature. This has sometimes been referred to as the stomachache theory of revolution: men and women with personal unhappiness attempt to share their unhappiness with the rest of the world by destructive or irrational acts. In its more crass form, this ad hominem approach would consider all student activists as immature, all right-wingers as sexually frustrated, or all women's liberationists as lesbians in disguise.

Much research and theorizing has been done in the area of the psychology of commitment to social movements. We shall try to wend our way through the complex maze with the hope that we can begin to generalize about the individual's personality and his or her propensity for a given social movement.

HOFFER'S AD HOMINEM?

One of the most popular books on the psycology of social movements was written not by a psychologist but by a longshoreman, and a unique longshoreman at that. Eric Hoffer, a truly self-made man of letters, did migratory farm work in California in the 1920's and 1930's

and became a dock worker during World War II. Hoffer schooled himself in German philosophy (although he distrusts intellectuals) as well as classical literature.

In 1951, Hoffer's *The True Believer*[8] was first seen by the public, and 20 years later it had sold nearly 500,000 copies. It was written as a series of aphorisms with one unifying thesis: commitment to a mass movement that advocates drastic change is symptomatic of fanaticism. Communism, Fascism, and Catholicism all came under the same anathema by Hoffer's analysis:

> All mass movements generate in their adherents a readiness to die and a proclivity for united action; all of them irrespective of the doctrine they preach and the program they project, breed fanaticism, enthusiasm, fervent hope, hatred and intolerance . . .[9]

Hoffer's true believer is an amalgam of psychological misfits, weak in self-direction, creativity, or compassion. Because of the fanatic's emotional weakness and lack of inner strength, he is seen by Hoffer as needing a group or herd identity. This loss of self in the mass movement relieves anxieties about one's identity and purpose in life. It makes no difference whether one is a leftist or a rightist; if he follows a drastic course, similarities emerge:

> The radical and the reactionary loathe the present. They see, it as an aberration and a deformity. Both are ready to proceed ruthlessly and recklessly with the present, and both are hospitable to the idea of self-sacrifice.[10]

The true believer Hoffer characterizes as full of hatred, and, in large part, this hatred springs from self-contempt.

> The fanatic is also mentally cocky, and hence barren of new beginnings. At the root of his cockiness is the conviction that life and the universe conform to a simple formula—his formula. He is thus without the fruitful intervals of groping, when the mind as it were in

---

[7] *Ibid.*, p. 302.

[8] (New York: Harper and Row, 1951.)
[9] *Ibid.*, p. ix.
[10] *Ibid*, p. 71.

solution—ready for all manner of new reactions, new combinations and new beginnings.[11]

This then is the woof and warp of the Hoffer construct: the true believer, a man driven by personal inadequacies to collective, radical mass actions. Since Hoffer's work cites few (if any) formal sociological or psychological studies, it may be in order to raise a few critical questions about his work.

Granted that fanatics exist, are they the cause or the result of social movements? Hoffer seemingly opts for the first position, yet this appears to be an open question. Further, are followers of totalitarian movements spurred on by purely aberrant personality drives or by social factors? Hans Gerth tells us that 97% of the schoolteachers in prewar Germany were members of the Nazi party.[12] Does this imply that German schoolteachers were nearly all psychologically disturbed, or is it more likely that bureaucratic pressures or status-seeking accounted for this seemingly remarkable fact?

Is Hoffer correct when he asserts that those committed to mass movements are without creativity? There is a certain logic to this statement, yet how are we to account for artistic groups or individuals with a high degree of political commitment, such as the French Surrealist poets, who as a group, were highly influenced by Marxist thought,[13] or Picasso whose painting *Guernica* is a highly political work, or for that matter, the massive numbers of artists and writers in America who involved themselves in the struggle against the war in Vietnam in the 1960's and 1970's?

Perhaps the most basic question we must ask ourselves about Hoffer's work has to do with

his analysis that commitment to a radical cause stems from psychological inadequacies. One concept in vogue in sociology at this time is the idea of the extreme situation. What is an extreme situation? One where hunger, imprisonment, loss of livelihood, or imminent death is at hand. If an individual reacts to one of these situations in an extreme way, are we free to call him a fanatic? Indeed, if ecologists are correct in their analysis of planet earth's early demise from industrial poisoning,[14] is radical action indicative of fanaticism? (Many concerned individuals are tagged ecology nuts in the United States at present.)

Our reading of Hoffer's ideas leaves us with many unanswered questions and some contradictions. Yet, *The True Believer* is a book any serious student of social movements must confront.

THE NEO-FREUDIAN VIEW OF
RIGHT-WING MOVEMENTS

The Nazi movement in Germany was a great blow to liberals' contention that man was at base rational and humane. It is no accident, then, that after the near triumph of European fascism, a nonrationalist understanding of many social movements would receive encouragement in intellectual circles. It was Sigmund Freud, of course, whose theories penetrated the nonrational core of everyday life. Many of Freud's politically aware followers had congregated around the left of center Frankfort school of sociology after World War II. Here German scholarship with strong traces of neo-Marxian and Freudian analysis attempted to understand atavistic movements such as Nazism.

We can deal here with only a sampling of the theories that came out of the Frankfort school. It is safe to contend, however, that all the theorists attached to the school saw the patriarchal family and the sexual repressions

---

[11] *Ibid.,* p. 141.
[12] Hans H. Gerth, "The Nazi Party: Leadership and Composition," *American Journal of Sociology* 14 (1940), pp. 517.
[13] See Robert S. Short, "The Politics of Surrealism, 1920-36," in Walter Laquer and George L. Mosse, editors, *The Left-Wing Intellectuals Between the Wars 1919-1939* (New York: Harper and Row, 1966), pp. 3-26.

---

[14] See Aldous Huxley, "The Politics of Ecology," *The Center Magazine* 2 (March, 1969).

associated with the family as key to the understanding of a social movement that nearly destroyed Western civilization.[15]

One of the most flamboyant of the German theorists was Wilhelm Reich whose curious blend of socialism and sexual libertarianism blinded many to the serious scholarship he produced in his early life. Although Reich began as an orthodox Freudian, he soon began to understand the world differently than his mentor. "Psychic health," Reich argued, "depends on orgastic potency . . . the capacity for sur-

render in the acme of sexual excitation in the natural sex act. . . . In the case of orgastic impotence from which a vast majority of humans are suffering, biological energy is dammed up, thus becoming the source of all kinds of irrational behavior."[16]

In essence, Reich is telling us that irrationality and destructiveness result from sexual frustration. Where then do we look for the source of this frustration? In the place any good Freudian would seek—the family structure. Like his contemporaries, Eric Fromm and Herbert

---

[15] For an analysis of the thought of prominent members of the Frankfort school, see Volker Eisele, "Theory and Praxis: The View From Frankfort," *Berkeley Journal of Sociology* 16 (June, 1971), pp. 94-105.

[16] Wilhelm Reich, *The Function of the Orgasm* (New York: Farrar, Straus, and Giroux, 1961), pp. xvii-xix.

The ideal "Aryan" family. (From George L. Mosse: *Nazi Culture*, New York: Grosset & Dunlap, 1968.)

26

Marcuse,[17] Reich believed that the patriarchal German family contained the seeds of totalitarianism. In 1933, during the ascendancy of the Nazi movement, Reich conceived his crucial work, *The Mass Psychology of Fascism*.[18] It was banned in Germany two years later.

> Since Authoritarian society reproduces itself in the individual structures of the masses with the help of the authoritarian family, it follows that political reaction has to regard and defend the authoritarian family as *the* basis of state, culture, and civilization. In this propaganda it can count on deep irrational factors in the masses.[19]

The führer principle of dictatorship is simply an extension of the patriarchal family to the state. We must obey the führer without question just as we must obey our father without question. Reich noted that the Nazi movement took an extremely puritanical view of sex in official propaganda but projected sexual neuroses with its political propaganda. Reich even perceived the swastika as a thinly veiled sexual symbol. Thus, neurotic sexual concerns and the patriarchal family contribute to a mass movement glorifying violence, thanatos (the death wish), and the assertion of power.

Reich's neo-Freudian theories of the psychology of totalitarianism received a mixed review by behavioral scientists. Perhaps the most crucial criticism of his work, like that of many Freudian theories, is that it lacks the kind of empirical evidence demanded by hard-nosed behavioral and social scientists.

Thus the challenge was to operationalize the neo-Freudian theories in a way that would meet the rigors of scientific discipline. This was attempted in a massive way by T. W. Aldorno, one of the leading intellectuals in the Frankfort school, who along with a number of other prominent social scientists attempted to investigate the essential question: Is there a fascist personality?

It was in 1950 that Adorno and others published the results of a massive study to answer precisely that question. The book created by the efforts of Adorno and colleagues at the University of California was entitled *The Authoritarian Personality*.[20]

The social scientists at Berkeley proceeded to create four attitudinal scales measuring political and economic conservatism, ethnocentrism, anti-Semitism, and potentiality for fascism (many of the items for the latter scale were taken from Nazi propaganda statements). A sample of several thousand Northern Californians were given these attitudinal scales, including students, labor unionists, prison inmates, nurses, veterans, and patients at a local psychiatric clinic. The researchers proceeded on two levels: first, to investigate the relationship between fascistic attitudes and other attitudinal clusters such as ethnocentrism or economic conservatism; second, to investigate the family structure of the individual demonstrating a fascistic character structure.

With regard to the first question, the researchers did find positive statistical correlations between the four attitudinal sets (although the strength of the relationship between certain variables such as conservatism and anti-Semitism is subject to some question).

For the more important of the two tasks, the investigation of the fascist character structure, Adorno and colleagues delineated the fascist syndrome—a personality system with the following traits:

1. *Conventionalism,* a rigid adherence to conventional middle class values
2. *Authoritarian submission,* a submissive, uncritical attitude toward moral authorities of the ingroup
3. *Authoritarian aggression,* a tendency to be on the lookout for and to reject and

---

[17] See Fromm's *Escape From Freedom* (New York: Farrar and Rinehart, 1941), for a similar analysis of the fascist character structure. See also Marcuse's more recent *Eros and Civilization* (Boston Beacon Press, 1955).

[18] (New York: Farrar, Straus, and Giroux, 1970.)

[19] *Ibid.,* p. 104

[20] (New York: John Wiley and Sons, 1964.)

punish people who violate conventional values

4. *Anti-intraception*, an opposition to the subjective, the imaginative, the tender-minded

5. *Superstition and stereotype*, the belief in mystical determinants of the individual's fate, the disposition to think in rigid categories

6. *Power and toughness*, a preoccupation with the dominance-submission, strong-weak, leader-follower dimension, identi-fication with power figures

7. *Destructiveness and cynicism*, a general-ized hostility, vilification of the human

8. *Projectivity*, the disposition to believe that wild and dangerous things go on in the world; the projection outward of un-conscious emotional impulses

9. *Sex*, exaggerated concern with sexual goings-on

If these are the character traits of the patho-logically prejudiced individual, how do we go about tracing his traits to the locus of his per-sonality—the family? One clue to the relation-ship between personality and family life became evident as researchers (through the aid of pro-jective techniques) found consistent though repressed hostility toward parents by subjects with an authoritarian personality. On the con-scious level, the authoritarian was quick to praise and slow to find fault with his or her mother or father. Yet latent hostilities were revealed when high scorers on the F (poten-tiality for fascism) scale were given intensive psychiatric interviews.

Adorno and his coresearchers began to dis-cern a consistent pattern in the early family life of the authoritarian personality. Typical was a home without the sharing of decisions (a hierarchical family). Typical also was the fact that parents in the home used harsh, unreason-ing discipline on the child, as well as cutting off the child emotionally when he or she failed to perform in a satisfactory way.

Was this study, then, the benchmark toward understanding the psychology of hate-ridden mass movements? In the decade that followed the publication of the study, students of soci-ology and psychology argued vehemently over the study and those it later generated.

In 1954, Richard Christie and Marie Jahoda published a book[21] pointing to the methodological weaknesses of the study (there were many), but confirming certain of its findings. In the same year, Hans Eysenck, a British psychologist, published a work[22] which agreed that a kind of authoritarianism did exist, but that it existed on the left as well as the right side of the political spectrum. Also, Eysenck attacked the Freudian assumptions of the Frankfort scholars. Eysenck's assumption was that communists and fascists were equal (or nearly so) in tough mindedness, a term he borrowed from William James. His studies on small samples of English Commu-nists and Fascists seemed to confirm his view.[23]

In 1960 Milton Rokeach, an American social psychologist, brought forth the idea that dogma-tism, a closed cognitive system tied to an au-thoritarian ideology, was crucial in understanding totalitarian movements.[24] Like Eysenck, Ro-keach did not accept the Freudian undergirdings of the California study.

At this point, it would be well to refer to a fascinating cross-cultural study done by the Harvard social psychologist, Thomas Pettigrew. Pettigrew gave the F scale to 620 white under-graduate students at the University of Natal in South Africa as well as to an equal number of white college students in the U.S.[25] As one

[21] *Studies in the Scope and Method of the Authori-tarian Personality* (Glencoe, Illinois: Free Press, 1954).
[22] *The Psychology of Politics* (London: Routledge and Kegan Paul, 1954).
[23] Richard Christie disagreed with this analysis. See his "Eysenck's Treatment of the Personality of Com-munists," *Psychological Bulletin* 53 (November, 1956), pp. 411-430.
[24] *The Open and Closed Mind* (New York: Basic Books, 1960).
[25] Thomas Pettigrew, "Personality and Sociocultural Factors in Intergroup Attitudes, a Cross National Comparison," *Journal of Conflict Resolution* 2 (Jan-uary, 1958), pp. 29-42.

would expect, Pettigrew found significantly higher antiblack prejudices among the students in racist South Africa. Yet their F scale scores indicated no higher degree of authoritarianism than their American counterparts. Pettigrew also found no difference in F scale scores between Northern and Southern individuals in the United States. Nevertheless, white Southerners carried significantly more antiblack prejudices than did the typical Northerner. Pettigrew did not reject out of hand the authoritarian personality studies, yet he did indicate that conformity to local norms was a much more reliable means of getting at beliefs such as irrational prejudice. Pettigrew's findings are consonant with a number of scholars' views (such as Rudolf Heberle and Hanna Arendt) that the supporters of European Fascism were not in the main unbalanced fanatics. Even in this most irrational of movements, men join because of economic uncertainty, to gain prestige, and out of their perception of their interests far more frequently than to assuage problems of a psychological nature.

Are we then indicating that the authoritarian personality does not exist? Not in the least, only that it has limited value in understanding why the masses flock to a given rightist movement.

Still the controversy goes on. In 1958, Herbert McClosky did a study of the political attitudes and personality traits of 1,211 adults in Minneapolis. His findings?

> The extreme conservatives are easily the most hostile and suspicious, the most rigid and compulsive, the quickest to condemn others for their imperfections or weaknesses. . . . Although aggressively critical of the shortcomings of the others, they are unusually defensive and armored in the protection of their own ego needs. Poorly integrated psychologically, anxious, often perceiving themselves as inadequate, and subject to excessive feelings of guilt, they seem inclined to project onto others the traits they most dislike or fear in themselves.[26]

Again we have evidence of the linkage between personality and politics, and again (proceeding in our usual dialectical manner) we will present an argument against the linkage.

Using a much smaller sample of Texans, Alan C. Elms examined the psychological make-up of a number of local ultrarightists. Some belonged to anti-Semitic groups, some to the Christian anticommunist crusade, some to the John Birch Society. In summation, he finds that his sample of rightists

> . . . cannot be explained as a group, and often not even individually by reference to a single influence such as neurotic conflicts or the displacement of status anxieties. They must be looked at not only in the context of these relatively extreme problems but also with regard to the ordinary everyday concerns and interests of surely a majority of the population: the need to be someone recognizable, to enjoy life, to get a firmer grasp of a complex world. They must also be considered with regard to the particular social environment they inhabit—in this case the Dallas environment, which is so accepting of rightist politics that Birchism can become a simple hobby to deal with these normal concerns and interests.[27]

Again we have a seeming contradiction—McClosky finds psychological problems with his ultraconservatives, whereas Elms does not. It may be, however, that the contradiction is only a superficial one. Perhaps conservatives living in a conservative area (Dallas) are better adjusted than conservatives living in a relatively liberal area (Minneapolis).

In any case, the psychological theory is a two-edged sword, and we shall proceed to use its cutting edge on the Left.

---

[26] Herbert McClosky, "Conservatism and Personality," *Political Science Review* 42 (April, 1958) pp. 27-45.

[27] Excerpted from "Right Wingers in Dallas" by Alan C. Elms in PSYCHOLOGY TODAY Magazine, February 1970. Copyright © Communications/Research/Machines, Inc. This article is based upon portions of *The People Science: Social Psychology and Social Relevance*, by Alan C. Elms. Boston: Little, Brown and Co., 1971.

PSYCHOLOGICAL EXPLANATIONS
OF LEFTIST ACTIVITY

There is often a crisis that stimulates social theorizing, and the crisis in the America of the late 1960's had to do with the war in Vietnam and the response to the war, on the streets and in college campuses. College students during that period demonstrated, sat down, sat in, blocked military recruiters, occupied buildings, and so on.

Lewis Feuer, a professor of sociology at the University of California, a major source of student fermentation, left his post at the university with the belief that learning at the school had been severely lessened due to student activism. In 1969, Feuer produced an immense tome analyzing the left-wing student movements— *The Conflict of Generations.*[28] It is an angry book. Feuer views student activists in much the same way Hoffer viewed true believing fanaticism. What is more important to our concerns is the fact that Feuer adopted a highly Freudian analysis of student rebels.

According to Feuer, student rebels were not opting for significant political change; they were in fact acting out unresolved oedipal complexes. They were attempting to reject or kill the symbolic father who represented authority, the university, the government, the police.

> A psychological parricide had taken place on a massive social scale; the fathers were in debacle, defeat, de-authorized, floundering; the fathers confessed that their values were wrong, but only under the physical compulsion of the sons. Freud once described the guilt which followed a primal parricide. Here the parricide was psychological and compounded by the elders' own abdication.[29]

Feuer's conclusions were not based on the kind of empirical research done on the authoritarian personality; still his analysis should be taken seriously. Are student activists more in rebellion against their own families than against social institutions?

Kenneth Keniston, a Yale psychiatrist, spent the summer of 1967 intensively interviewing a small number of New Left antiwar activitists in Cambridge, Massachusetts. Keniston's resultant book, *Young Radicals,*[30] does have something to tell us about Feuer's hypothesis.

> "... perhaps," Keniston explains, "the most striking feature of these young radicals was their relative detachment, compassion, and ability to view their parents in the "round" as complex and differentiated human beings. And perhaps related to this current sympathy for their parents was a portrait of early family relationships and of family atmosphere most often characterized by parental warmth, closeness, and idealism."[31]

Keniston's study finds these socially committed radicals to be given to social action not because of aberrant psychological needs but because they are attempting to live out what they feel are their families' basic values.

> Becoming a radical, as seen in this group, involves no fundamental change in core values. To be sure, the formal political beliefs of parents invariably differ, even in the children of radical families. But each of those interviewed was brought up in a family whose core values are fully congruent with present radical activities. For example, the great majority of these radicals' parents currently applaud, approve, or accept their activities ...[32]

As we have seen, Keniston's research does not support the Feuer hypothesis concerning activism. Yet Feuer's assertions are joined by other theorists in the Freudian analysis of left-wing activities.

James Vander Zanden, an Ohio State sociologist, analyzed the early civil rights struggle in the following way.[33] His first assumption was that to be a black man or woman in the

---

[28] Lewis S. Feuer, *The Conflict of Generations* (New York: Basic Books, 1969).
[29] *Ibid.*, p. 480.
[30] Kenneth Keniston, *Young Radicals: Notes on Committed Youth* (New York: Harcourt, Brace, and World, 1968).
[31] *Ibid.*, p. 51.
[32] *Ibid.*, p. 113.
[33] James Vander Zanden, *Race Relations in Transition* (New York: Random House, 1965).

southern United States was to be placed in a situation of unavoidable hostility. The white social system was organized around rituals of etiquette designed to keep the Negro in his place and to constantly remind him of his inferiority. To survive, blacks were forced into subservient games in which they showed deference to whites while secretly feeling either latent or overt hostility toward the dominant whites. Vander Zanden quotes one psychiatric observer who maintains: "I have yet to see a Negro who did not unconsciously have a deep fear of and hostility toward white people."[34]

Vander Zanden goes on to describe the paradox of the Southern black. Not only is he in a situation where the avoidance of prejudice is impossible, he is taught by his fundamental Christianity that it is sinful to hate. The result of this situation is guilt, and Vander Zanden sees Martin Luther King's nonviolent resistance movement in the early 60's as motivated by this guilt over feelings of hostility to the white man.

> Prevailing guilt feelings caused by aggressive and hostile impulses seek satisfaction in the need for punishment. This probably accounts, in part, for the considerable premium assigned by the non-violent resistance movement to suffering. . . . [Martin Luther] King declares: "We will match your capacity to inflict suffering with our capacity to endure suffering. . . . Do to us what you will and we will still love you. . . . But we will soon wear you down with our capacity to suffer!"[35]

Vander Zanden concludes that, "At times it appears that some members engage in subtle provocations, in a masochistic fashion, whereby they expect to bring about pain and degradation; they offer their 'cheek' with the prospect of receiving a slap."[36]

Vander Zanden does not, of course, account for the genesis of the entire civil rights movement with his hostility-guilt-punishment seeking thesis. Nevertheless, he postulates it as a

basic motivation for many members of Dr. King's movement.

Was the nonviolence technique a way of seeking punishment and alleviating guilt or more simply a tactical move by people with very few resources in case of violent conflict? Stokely Carmichael, an early follower of King's nonviolent direct action, very rapidly dropped his support for nonviolence as a method. It is clear that, for him, nonviolence was a tactic rather than a principle. As for the others in the early civil rights movement, the question is still open.

One last study will end our investigation of the psychology of social movements. This is Seymore Lipset's classic study entitled *Political Man*.[37] One of the sections of Lipset's book is devoted to an idea that working class (blue collar) families are authoritarian in their child-rearing patterns, prejudices, and political preferences. Because of this authoritarianism, blue collar workers are "more likely than other strata to prefer extremist movements which suggest easy and quick solutions to social problems and have a rigid outlook."[38] For this reason, Lipset sees European workers as attracted to communist or other radical political parties rather than reformist left-wing groups. Moreover, Lipset indicates that in Sweden, higher paid workers are more likely to vote communist than those with lower incomes.

Yet in an article in the *American Sociological Review*,[39] a Swedish sociologist, Walter Korpi, takes issue with Lipset and reanalyzes his data.

> If anything, the communist workers tend to have lower incomes than the Social Democrats except for those in the largest cities. Lipset's hypothesis is also refuted when we look at the composition of Communist and Social Democratic workers with respect to degree of occupational skill. The Communists recruit their support among the unskilled workers in urban occupa-

---

[34] *Ibid.*, p. 63

[35] *Ibid.*, p. 64-65.

[36] *Ibid.*, p. 65.

---

[37] (London: Mercury Books, 1960).

[38] *Ibid.*, p. 100.

[39] Walter Korpi, "Working Class Communism in Western Europe: Rational or Nonrational," *American Sociological Review* 36 (December, 1971), pp. 971-984.

tions to a larger extent and from the skilled workers to a smaller extent than the Social Democrats.[40]

Korpi is arguing here that extreme deprivation, not authoritarianism creates extreme political choices. Korpi concludes his analysis:

> The available evidence does not falsify the assumption of rational, self interested behavior among voters basic to Lipset's theory when we come to Communist workers. Lipset's argument that workers voting for the Communist party act to receive immediate gratifications can be applied to the upper strata in a society with even greater force. Since the stratification system brings them continuous rewards, a vote for conservative parties safeguarding the maintenance of this system is a vote for continued and immediate gratification.[41]

It may seem discouraging to wind through the maze of psychological studies just mentioned; nonetheless, amidst the confusion generated by those studies, certain truths begin to emerge. The first and most basic is that social movements cannot be understood as the collective psychology of their membership. In other words, personality theory cannot give us the really important answers we need to comprehend the rise and fall of social movements.

While we may condemn some movements for their antihumanistic tendencies or praise others for their altruistic principles, it would be dangerous and unwise to attempt to understand any group through abnormal psychology. Part of the difficulty here stems from our in-

ability to get inside the head of an individual to assess his true motivation. Moreover, there is a tendency in all of us to believe that if we can account for the motivation of an individual, we do not have to confront the validity of his ideas. Conservatism and socialism do have appeals to certain social classes. Yet having said this, we must deal with the ideas of government proposed by these groups. Liberalism developed through the needs of the entrepreneurial classes, yet its ideas concerning individual liberty and the like should be argued on their own merit rather than by reference to their origins.

While we have consistently argued that a social movement cannot be understood by adding up the individual personalities of its membership, we do not mean to imply that social movements do not influence or attract certain personality types.

When Robert Welch of the John Birch Society states emphatically that "... we are not going to have factions developing on the two-sides-to every question theme,"[42] he is, without a doubt, appealing to dogmatic individuals. Yet, it would be specious to say that the reason individuals join the John Birch Society is because of their dogmatism or authoritarianism. The Birch Society has definite views on economics, foreign policy, as well as other governmental functions. Indeed, a wealthy individual may perceive the Birch Society's goal as congruent with his own (that is, preserving the privileged position of the wealthy in our society).

---

[40] *Ibid.*, p. 977.
[41] *Ibid.*, p. 981.

[42] Robert Welch, *The Blue Book of the John Birch Society* (Belmont, Mass.: John Birch Society, 1961), p. 161.

CHAPTER 3 SOCIOLOGICAL PERSPECTIVES ON SOCIAL MOVEMENTS

We have argued that a psychological explanation for the development of social movements will not suffice. We cannot reduce movements to a series of personality traits that may be in individual behavior. Sociologists are prone to take social institutions or classes or, at the very least, human interaction as a unit of analysis. We will attempt in this chapter to present theories of mass action, the politics of class and status, as well as the human interaction involved in what is called the conversion process.

SMELSER'S THEORY OF COLLECTIVE BEHAVIOR

No social movement begins in a period of social tranquility and stasis. Movements, like insomnia, are born of unrest. Neil Smelser[1]

has dissected this premovement social unrest with what he calls a value added theory of collective behavior. A value added theory derives from economics where raw materials gain in value or utility when they pass through molding and refining processes. If at any point in the processing the sequence of events stops, the final product will not have its ultimate social utility. If, for example, iron is refined and blended as steel, it will still lack utility until it is molded, shaped, and combined with other material to make tools. Collective behavior, a riot, lynching, or spontaneous uprising, also depends on an elaborate series of determinants, which must take place sequentially if the collective behavior is to occur.

The determinants of collective behavior are six in number and, of course, all must operate to produce a burst of collective activity.

The first of these is what Smelser terms *structural conduciveness*—which simply means that a society holds the possibility for a given action to occur. We would not, for example, expect mass action in areas that are sparsely populated.

---

[1] Neil Smelser, *Theory of Collective Behavior* (New York: The Free Press, 1963).

33

On the other hand, urban areas, universities, and factories are densely populated. The potential for spontaneous mass action lies in those areas.

A second and more specific determinant of collective behavior is *structural strain* among values or norms in a society. Another term for this phenomenon is internal contradictions. A dynamic society like the United States is rife with internal contradictions or structural strain. In 1968, the Citizens Board of Inquiry released its findings on the scope of hunger and malnutrition in the United States. The Board found

> ... that in the wealthiest nation in the history of the world, millions of men, women and children are slowly starving ... that nutritional anemia, stemming primarily from protein and iron deficiency, was commonly found in percentages ranging from 30-70 per cent among children from poverty backgrounds ... and that the aged living alone, subsist on liquid foods that provide inadequate sustenance.[2]

In the same year the federal government diverted 35 million acres from production by paying large farmers not to produce feed and grains.

This is only the most dramatic of many structural strains in America. Others relate to the American ideal of equality of opportunity and its antithesis of institutional racism or institutional sexism.

The third determinant is the *spread of a generalized belief*. The social strain we discussed above gives rise to ambiguities in individual belief systems. This facilitates the growth of anxiety within the individual. At this point the individual may opt for a belief system (based perhaps on rumor) that certain individuals, classes, or races are responsible for the sorry state of affairs. Once this stage is reached, a mobilization of aggression toward the enemy is effected. Oftentimes, a generalized faith in the omnipotence of the cause accompanies the belief system.

In 1969 when antiwar sentiment was beginning to peak in the United States, a massive march on Washington, D.C. (estimated at over one million in size) was formed. Most in the march were content to listen to the speakers' denunciation of the war and the Nixon regime. Some, however, claimed later that they felt (emotionally at least) that they could "take over the White House and kick the war-lords out."

This hostile belief Smelser says, "involves wish-fulfillment of two sorts: (a) an exaggerated ability of the attackers to punish or harm the agent of evil and (b) an exaggerated ability, therefore, to remove the evils which have been ascribed to this agent."[3]

The next determinant is the *precipitating factor*. This may be any highly emotionalized event that serves to point up in a dramatic way the strains in the society. In the Watts riots of 1965, a patrolman attempted to arrest a black man for supposed drunken driving. Rumor spread around the black community that the patrolman had insulted and physically abused the mother of the black man. Rock throwing escalated into shooting and looting as the National Guard invaded the black community.

The fifth factor is the *mobilization of the participants for action*. This is a function of communication and persuasion of the masses that they should take drastic collective action. Here emergent leadership becomes most important. Charismatic figures urge the masses to concrete action, telling them the time for redemptive action is now and that the goals are within reach. Anxieties and tensions are politicized and translated into slogans of solidarity against the enemy, which may be capitalism, an ethnic group, elites, deviants, or any other distinguishable class of people.

The last determinant is the *failure of social control*. If, in a situation of crowd or mob behavior, the elites are divided on tactics or philosophy, social control will break down and the mass action has greater probability for suc-

---

[2] Citizens Board of Inquiry, *Hunger U. S. A.* (Boston: Beacon Press, 1968), pp. 7, 9.

[3] Smelser, *op. cit.*, p. 103.

cess. Authorities in Europe and America have, at given periods of time, winked at violence from the reactionary Right since this kind of mob activity is directed toward holding down insurgent groups or individuals. Examples of this are legion and relate to the dominance of the Ku Klux Klan in many black belt areas of the American South, or the nonpunishment of Fascist violence by conservatives in pre-World War II Europe.

Smelser's analysis of collective behavior is an analysis of potentially political behavior. That is to say, spontaneous uprisings on either the Right or Left can sometimes be translated into social movements if the collectivities of like-minded individuals persist over time, develop long range tactics and goals, and translate their anxieties into political consciousness.

It would be interesting at this point to compare the theories of Smelser with the rather less orthodox theories of Franz Fanon. To be sure, Smelser and Fanon represent polarities in their ideological perspectives. Smelser's work approaches the ideal of the value-free intellectual, whereas Fanon's work is a fiery polemic as well as an analysis of mass action. Yet both share an interest in spontaneous mass uprisings.

Fanon's best known work, *The Wretched of the Earth,*[4] is an analysis of the spontaneous violence and uprisings in the colonized world. Fanon sees the position of the native in the colonial situation as indeed one of social strain and contradiction. The native is continuously assured of his inferiority by the colonizer who exploits his labor, his women, and his land.

> The settler keeps alive in the native an anger which he deprives of an outlet; the native is trapped in the tight links of colonialism. But we have seen that inwardly the settler can achieve a pseudo petrification. The native's muscular tension finds outlet in bloodthirsty explosions—in tribal warfare, in feuds between sects, and in quarrels between individuals.[5]

In a psychological sense then, we would say that the native internalizes aggression toward himself as well as those closest to him. Violence is unavoidable in the colonial system. Later when critical incidents occur, spontaneous mass violence begins to emerge. In Smelser's terms, a generalized belief system begins to create the idea that the colonizer has committed a massive outrage. Mobilization occurs in the native community, and mass terrorism is the result. Often members of the colonizer's race are chosen at random for assassination or brutalization.

Up to this point, according to Fanon, the colonizing power has always invoked equality, community, democracy, or some other shibboleth to create a sense of fraternity between the oppressors and the oppressed. When spontaneous violence begins, the native learns to demystify these concepts, especially when repression and massive retaliation become part of the system of control. The native's belief about himself begins to change at this point also. The wish fulfillment of the native begins to sharpen. For the first time, he can imagine himself as dominant in his land. Images of revenge are spoken of among groups of men and women.

It is possible that the spontaneous uprising will be contained at this stage if the colonial means of social control (that is, force) is still effective. The leadership of the movement (and it can now legitimately be called a movement) goes underground to operate revolutionary tactics as a fish in the sea of the peasantry. In this way, Fanon demonstrates his belief that violence transforms a personal act into a mode of social revolution.

Only history can tell if Fanon's theories will prove prophetic in the third world. However, they do provide a link between the spontaneous collective behavior described by Smelser and the social movements described later in this book. It is important to remember that political goals are long-term affairs and are not achievable by spasmodic mob action. Can mob action change the self-concept of the powerless, as Fanon argues? Or is it merely a placebo to give

---

[4] Franz Fanon, *The Wretched of the Earth* (New York: Grove Press, 1968).
[5] *Ibid.,* p. 54.

the individual a moment of psychological glory? The answers to these questions are not clear, but it is probably correct to assume, as does Smelser, that at each stage of events in the culmination of collective action the possibilities for the failure of that action exist. In any case, sociology has not reached the scientific status to be able to predict the failure or success of a collective activity.

SOCIOLOGICAL THEORIES OF RADICAL SOCIAL MOVEMENTS

James C. Davies, an American sociologist, has examined the comparative revolutionary theories of Karl Marx and the French conservative Alexis de Tocqueville. Davies argues that Marx did not accept the idea of the increasing misery of the working classes entirely, and he quotes Marx to prove this point:

> A noticeable increase in wages presupposes a rapid growth of productive capital. The rapid growth of productive capital brings about an equally rapid growth of wealth, luxury, social wants, social enjoyments. Thus, although the enjoyment of the workers has risen, the social satisfaction that they give has fallen in comparison with the increased enjoyment of the capitalist, which are inaccessible to the worker, in comparison with the state of development of society in general. Our desires and pleasures spring from society; we measure them, therefore, by society and not by the objects which serve for their satisfaction. Because they are of a social nature, they are of a relative nature.[6]

In contrast to this Marxian idea of revolution occurring when the gap between the proletariat and bourgeois widens, de Tocqueville postulates the seemingly untenable idea that revolution is encouraged as situations become better. In his study of events leading to the French revolution, de Tocqueville concludes that

> ... it would appear that the French found their condition the more unsupportable in proportion to its improvement. ... Nations that have endured patiently and almost unconsciously the most overwhelming oppression often burst into rebellion against the yoke the moment it begins to grow lighter. The regime which is destroyed by a revolution is almost always an improvement on its immediate predecessor. ... Evils which are patiently endured when they seem inevitable become intolerable when once the idea of escape from them is suggested.[7]

The ideas of Marx and de Tocqueville seem to be at cross purposes; certainly the motives of the two scholars differ. Yet Davies, in his "Toward a Theory of Revolution,"[8] attempts rather successfully to synthesize the two. First, Davies makes clear his agreement with de Tocqueville's statement that societies do not revolt when they are generally impoverished. Davies cites studies such as those done at the University of Minnesota[9] in World War II, which indicated that under conditions of experimental starvation men became private in their thoughts, withdrawn in their social relations, and given to fantasy about food. It would seem that the need for individual survival overwhelms external concerns when the individual is faced with gradual extinction. We would, therefore, not expect to find a great deal of revolutionary consciousness in areas where most waking hours are devoted to simple survival.

It is Davies' view, as we have mentioned, that neither Marx nor de Tocqueville is wrong, yet neither is complete. Another student of comparative revolutions, Crane Brinton, in his classic *Anatomy of Revolution*[10] describes several similarities in the revolutionary situation. They are

[6] Karl Marx and Frederick Engels, "Wage Labour and Capital," in *Selected Work in Two Volumes,* Vol. 1 (Moscow: Foreign Languages Publishing House, 1955), p. 94.

[7] Alexis de Tocqueville, *The Old Regime and the French Revolution* (New York: Harper Brothers, 1956), p. 214.
[8] James C. Davies, "Toward a Theory of Revolution," *American Sociological Review* 27 (February, 1962), pp. 5-19.
[9] See Ancel Keys and others, *The Biology of Human Starvation* (Minneapolis: University of Minnesota Press, 1950).
[10] Crane Brinton, *Anatomy of Revolution* (New York: Vintage Books, 1952).

(1) governmental financial problems, (2) ineffective efforts at reform, (3) a desertion by the intellectuals, (4) a split in the ranks of the ruling class, (5) an increase in class antagonisms, (6) increased and, as generally regarded, unfair tax levies, and finally, (7) the emergence of a revolutionary myth.

As Davies views all these theories, he develops the idea that economic progress does precede revolutionary activities, but that sudden reversals in that progress produce anger and frustration in those who had gained hope from reforms. Davies perceives the revolutionary process as a kind of J-curve when rising need satisfactions gradually ascend and are subject to severe reversals. Davies' "Rebellion in the United States," "The Russian Revolution in 1917," and "The Egyptian Revolution in 1952" support his ideas. We should note here that the revolutions discussed by Davies are all egalitarian, unlike the fascist revolutions from above.

Although Davies does not specifically say it, we are led to the conclusion that reforming a given society is dangerous if elites in that society are not prepared to follow through on those reforms. Or, as Michael Harrington argues, social reform is a necessary prelude to revolution.

If, as Davies believes, revolution is the result of expectations outstripping social and economic change, we can conclude that it is essentially a psychological phenomenon. It is important to qualify this view with the idea that all social events are psychological and that many of the frustrations felt by collectivities of men do not lead to revolution or even collective behavior. What of the frustrated expectations of Christians who for centuries expected the imminent return of Christ? Their disappointments were on occasion real, as for example, when the Millerites sat on roof tops in ascension robes in the fourth decade of the nineteenth century waiting for the Messiah. Of this we may be sure, the frustrations of this expectation did not lead to revolutionary action. The difference between this kind of frustration and the variety discussed by Davies is that the latter involved direct economic exploitation as well as an identifiable devil to focus hostilities toward.

It has been said that social movements can function adequately without heroes but not at all without devils. A focus for hostility is a unifying force, and that unity is necessary for the long struggle involved in revolutionary change.

We can sum up Davies' position with the following quotation:

> Revolutions are most likely to occur when a prolonged period of objective economic and social development is followed by a short period of sharp reversal. The all-important effect on the minds of people in a particular society is to produce, during the former period, an expectation of continued ability to satisfy needs—which continue to rise—and, during the latter, a mental state of anxiety and frustration when manifest reality breaks away from anticipated reality. The actual state of socioeconomic development is less significant than the expectation that past progress now blocked, can and must continue in the future.[11]

Davies' position on revolution is an important one, but it is not the only current perspective on revolution or other radical social movements. Gerhard Lenski has developed the idea of status consistency to understand participation in social upheaval. Lenski sees status inconsistency as the simultaneous occupancy of a high and low status. An example would be an individual who has high status in education or income but is accorded low racial or ethnic status. Such a situation could produce a good deal of dissonance within the individual. One way to resolve this dissonance would be to change the system or institutions that produce the tension. The individual with status incongruity, or the marginal man, as E. Franklin Frazier called him, is a potential constituent for revolutionary causes. Indeed, it has been the educated black man in America who has led the struggle for racial equality.

If we were to contrast the rise and fall theory of Davies to the marginality theories of Lenski

---

[11] Davies, *op. cit.*, p. 9.

or Frazier, we would conclude that the latter theories tell us where to look for revolutions (that is, among what classes of people), while Davies' thesis gives us a rough indication of when to expect one.

In an article in *Social Forces* James A. Geschwender sums up the varying theories of revolution in a series of axiomatic statements:

> Individuals whose present socioeconomic circumstances are at a lower level than past circumstances will be aware that they have experienced a worsening of conditions and will be fearful of further deterioration. A comparison of present circumstances and past circumstances will produce dissonance . . . change oriented, dissonance-reducing attempts on the part of status inconsistents will take a rightist orientation when high ethnic status is combined with lower levels of occupations or income; they will take a leftist orientation when high educational status is combined with a lower level of occupation or income.[12]

We have discussed, in a cursory way, the social conditions that make for revolutionary change in a society. How are we then to differentiate revolution from reform or even the so-called palace coup? It is obvious that reform calls for less sweeping changes than revolution. In a sense, however, this begs the question of which areas are important to social and political change: tactics? Perhaps it is true that reformers more often than not favor working through the existing political system for change. Nonetheless, many violent political confrontations in Latin America have come and gone, leaving the society much as it has always been. The use of violence is not the total prerogative of revolutionists. The history of labor relations in the United States is filled with violent men who wanted not a revolutionary society or an end to capitalism but simply a secure job, an end to scab labor, or a union shop.

If violence is not the differentiating factor between revolutionaries and reformists, what is the difference? Basically, we would argue, it lies in the degree of mobilization of the masses of people. Many successful reforms have been effected without great commitment by the masses. The case is different with a successful revolution. In this case the masses must be mobilized to overturn the elites and to make basic institutional changes. In a reformist situation, elite and wealthy influentials such as the British Tory Socialists create policies in social security, preservation of the environment, and the like. The British Fabians, another elite and educated group, were very instrumental in British labor reform. The problem of revolutionary change is of a different magnitude. Consider Mao Tse-Tung's exhortations to his revolutionary cadres:

> The mobilization of the common people throughout the country will create a vast sea in which to drown the enemy, create the conditions that will make up for arms and other things. . . . To win victory, we must persevere in the War of Resistance, in the united front and in the protracted war. But all these are inseparable from the mobilization of the common people. . . . What does political mobilization mean? First it means telling the army and the people about the political aim of the war.[13]

Revolution, then, tries to politicize the masses in an intensive way. In order to create a new institutional order of things, indoctrination of the common folk is crucial. Revolutionaries have had varying successes in their attempts to politicize the consciousness of the masses. As Chè Guevara found to his dismay and ultimate demise, a peasantry even in a miserable state of affairs is not automatically a revolutionary force.

To be sure, a revolution such as the Russian experience has made drastic changes in the institutional life of its citizens, especially in economics. However, the Russians have been more reformist than revolutionary in their attitude toward the institution of the family. Failing to mobilize the masses, the Russians have acquiesced to the traditional system of marriage, their

---

[12] James A. Geschwender, "Explorations in the Theory of Social Movements and Revolutions," *Social Forces* 46 (June, 1968), p. 480.

[13] Mao Tse-Tung, *On Protracted War* (Peking: Foreign Languages Press, 1967), p. 49.

only changes being a secularization of the marriage and divorce procedures.

The relationship between reform and revolution is in fact a complex one. Sometimes reforms are used to prevent revolution; in other cases they have paved the way for deeply radical change. Many political scientists have argued that most revolutionary movements, of necessity, shift to reformist goals after a time because of the natural inability of the masses of people to remain mobilized over time. History will prove or disprove this thesis.

PROCESSES OF COMMITMENT
TO MOVEMENTS

It is true that humans come into the world little more than a tabula rasa or empty slate in a social sense. Certainly no one was born an Anarchist or a Republican. The world is interpreted for all of us by those who have gone on before us. Hans Toch has described the process by which the child becomes ideologically indoctrinated into the religious and political beliefs of the parents.

First, as Toch points out, the child is vulnerable to the beliefs of the parents because

> . . . the child's early view of society is one in which the godlike figures of his father and mother tend to loom immensely large. . . . The most casual remarks of parents in this context can easily acquire the weight of infallibility.[14]

Moreover, Toch cites the dependence of the child on adults and the child's realization that conformity is necessary to survive adult demands, as reasons for the child's acquiescence to an adult belief system. Finally the child identifies with his parents; that is to say, he uses them for role models. As Adorno and others indicated, bigotry derives partly from the child's perception of authoritarian parents.

These are all reasons why the child falls "naturally" into the belief system of his parents. It is true enough that in times of social stability children do tend to accept their parents' beliefs as "the way the world is."

Why is it that some generations of the young do not follow the beliefs and tendencies of their parents? Karl Mannheim offers a partial answer to this question in his famous essay on the sociological problem of generations.[15] Mannheim shows that, regardless of the careful indoctrination each generation gives to the next, a certain social location is endemic to any generation. Put another way, each generation has a new enemy to fight and a new set of problems to confront in a dynamic society. It is easy to see that the builders of the nineteenth century communal experiments had a different set of tasks than those who followed them. The dream of one generation sometimes became the constrictive prison of the next.[16] Another case in point would be the revolutionary; he may spend his entire life attempting to gain power, whereas the tasks of the following generation may revolve around the tasks of maintaining power, creating (or fighting) new bureaucratic structures. It is clear that a different style is required to maintain a society than to create one. This is why even careful indoctrination of children by their elders does not result in the child's becoming a perfect replication of the parent. We mention this not to dispute Toch's contentions but to place limits on them.

Of course, Toch points out that transmission of a point of view to children is not the only way to maintain a movement. Individuals are also converts to movements either in a subtle or dramatic sense of the word. Usually the period of conversion to a movement is a gradual, almost imperceptible sequence of attitudinal changes. The true believer, as outlined by Hoffer, is an interesting exception to the rule.

---

[14] Hans Toch, *The Social Psychology of Social Movements* (Indianapolis: The Bobbs-Merrill Co., 1965), p. 111.

[15] Karl Mannheim, *Essays in the Sociology of Knowledge* (London: Routledge and Kegan Paul Ltd., 1952).
[16] See Ron E. Roberts, *The New Communes,* especially "Early Communitarianism in America" (Englewood, N. J.: Prentice-Hall Inc., 1971).

Annie Besant, for instance, turned from self-flagellation to organized atheism, and migrated through Malthusianism, feminism, socialism, and theosophy. Her writings include "On the Deity of Jesus of Nazareth," "My Path to Atheism," "Why I am a Socialist," "Why I Became a Theosophist," "Occult Chemistry," and "Self-Government for India." [17]

As we pointed out earlier, social movements are not composed chiefly of fanatics looking for a cause. Most individuals are placed in a situation where they are psychologically susceptible to the appeals of a certain group. "What matters," Toch shows, "is that the person feels walled in, irrespective of objectively specifiable alternatives. He perceives the workaday to be closed, and he therefore looks for a way out. He is motivated by a feeling of futility and despair." [18]

As Toch correctly points out, the social movement offers the individual a collective solution to his or her individual problem. Toch sums up the situation nicely: "When a person resorts to a social movement for the solution of a private problem, his actions have inescapable social consequences. To the extent to which he participates in the collective effort, he changes society as he changes himself." [19]

Let us try to sum up some of the sociological perspectives on social movements. Remember that none of these theories postulates a special personality type to be associated with any social movements. To the contrary, sociologists postulate that certain universal needs, felt in all humans, contribute to the genesis of social movements. As we shall show later, social trends such as industrialism, imperialism, and bureaucratization disorient and intensify anxiety within the individual. In specific terms, individuals confronted with these trends frequently fear for their livelihoods, their families, their physical or mental health, as well as their traditions.

Often when these essentials are threatened, men and women resort to collective behavior, mob behavior, insurrection, or spasmodic violence. Collective behavior is often a prelude to the sustained action we call a social movement. We are most likely to find social movements among people who have found recent progress in their economic or social standing threatened as well as in individuals who occupy contradictory statuses in their society. While it is true that many individuals are "born into" social movements, it is equally true that attitudinal change and conversion commits many others. Conversion is usually gradual and occurs when a psychologically susceptible individual confronts an ideology that promises to solve his personal problems in a social and political way.

---

[17] Toch, *op. cit.*, p. 123.
[18] *Ibid.*, p. 23.
[19] *Ibid.*, p. 85.

CHAPTER 4 COLLECTIVE NONMOVEMENTS AS OPTIONS

We have discussed the social trends that uproot individuals from folk society, economic security, or even emotional security. Yet we find that while many individuals' lives have been drastically changed by bureaucratization, imperialism, or industrialization, many, perhaps most, individuals do not opt for the changes represented by social movements. It appears that other options compete with movements that have as their aim the transformation of labor and property relationships. For to participate in a movement means to struggle for political power. The game of politics, especially in a time of crisis, may involve sacrifice, compromise, boredom, and commitment. Not all are willing to pay these prices, especially when the possibilities for winning a political struggle may seem remote. Moreover, political goals are finite, and often the accomplishments are rescinded after they are achieved.

Some solutions to social contradictions are personal, such as excessive drinking or drug use. R. D. Laing argues that schizophrenia is a possible option for the individual placed in an insoluble social dilemma.[1] We will not discuss here all the personal options for facing social strain. Some of the options are creative; some are tragic. Suffice it to say that individual modes of coping with social crises often lead to loneliness and despair.

It is of some interest to explore several collective nonmovements open to individuals who may find themselves victims of the "progress" of industrialization, bureaucratization, or imperialization. *A collective nonmovement refers to a social or collective solution to a problem which does not attempt to influence the labor or property relations of a given society.* Stated another way, collective nonmovements depend on psychological reorganization rather than social change to solve social problems.

---

[1] See R. D. Laing, *The Divided Self* (London: Penguin Books, 1970) for his argument on family life and schizophrenia.

JESUS PEOPLE

A case in point is the Jesus movement (or in our terms nonmovement) in the United States and Europe in the early 1970's. Any description of the turmoil in the United States during this period would probably understate its extent, with drugs, war, riots, and sexual upheavals leading the list of conflicts. For some of the precocious young, the Jesus movement with its simple philosophy, its emphasis on warm emotion and its other-worldliness seems to be the answer. The Jesus movement is not generated in the main by established churches. In fact, the faddish aspects of the Jesus movement ("Honk if you love Jesus") irritate the sensibilities of establishment theologians.

Frederick Elkin describes the faith of the Jesus people as well as the fundamentalist beliefs of their forefathers in the following:

> God exists and watches over us . . . we should have faith in him and not be afraid. . . . If you have faith in God and live according to his word, all will be well in the world. There will be no bitterness between an employer and an employee, between a husband and his in-laws, between a policeman and a citizen, and presumably, between one nation and another. With such faith and a good life, a son will not try to worry his mother, a pregnant woman will bear her child without difficulty, and perhaps even a defective automobile starter will begin to work properly.[2]

One of the perspectives of large segments of the Christian faith is an individualistic attitude toward morality. Ernest Campbell and Thomas Pettigrew[3] found in a study of Little Rock ministers during the racial desegregation crisis that few were able to speak to the issue of racial conflicts since most saw their tasks as involving condemnation of individual sins such as drinking or adultery. Social issues were regarded as controversial as well as threatening to the unity of the church.

Many of the young in the Jesus movement have come to perceive issues such as war, poverty, and racism in an individualistic perspective as well. All are seen as resulting from inadequate individual morality. This is diametrically opposed to the views of most of the egalitarian movement activists described in this book. To them, social problems are caused by systematic inequities in the institutions of society. Often members of egalitarian movements attribute war, oppression of women or blacks, and chronic poverty to economic exploitation or bureaucratic structures. Inequality, in this view, must be attacked before social evils can be alleviated.

This is not so for members of the Jesus movement. In a nationally distributed newspaper circulated by the Jesus people, the author attacks a fellow minister who made a plea for a redistribution of wealth.

> We are already trying that and have been for years. Does he want more of it? Does he not know that in the countries where the most effort has been made to redistribute the wealth, we find the greatest poverty and the least freedom. What does it matter if the top one-fifth controls forty percent of the wealth if they can and do use it more effectively to produce more wealth than would be the case if the wealth they have were distributed to the poor? It isn't how much a man owns, its what he does with it that means weal or woe for society. . . . Redistribution of wealth, therefore, cuts off production at both ends of the spectrum.[4]

This statement appears closer to the ethics of the National Association of Manufacturers than Jesus' saying, "Woe unto you that are rich for ye have received your consolation."[5] The Jesus people oppose other egalitarian movements as well. In another issue of the Jesus peoples' newspaper, a critique of the Women's Liberation movement is given.

---

[2] Frederick Elkin, "God, Radio and the Movies" in Bernard Rosenberg and David White, editors, *Mass Culture* (New York: Free Press, 1957), p. 310.
[3] Ernest Campbell and Thomas Pettigrew, *Christians in Racial Crisis* (Washington: Public Affairs Press, 1959).

[4] Howard Kershner, "Wants Revolution But Lacks Goal," *For Real* (June, 1972), p. 10.
[5] St. Luke 7:24.

The thing with the radical feminists is that they're not satisfied with being equal with their husbands—to be under his arm to be protected and near his heart to be beloved. The new breed is the Women's Lip Movement shooting off at the mouth for headship to rule over all male chauvinist pigs. What's a chauvinist pig anyhow? [6]

Ethnic movements are also non grata in the eyes of the Jesus people. In *Student Action,* another publication of the Jesus people, a former activist in the Chicano movement describes his disaffiliation with activism as he became associated with the Jesus people.

I began to involve myself in the activities of the movement. I studied leaders: Ché, Castro, Mao, Marx. I tried to follow these leaders. I had to put everything into practice, which meant trying to get the young Mexican-American people to rebel. Brown power became very important to me. It satisfied my ego. I could do anything I wanted. Now I was demanding things and sometimes I didn't know why I asked for them. . . . Then last year I found Christ. . . . I asked Christ into my life because I didn't have anything to lose. When he came into my heart, I finally saw the Mexican movement, the ego tripping, and the booze parties for what they were. . . . Many Mexican-American students are being misled into a revolution they know nothing about. They really don't know their leaders or, in many cases, what they are protesting. They just participate in the walk-outs, protests and name calling that are being used to get what the movement needs to change the system. [7]

It is important at this point to understand the ideological differences between the salvation-oriented religious groups and egalitarian social movements. The crux of the matter is that both aim at social improvement by different means. The unit of concern for the salvation-oriented groups is, as we have mentioned, the individual. The ideal in this way of thinking is to revitalize the individual personality through religious experience while ignoring the human and corruptible institutions of politics and economics.

This view is well stated in the pop-religious song, "If we all just lit one little candle, what a bright world it would be."

The result of this attitude is generally a conservative view toward institutional change. Egalitarians involved in social change argue, of course, that institutions, not isolated individuals, shape the life chances of the masses of individuals and that problems such as war, unemployment, or other threats to human existence are best corrected by institutional change.

Two other factors separate the social activists from the salvation-oriented religions. The first is that members of many religious sects perceive egalitarian social change as a threat to a mystical and spiritual view of life. If, indeed, the inner world of the spirit is the true one, social experimentation can only drain off energy from spiritual concerns. Hence, it is better to play one's socially assigned role without bitterness or rebellion. Billy Sunday, the most popular Protestant preacher of the World War I era in America, was not an advocate of changes in the role of women:

All great women are satisfied with their common sphere in life and think it is enough to fill the lot God gave them in this world as wife and mother. I tell you the devil and women can damn the world, and Jesus and women can save it. It remains womenhood today to lift our social life to a higher plane. [8]

If social experimentation is harmful to the spiritual side of man, it is also seen as futile by those with a messianic viewpoint, for to them the age of man is nearly finished on the planet. Billy Graham identifies many evils of the world today as cited in Biblical prophecy. They are unfortunate, he believes, but as inevitable as the end of the world.

These are apocalyptic trends, marked by the war, famine, pestilence and death that we know so well are riding around the world at this very moment. Time . . . may give us ten years, a hun-

[6] David Kerby, "Turn On, Tune In, Drop Out," *For Real* (May, 1972), p. 4.
[7] "Mexican Americans Set Free," *Student Action* (no date given).

[8] William T. Ellis, *Billy Sunday: The Man and His Message* (Philadelphia: The John C. Winston Co., 1914), p. 229.

dred years, a thousand years; but it may also give us only a day, a week, a month. It may well be true now "that this generation shall not pass, till all these things be fulfilled." . . . All of history is moving toward that climactic day when all enemies shall have been put under His feet and Christ shall have been crowned. . . . In that day war and strife shall cease. Sin and want shall be no more. In that day sorrow and pain will be unknown.[9]

As we shall see later, the messianic view of life does not preclude political or even revolutionary activities. The medieval Anabaptists and more recent nativistic movements are cases in point. Nonetheless, the messianic view can function as an alternative to a social movement in explaining social discord and personal unhappiness. Moreover, unlike most political activity, it offers a guarantee of success, an appeal that is well-received by those with rigid cognitive functioning.[10]

COUNTERCULTURALISTS

Many ideas compete for the allegiance of youth in the United States and Europe. Some mystical ideologies such as astrology, transcendental meditation, Yoga, and Hari Krishna are modish on university campuses where awareness of the social situation has led to despair rather than action. As we have stated, individual modes of adaptation to distressing social change have often been found. D. H. Lawrence's reaction to the dehumanization of industrialism was that man's and woman's salvation lies in the celebration of the sex act. Other forms of personal salvation, as we have mentioned, are less happy—drugs, alcohol, or other forms of chronic suicide.

Another collective response (as opposed to an individual one) to social disorder and personal contradiction can be found in the Bohemian or

Counterculture vs Hardhat. (From *The Nation*. October 26, 1970, by permission.)

countercultural communities. It is important to realize that so-called deviants have always banded together for mutual protection against a hostile society. In Europe and America, groups of Bohemians such as artists, writers, and other "unappreciated" intellectuals gained a kind of collective identity on the left bank of Paris or in Greenwich Village in New York. For the most part, counterculturalists such as the Beat generation of the 1950's were apolitical. They, like those of an orthodox Christian point of view, saw the world as a hopeless place full of hypocrisy. For the Beat generation and for many of the counterculturalists who followed, it could be said that "opium is the opiate of the people."[11] Ingesting forbidden drugs was seen as a personal negation of bourgeois society. So also was interracial sex, strange dress, and a near patois of the English language.

Later counterculturalists, such as the Provos of the Netherlands and the Yippies of the United States, did exhibit a good deal of political consciousness. This is not to say that they used electoral or even revolutionary (in the traditional sense) techniques.

---

[9] Billy Graham, *Peace With God* (Garden City, New York: Doubleday and Company, Inc., 1953), p. 215.
[10] For an analysis of the "dogmatic" individual, see Milton Rokeach, *The Open and Closed Mind* (New York: Basic Books, 1961).

---

[11] This statement is attributed to Richard Kaplan.

Basically, the avant-garde young were committed to the idea of cultural revolution and revolt through deviant life style. When one adds the actions of those dropping out of the system (just as one adds the personalities of those experiencing religious conversion), revolutionary changes occur.

In an article in the *Berkeley Barb,* a West Coast publication, counterculturalists explain the mentality as well as the tactics of the Hippie nonmovement.

> Almost anyone over thirty-five, as Dr. Dylan said, couldn't be trusted. You knew only too well the concessions, the lies, the crimes they had committed in order to be where they were. . . . So we left, dropped out, lit up our pipes and popped our acid. There was nothing left to do. So few seemed to understand, so many were afraid of losing that air-conditioned life of luxury without feeling in the wasteland of America called the suburbs.
>
> People's minds, it seemed, had been destroyed by too many words, their values too destroyed, their fears too great. We were waiting, trying to live out the time until it was all over. Until we could just forget and somehow live in a world too horrible to endure any longer. Yet we pumped the nation full of acid, pot and what have you. We created a new perspective, new forms, a new culture; a clear-cut tribute to the decadence and horror of the America we refused to take part in. . . . America had become a nation of scared individuals believing that they were insane with desires and feelings that must be suppressed in order to conform. Conform, conform, in your heart of hearts and obey. What other choice was there? The question created us and we created a choice.
>
> There would probably be no Haight-Ashbury without the war and perhaps the antiwar movement would not have reached the cold brutal turning point from disobedience and submission to rebellion and violence had there been no hippies, the pre-hippies, hippies, and past hippies who marched, got arrested, sang, screamed and cried; who philosophized, ignored the law and were pushing all the time. Hippies are more than just people who walk down Haight Street with beads, bells, long hair, stoned on drugs. They are a concept, an act of rejection, a militant vanguard, a hope for the future.[12]

[12]"From the Haight," *Berkeley Barb* (October 26, 1967).

That Hippies represent an act of rejection of the mainstream of American culture there can be no doubt. The question that remains is, is that act of rejection a political one? Put another way, is the Hippie nonmovement a threat to the powers that be or is it a force, which like other trendy fads, will be co-opted into the commercial status quo? Not long after this defense of the Hippie nonmovement was made, faded blue jeans were sold at the largest department stores in America and Europe, long hair for men was no longer outré, and fraternities as well as communes became centers of drug use. With the Hippie nonmovement as well as with the Jesus people nonmovement, the question is still open as to whether they will change the old regime. It is, of course, possible that America will continue to function despite individual dropouts. In fact, with automation producing more and more of the goods and services for the great masses, it stands to reason that fewer and fewer individuals will be needed to run the economy or for that matter the war in Southeast Asia. Hence, one could easily conclude that dropping out is more in the nature of an existential act than a political one.

The Hippies were only one variant of the counterculturalists in the late 1960's and early 1970's in America. Later variations on the central theme were provided by the Yippies (Youth International Party—actually a nonparty) in 1968, and the Zippies who demonsrated during the Democratic and Republican party conventions in 1972.

The Yippies, who were led by many such charismatic figures as Abbie Hoffman and Jerry Rubin, organized demonstrations and guerilla theater in the streets of Chicago during the infamous "police riots" associated with the Democratic convention. In the Chicago conflagration, the Yippies, who ran a pig for the presidency, hoped to show the masses of Americans the absurdities and contradictions in the American social system. "I believe in compulsory cannibalism," Abbie Hoffman pontificated in his semiserious way, "If people were forced to eat what they killed, there would be no more wars." [13]

In a more sedate vein, Hoffman argues for his *Revolution for the Hell of It*. The revolution put forth by Hoffman is cultural rather than political. "Cultural revolution means a disavowal of the values; all values held by our parents who inhabit and sustain the decaying institutions of a dying Pig Empire." [14]

Hoffman and the other Yippies had no programmatic statement dealing with the establishment and no traditional strategy for gaining power. A mimeographed pamphlet put out before the 1968 elections by the Yippies is a curious mixture of despair, whimsy, anger, and hope.

> Come into the streets on Nov. 5 election day. Vote with your feet. Rise up and abandon the creeping meatball! Demand the bars be open. Make music and dance at every red light. A festival of life in the streets and parks throughout the world. The American election represents death, and we are alive.
>
> Come all you rebels, youth spirits, rock minstrels, bomb throwers, bank robbers, peacock freaks, toe worshippers, poets, street folk, liberated women, professors, and body snatchers: it is election day and we are everywhere.
>
> Don't vote in a jackass-elephant-cracker circus. Let's vote for ourselves. Me for president. We are the revolution. We will strike and boycott the election and create our own reality.
>
> Can you dig it: in every metropolis and hamlet of America boycotts, strikes, sit-ins, pickets, lie-ins, pray-ins, piss-ins at the polling places.
>
> Nobody goes to work. Nobody goes to school. Nobody votes. Everyone becomes a life actor doing his thing, making the revolution by freeing himself[from] the system. Ministers in the streets. Thousands of kazoos, drums, tambourines, triangles, pots and pans, trumpets, street fairs, firecrackers—a symphony of life on a day of death. L.S.D. in the drinking water. . . . Stall for hours in the polling places trying to decide between Nixon and Humphrey and Wallace. Take your clothes off. Put wall posters up all over the city. Hold block parties. Release hundreds of greased pigs in pig uniforms downtown.
>
> . . . On election day let's pay tribute to rioters, anarchists, commies, runaways, draft dodgers, acid freaks, snipers, beatniks, deserters, Chinese

spies. Let's exorcise all politicians, generals, publishers, businessmen, popes, American Legion, A.M.A., F.B.I., narcos, informers.

> And then on Inauguration Day, January 20, we will bring our revolutionary theater to Washington to inaugurate pigasus, our pig, the only honest candidate, and turn the white house into a crash pad. They will have to put Nixon's hand on the Bible in a glass cage. . . . Every man a revolution! Everyone group a revolutionary center! We will be together on election day. Yippee! [15]

A few Yippies did congregate on the streets of a few major cities in the United States. Yet little notice was paid to the Yippies, except for the U. S. Justice Department, which proceeded to prosecute Hoffman, Rubin, and several others for conspiracy. Unlike the fabled walls of Jericho, the United States did not crumble at the sounds of the Yippies' trumpet. The war in Vietnam persisted along with the continued ghetto existence of blacks in cities. In short, the problems that generated the Yippie spasm remained after the demise of Yippie tactics.

BLACK CULTURAL NATIONALISM

Other groups see a reality greater than the traditional political one. Like the Jesus people and the Yippies, groups of Black Nationalists have gravitated to the idea that collective change is not at base political in the traditional sense. Ron Karenga, the black leader of the U. S. organization, believes that collective black pride is a more important goal than political achievement.

> For Karenga, culture takes place over everything else. He maintains that for Black people, blackness is their ultimate reality, as the ultimate reality for whites is their whiteness. To his way of thinking the black freedom struggle is a fight for the right of self determination, race pride and the pursuit of blackness. [16]

Karenga sees part of the liberation of black people as the development of black art forms, communality of dress with African robes, dashi-

---

[13] Abbie Hoffman, *Revolution for the Hell of It* (New York: Pocket Books, 1970), p. 183.
[14] *Ibid.*, p. 3.

[15] From a mimeographed pamphlet.
[16] Robert L. Allen, *Black Awakening in Capitalist America* (New York: Anchor Books, 1970), p. 166.

kis, and afros, as well the attempt to develop a positive mystique about the idea of blackness. He does not propose basic economic changes save for the idea that black people should supplant whites in institutions.

Huey Newton, Minister of Defense of the Black Panther Party and ideological rival of Karenga, criticized the nationalist position in the following statement:

> Cultural nationalism, or pork chop nationalism, as I have called it, is basically the problem of having the wrong political perspective. It seems to be a reaction instead of responding to political oppression. The cultural nationalists are concerned with returning to the old African culture and thereby regaining their identity and freedom. In other words, they feel that the African culture will automatically bring political freedom. Many times cultural nationalists fall into line as reactionary nationalists.
>
> Papa Doc in Haiti is an excellent example of reactionary nationalism. He oppresses the people but he does promote the African culture. He is against anything other than black, which on the surface seems very good, but to him it is only to mislead the people. He merely picked out the racists and replaced them with himself as the oppressor. Many of the nationalists in this country seem to desire the same ends.[17]

Not all nationalism is purely cultural, as we shall later show in our discussion of imperialism. Yet, refusal to reorganize property and labor arrangements is a possible option for nationalists. To the degree that Black Cultural Nationalists fail to specify economic reorganization, they mirror aspects of the Yippies or Jesus people. Stated another way, these nonmovements view man as an essentially noneconomic creature; for this reason they attack other than economic institutions.

Another way to view the phenomena we have discussed is to examine Herbert Blumer's concept of expressive movements.[18] Blumer sees expressive movements as resulting from the social disorganization and contradictions in the life of an individual. The expressive movement according to Blumer is characterized by intense intimacy and esprit de corps. Further, individuals are drawn to these "movements" because of the emotional satisfaction and exaltation they receive from group activities. Collective feelings are projected onto symbols of power. The result of all this is a great emotional catharsis along with little or no sociopolitical change.

It is not difficult to perceive that Blumer is discussing what we are terming collective nonmovements. We would add to his analysis two other characteristics of the nonmovements. First, nonmovements are characterized by charismatic leadership, that is, leaders who are accorded special powers of persuasion. They are in this sense dynamic and not given to long-term organization. For this reason, many collective nonmovements have little direct effect on the larger society. Then, too, the idea that the individual can be fulfilled immediately by certain actions (for example, being saved, freaking out, or thinking black) may assuage the tension needed to build a lasting social movement. In other words, if the nonmovement is successful in reorganizing the ego structure of the individual, he or she may see little reason to change the world. Inner peace may supplant the need for struggle in the political world.

We are not suggesting here that social movements do not attempt to reorganize the innards of their membership. Quite to the contrary, many successful movements have attempted this. Of special interest is the Marxist concept of the new socialist man or the sabra of the Israeli kibbutz. In both of these cases, social movements attempted quite consciously to develop noncompetitive but self-directing individuals who had collective concerns merged with their self-interests. Techniques such as mutual criticism were used along with indoctrination to accomplish this task. Other political groups, such as women's liberationists, attempt through consciousness raising techniques to actually change psychosexual personality characteristics while attacking the political problems of women's oppression in a male-dominated society.

---

[17] *The Movement*, (August, 1968).
[18] Herbert Blumer, "Social Movements," in A. M. Lee, editor, *New Outline of the Principles of Sociology* (New York: Barnes and Noble, 1951), pp. 199-220.

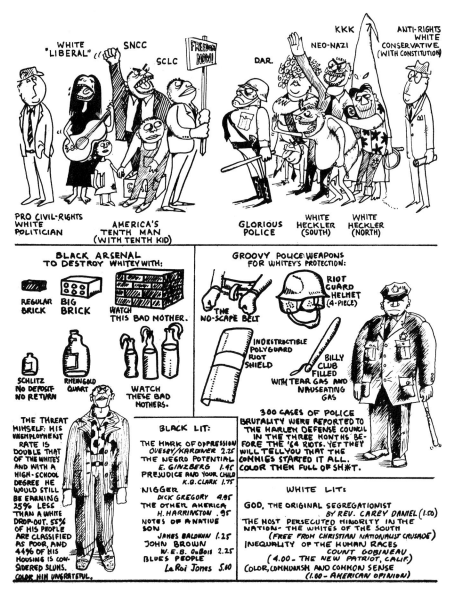

A satire on the racial conflict of the 1960's in America. (From *The Realist*, no. 72, December, 1966.)

These techniques represent attempts to change the lives of individuals while working on institutional change. Other social movements ignore individual change, but to do so invites betrayal of their ideals. It is true, for example, that socialist man has not yet been created in the U.S.S.R. Members of social movements can learn much from the techniques of collective nonmovements about individual change. It may also be fair to assume that members of collective nonmovements should investigate institutional analysis before they reject it out of hand.

PART TWO
TRENDS AND SOCIAL MOVEMENT TENDENCIES

It is not the purpose of sociological science to discover, or rediscover, solutions, since numerous problems of the individual life and the life of social groups are not capable of "solution" at all, but must ever remain "open." The sociologist should aim rather at the dispassionate exposition of tendencies and counter-operating forces, of reasons and opposing reasons, at a display, in a word, of the warp and woof of social life.

Robert Michels

The point has been made previously that social trends—industrialization, urbanization, secularization, politicalization, democratization, and so forth—create new collectivities. These collectivities, in turn, help to further changes in the trends. Many lists of trends have been developed by scholars (Table 1). Becker and Barnes say that the most dominant one is the shift from a sacred view of the world to a secular one.[1] Nisbet says that modernization, or the historical conflict between traditionalism and modernism, is the leading trend: "The conflict is one between two sets of dialectically opposed values: on the one hand, hierarchy, community, tradition, au-

thority, and the sacred sense of life; on the other hand, egalitarianism, individualism, secularism, positive rights, and rationalistic modes of organization and power."[2] Weber sees the dominant trend of our times as the process of rationalization, that is, social change as the shift from traditional authority to rational-legal authority.[3] Others see urbanization, increase in political scale (planetarianization, globalization), and bureaucratization as leading trends of our epoch.

---

[1] Howard Becker and Harry Elmer Barnes, *Social Thought from Lore to Science* (New York: Dover Publications, 1961).

[2] Robert A. Nisbet, *Tradition and Revolt: Historical and Sociological Essays* (New York: Random House, 1968), p. 4.

[3] Hans Gerth and C. Wright Mills, editors, in *From Max Weber, Essays in Sociology* (New York: Oxford University Press, 1946). More on this in Chapter 4 on Bureaucracy.

TABLE 1. CONCEPTS OF SOCIAL CHANGE

LABELS OF SOCIAL PROCESS TRENDS AND TENDENCIES	LABELS OF COLLECTIVE RESPONSE GROUP ACTIONS
Modernization	Retribalization
Civilization	Primitivization
Industrialization	Revitalization
Mechanization	Revolution (Revolt)
Bureaucratization	Reform
Secularization	Restoration
Urbanization (sub-)	Reparation
Alienation (dis-)	Repatriation
Rationalization	Relief
Politicalization	Recovery
Colonialization (de-)	Reaction
Globalization	Rebellion
Planetarianization	Riot, Insurrection
Imperialization	Repression
Democratization	Reorganization
Oligarchization	Arbitration
Militarization (de-)	Compromise
Development	Negotiation
Nationalism	Coalition
Internationalization	Protest
Disorder	Dissent
Decay	Withdrawal
Progress (re-)	Boycott
Desanctification	Strike
Unionization	Reconstruction
Pacification	Insurgency (counter-)
Decline	Resistance
Evolution	Redevelopment
Diffusion	Regulation
Formalization	

MASTER TRENDS

One list that has bearing on our perspective is by Gerth and Mills, who see the "master trends" of the twentieth century as: (1) The coordination of political, economic, and military orders toward interlocking bureaucracies; (2) the buildup of a centralized, interdependent bureaucracy that puts stress on the individual when world breakdown yields mass unemployment and insecurity; (3) the decline of liberalism (the style of thinking that assumes a friendly universe of equal and open opportunities with men born free and equal)

because of its incongruity with the modern social facts of mass unemployment, impoverishment, and the closing of various kinds of frontiers by imperialism; and (4) changes in character structure in a polarized world between the greatest land power, the U.S.S.R., and the greatest industrial and naval power, the U.S.A.

> Regardless of the enormity or institutional diversity and psychological types, the trend with the widest scope and the most far-reaching ramifications is the *industrialization of the world* [italics added].[4]

These four master trends of Gerth and Mills offer us a departure point for the choice and discussion of our selected trends and movements. And the previous quote brings out the very real social context in which we as writers must operate—the industrialization and militarization of the world by two super-powers whose decisions influence the framework of the master trends of industrialization, bureaucracy, and cultural imperialism as an increase in political scale. Every major social movement in the world today flows from the involvement of these two nation-states within these trends, both when they operate in consensus and when they are in conflict. For the first time in history, these super-powers have brought forth an international cold war as the world decolonializes, anticolonizes, and reconstructs itself after two world wars and a world depression. It is in the "best interests" of these sovereign powers to develop policies of containment for all third world revolutions among allies, captives, and neutrals. And with their various doctrines and international intelligence agencies, they are able to speak softly and carry rather big sticks—whether they are in the Berlin of 1948, the Suez of 1956, the Cuba of 1961, or the Vietnam of 1972.

It is not the purpose of this book to analyze these two super-powers and their international control over much of the world. But we must

---

[4] Gerth and Mills, *Character and Social Structure: The Psychology of Social Institutions* (New York: Harcourt, Brace and World, Inc., 1953), pp. 456-476.

note their place in international industrialization, be it in the form of multinational corporations or technical aides in Africa; we must note their place in international bureaucratization, be it in the form of bureaucratic collectivism or international cartel; we must note finally their tremendous involvement in cultural imperialism or increase in political scale, be it the forces of industrial capitalism or industrial communism.

We have selected industrialism, bureaucracy, and cultural imperialism as our master trends or structural transformations. They are radical trends because they have created and are creating massive stirring, unrest, and discontent for some and tremendous affluence and power for others. These master trends, which are seemingly ubiquitous and irreversible, may be said to have both liberative as well as repressive possibilities.

Chapter 5, "Bureaucratic Trends and Antibureaucratic Movements," is analyzed in terms of its advantages and disadvantages for the new groups in the world. Antibureaucratic movements, such as student movements East and West, the Chinese Cultural Revolution, and the ecological movement, exemplify reactions to the repressive tendencies inherent in the bureau-

cratic gargoyles of objectification and abstraction of the world, alienation, goal displacement, and new concentrations of power.

Chapter 6, "Cultural Imperialism: Nativistic and Nationalistic Movements," centers on the dialectical relationship between imperialism—as the hegemony of one nation-state over another and the forceful impingement of one value structure on another—and the movements reacting to it: the revitalization movements (Ghost Dance, Cargo Cults, Africanism) and movements of national liberation (reformist nationalism and revolutionary nationalism).

Chapter 7, "The Industrial Trend: Oligarchy and Egalitarian Social Movements," deals with these repressive and humanistic possibilities around the issues of inequality, increasing deprivation, and poverty. Egalitarianism as a combination of ideology, planning, and action is seen as the master or radical international social movement in response to the industrialization of the world. Democratic planning as a major egalitarian movement against poverty is seen as having liberative possibilities or potentials because it may be in consonance with the liberative tendencies of industrialization.

CHAPTER 5   BUREAUCRATIC TRENDS AND ANTIBUREAUCRATIC MOVEMENTS

Bureaucracy is . . . all powerful and at the same time incapable of determining how its power should be used.

Ernst Van Den Haag

BUREAUCRATIC TENDENCIES

The word bureaucrat is of French derivation and was probably coined somewhat later than the term aristocrat. "Bureau" refers to office or governmental unit, and the suffix "crat" means to rule by a certain mode. While the terms bureaucrat and aristocrat are of relatively modern French origin, they are obviously not comparable in other ways. The word aristocrat may be used in a positive or negative sense, yet it would be highly unlikely that the term bureaucrat would be used in a flattering sense in today's world. For the bureaucrat today is often perceived as a rigid, humorless person lacking in creativity, efficiency, or perhaps even intelligence.

Yet, it must be said that bureaucratic positions are proliferating all over the world. In the developed nations, few youths can look forward to a nonbureaucratic career (with the exceptions of street artists, subsistence farmers, vagabonds,

or day laborers). In the nondeveloped world, the most promising young men and women often leave the security of village life for the chance to become a part of the local government or industry.

We must look at the idea of bureaucracy to understand its effects on the lives of those involved directly or indirectly in its activities.

A bureaucracy is at once both an attitude toward the world and a set of social relations. What is the bureaucratic attitude toward the world? Simply that a bureaucratic organization can utilize the untapped resources in men and materials. Bureaucracy can order or reorder nature in consonance with man's desires. Americans and Russians spoke of *conquering* space rather than living with it. Men and materials are perceived as resources in the task of reordering the world in a more rational way. The earth is no longer a magic, mystical unity; it is rather a gigantic puzzle that can be unraveled, given enough time and expertise. This process Max

Weber called the "disenchantment of the world" (Entzauberung der Welt).[1]

The hallmark of any bureaucracy is the ideal of rationality. A rational act is one that occurs when an individual rigorously defines his goals, outlines the possible means to those goals, and proceeds to choose the most efficient or productive means to an end. Usually, the most efficient means of solving large-scale social problems or conflicts involves specialization of tasks or a division of labor. We can say, then, that task specialization involves functional rationality, that is, large numbers of men and women organized rationally and with specific functions. Thus, we can say that the bureaucracy we call General Motors is functionally rational. Specialists who have undergone training in professional, skilled, and semiskilled jobs produce hundreds of thousands of vehicles for the corporation.

Karl Mannheim[2] has argued that this efficiency and specialization we call functional rationality can have negative consequences. Mannheim maintains that as functional rationality and specialization increase, substantive rationality decreases. Substantive rationality involves the ability of individuals or groups to evaluate their goals in light of other goals they hold. Thus, while General Motors can manufacture cars at an increasingly efficient rate, we must ask: do we need more cars on the highways in light of pollution, noise, increasing fatalities, and the like? The answer to this question may be yes or no, but it involves substantive rationality, and it is unlikely that those immersed in the production or sales of their product are ever in a position to make such a query.

It was Max Weber, of course, who clearly delineated the social relations in a bureaucracy. In Weber's approach, a bureaucracy is (1) "a continuous organization of official functions bound by rules"; (2) "a specific sphere of competence"; (3) "[an] organization of offices [that] follows the principle of hierarchy; that is, each lower office is under the control and supervision of a higher one"; (4) "[a set of] rules which regulate the conduct of an office . . . [through] technical rules and norms"; (5) ". . . complete separation of the property belonging to the organization, which is controlled within the spheres of the office, and the personal property of the official. . . ."; (6) "administrative acts, decisions and rules [which] are formulated in writing."[3]

Bureaucracies, according to Weber, are the result of revolutionary and charismatic movements such as early Christianity. In fact, bureaucracy is not strictly limited to economics, even though Weber usually associates it with the growth of capitalism. Churches, labor unions, universities, governmental institutions, and voluntary associations have all grown more bureaucratic in the last century.

ADVANTAGES OF BUREAUCRATIC ORGANIZATION

Perhaps the most compelling argument for usefulness of bureaucratic organization came from the classic French sociologist Emile Durkheim.[4] It was Durkheim's contention that population growth makes for such complexity in terms of human interaction that bureaucracy is needed to give order to the increasing problems of "dynamic density." Durkheim was not unaware of the problems endemic to the bureaucratic (or "organic" as he called it) organization of society. But as societies grow, more rules are needed, more administrators are needed to carry out those rules, and centralization of power is inevitable. Much human history would tend to bear out Durkheim's contention; yet there are

[1] Max Weber, *The Theory of Social and Economic Organization*, A. M. Henderson and Talcott Parsons, translators (New York: Oxford University Press, 1947), pp. 329-330.

[2] Karl Mannheim, *Man and Society in an Age of Reconstruction* (New York: Harcourt, Brace and World, 1940).

[3] Weber, *op. cit.*, pp. 329-330.

[4] Emile Durkheim, *The Division of Labor in Society*, George Simpson, translator (Glencoe, Ill.: Free Press, 1947).

some who would argue that bureaucratic centralization is not only not inevitable but is disastrous for contemporary societies. This view, as we shall see later, has been held by the proponents of the Cultural Revolution in Communist China.

A second advantage claimed by those who see bureaucracy as a blessing rather than a curse is the idea that bureaucratic organization is the only way to raise the standard of living of large masses of people. There may be more art in the work of the cobbler than in the mass production of shoes in today's factories, but no one could suggest that the number of goods produced by the old time cobbler would be sufficient for the needs of large masses of people. In places where kinship or racial loyalties blind individuals to the advantages of bureaucratic specialization and cooperation, we are likely to find a stagnant economic situation as well as great poverty for the masses.

Looking directly at specifics, we could hardly imagine adequate health care or such breakthroughs as a cure for polio or cancer without the specialized training and control of resources we call bureaucracy.

A more controversial argument is that bureaucracy is a necessary adjunct to democratic political processes. (This was especially true in the early 1970's in the United States when secrecy of crucial decision making was sanctioned for bureaucratic functionaries.) The argument here is that the will of the people cannot come to fruition without an effective civil service which can function only through an effective bureaucracy. A case in point here was the assignment of Federal Voter Registrars (bureaucrats par excellence) into the Southern United States to assure the participation of black voters in areas committed to white supremacy.

BUREAUCRATIC GARGOYLES

While most sociologists and economists would argue that bureaucracy is a necessity in some degree to modern life, few would maintain that

it is without serious ethical and political implications. The following are some of the crucial problems associated with the worldwide trend spoken of as bureaucratization.

OBJECTIFICATION AND ABSTRACTION. Bureaucrats must by definition avoid emotional decision-making. Rules govern their working lives, and rules must govern their decisions. Both men and resources are regarded as material for a long-term goal—profits, attitudinal changes, military victories, or whatever. This necessitates that the bureaucrat, whether social worker or shoe salesman, treat individuals without much relationship to their individual uniqueness. In a word, people become objectified in the bureaucratic mind as a potential profit, a potential impediment to carrying out rules, or, in the more extreme case of war, as a body to count for a successful kill ratio.

> They, the people to be administered, are objects whom bureaucrats consider neither with love or hate, but completely impersonally; the manager-bureaucrat must not feel, as far as his professional activity is concerned; he must manipulate people as though they were figures or things.[5]

In some cases, looking at an individual as an object is to be desired. (We would not have faith in a doctor who wept at the sight of broken skin.) In other cases, perceiving the individual as an object is a mere inconvenience. Yet in some situations it is boundless tragedy.

The *National Catholic Reporter* carried stories of the American air war over Southeast Asia in 1972:

> Planes drop sensor devices which can pick up body heat, urine or body smells, or footsteps. These "people sniffers" then signal computers as to the gathering of animate life. They are unable to discriminate between civilians and soldiers, children and adults, or even between human and animal life.
>
> The computers then return signals that send off bombing missions to these localities. The bombs are essentially antipersonnel weapons. They include such devices as the "pineapple"

[5] Erich Fromm, *The Sane Society* (New York: Fawcett Books, 1965), p. 116.

which explodes above the ground shooting 20,000 steel pellets in all directions. These tiny "bomblets" cannot destroy any physical target. They rip only into unarmed human flesh. The "gravel mine" looses camouflaged bombs which look like leaves or animal droppings but explode to rip off an arm or leg. . . .

The code name for one automated weapon is Puff the Magic Dragon. It is indeed a magic dragon, though it hardly makes people vanish in a "puff," but rather with terrible agony and blood. Such phrases, along with other such terminology that has proliferated in this war (i.e. "wasting" meaning massacre, or "to terminate with extreme prejudice" meaning secret assassination of political dissidents) point to the linguistic depersonalization that has mushroomed with the mushrooming of dehumanized psychology and technology, and which is designed to make the realities of the war invisible and undiscussable.

The automated battlefield is supported by hierarchies of technology; levels upon levels of aircraft, and level upon level of grids, manned by more and more remote human operators.[6]

Modern automated warfare is probably the extreme in technological dehumanization or objectification. Military professionals are separated from the consequences of their deadly acts; hence, they are easier to perform. Yet the same phenomenon on a less vicious scale occurs in many facets of an individual's life. The college instructor in a classroom of two hundred students has no way of knowing what the human results are of assigning a failing grade to the student in seat number 135. He, too, is separated from the consequences of his actions.

A problem related to objectification is Erich Fromm's rather awkward sounding term "abstractification." What Fromm means is that bureaucracies can deal only with measurable commodities. "If you can't measure it, it doesn't exist," is an extreme of this position. Things that can be measured include individual test scores, accumulations of money or debts, or physical properties. This means that qualities of humanistic import that cannot be measured with pre-

cision are often ignored in the bureaucratic framework. Aesthetics, humor, and personality differences are all given little regard in the bureaucratic mentality unless they relate to quantifiable goals.

It is interesting to observe individuals who enter art galleries for the first time. Often their only mode of communication about avant-garde art concerns its price tag. Five hundred dollars is more easily understandable than the seemingly chaotic work facing the novice in artistic appreciation. The work of art has become a commodity.

As professional sports become more bureaucratized, players are lionized by their salary scale as well as their sports performance. The extreme of this position occurs when individuals are seen as commodities for the open market. Again quoting Fromm:

> This abstractification takes place even with regard to phenomena which are not commodities sold on the market, like a flood disaster; the newspapers will headline a flood, speaking of a "million dollar catastrophe," emphasizing the abstract quantitative element rather than the concrete aspects of human suffering . . . the abstractifying and quantifying attitude goes far beyond the realm of things. People are also experienced as the embodiment of quantitative exchange value. To speak of a man as being "worth one million dollars" is to speak of him not any more as a concrete human person, but as an abstraction, whose essence can be expressed in a figure.[7]

What Fromm is expressing here can be documented in many aspects of the bureaucratic mentality when individuals, including oneself, are seen as a commodity. Consider, for example, one of the selling points of the Dale Carnegie Personality Improvement courses, "How to sell yourself to other people." Here the self of an individual is experienced as a useful commodity.

Fromm quotes two American religious leaders to show how abstractification occurs in the sacred aspects of religious experience. He first quotes Bishop Sheen. "Our reason tells us that

---

[6] Rosemary R. Ruether, "The Automated Asian Air War," *National Catholic Reporter* (April 21, 1972), pp. 11, 12.

[7] Fromm, *op. cit.*, p. 109.

if any one of the claimants come from God, the least that God could do to support his representative's claim would be to pre-announce his coming. Automobile manufacturers tell us when to expect a new model." Fromm then quotes evangelist Billy Graham as saying, "I am selling the greatest product in the world; why shouldn't it be promoted as well as soap?"[8]

When the most profound emotions, religious experiences, death, love, or beauty become abstracted or turned into saleable commodities, they become trivial. For this reason the bureaucratic mentality deeply disturbs the sensibilities of many individuals.

ALIENATION. The word alienation, like its counterpart, charisma, has been so misused that one is tempted to abandon it. News commentators maintain that young and old, poor and middle class, ethnic and native are alienated. The word begins to take on the nebulous connotations of a sick headache.

Nevertheless, the concept has a definite value in philosophy and sociology. Rousseau conceived of alienation as the ownership, formal or informal, of one human over another; Hegel saw alienation as the lack of knowledge of one's place in historical processes. But it was Marx who took the concept and related it to specifics in the social structure. When Marx used the word alienation, he implied that it was a specific kind of separation. In his *Economic and Philosophical Manuscripts of 1844,* Marx outlined three varieties of alienation. Of course, all were intrinsic to his critique of capitalism.

First, Marx believed, man is alienated from nature; that is to say that the worker is separated from the physical, sensual product of his labor. He is separated from his own creation and reordering of the world through mass production.

Second, man is alienated from himself (that is, his own activity) because as a worker he produces only for the satisfaction that his work will give to another, not for the intrinsic joy of

creation. The worker is paid in abstractions such as money rather than by the pride of craftsmanship that is an extension of the self.

Finally, according to Marx, men are alienated from other men through exploitation and the division of labor in capitalism:

> What applies to man's relationship to his work, to the product of his labour and to himself, also holds of man's relation to the labour and object of labour. In fact, the proposition that man's species nature is estranged from him means that one man is estranged from the other.[9]

Marx saw the division of labor necessary to capitalist bureaucracy as separating men from the fruits of their labor, their creativity, and their social cooperation and human exchange. We now have the benefit of hindsight, and we can see (as Marx did not have the opportunity to do) that capitalism is only one of many bureaucratic forms that can alienate the individual and produce a sense of self-estrangement. We shall return to this point later.

It is not true that all bureaucracies are equally alienating or that alienation must lead to a dramatic social movement. Yet painful boredom often symptomizes the bureaucratic endeavors on the lower levels. Daniel Bell describes it thus: "In his travel to and from work the worker is chained by time. Time rules the work economy, its very rhythms and motions."[10] Eli Chinoy comments further on the automobile workers' "slavery to the clock. . . . Its coerced rhythm, the inability to pause at will for a moment's rest, and the need for undeviating attention to simple routines make it work to be avoided if possible and to escape from if necessary."[11]

Bell quotes another factory worker: "After a few months . . . the regularity of the break and

---

[8] *Ibid.,* p. 109.

[9] Karl Marx, *Economic and Philosophical Manuscripts of 1844,* Martin Milligan, translator (London: Laurence and Wishard Ltd., 1959), p. 77.
[10] Daniel Bell, *Work and Its Discontents* (New York: League for Industrial Democracy, 1970), p. 5.
[11] Eli Chinoy, *Automobile Workers and the American Dream* (New York: Random House, 1955), p. 71.

your dependence on it as a means for destroying the day, utterly rob it of its purpose. . . . Your first break on Wednesday . . . means that you have six hours left for that day and twenty-two for the rest of the week. Not half the required forty hours is yet past and only one-fourth of Wednesday's."[12]

Alienation is not by any means confined to the assembly line. C. Wright Mills[13] described graphically the attempts by management to enhance the morale of the "cheerful robots" called white collar workers. Managerial seminars in the creation of "positive thinking" and "team effort" attest of the alienation of many in the grey flannel suit.

Robert Presthus, in a fascinating study[14] of bureaucratic operation in the military-industrial-research area, outlines three basic reactions to work in the bureaucratic milieu. The upward mobiles are individuals who strongly identify with the goals of the bureaucracy. They are on the move and their morale is high. Next Presthus describes the "indifferent" who is alienated from his work but generally contented with job security, family life, and free time. Last is the "ambivalent" whose "personality is typically an introvert, with intense intellectual interests and limited interpersonal facility."[15] The ambivalent also has difficulty in playing the contradictory roles required of bureaucrats in dealing with subordinates, superordinates, and the rest.

Alienation in a bureaucratic society does not create or impede social movements. However, alienation as a state of separation from one's self, one's labor, or one's fellow man creates an atmosphere conducive to the growth of mass movements. Bureaucracies often break up kinship relations and rob individuals of stability in other human relationships. This is especially true of capitalism in its early stages of growth, as well as, one would think, socialist organizations in newly developing countries.

GOAL DISPLACEMENT. Perhaps the most direct relationship between bureaucratic trends and the genesis of social movements has to do with one crucial fact. This is that bureaucracies, the most rational and efficient method of social organization organized by large groups of men, often lose sight of or betray their original reason for being.

As we have mentioned before, most bureaucratic organizations claim to function in the public interest. (Even certain Mafiosi have made this claim!) Nevertheless, altruistic goals have a way of becoming lost in the maze of self-interested functionaries.

Robert Merton states it well: "Adherence to the rules, originally conceived as a means, becomes transformed into an end-in-itself; there occurs the familiar process of displacement of goals whereby an instrumental value becomes a terminal value."[16]

Phillip Selznick's study[17] of the Tennessee Valley Authority showed how the original and rather radical aims of the New Deal experiment were subverted by local conservatives in its own organization. Robert Michels' famous study of radical unions and social-democratic parties in Germany showed how bureaucratization and elitism frustrated the desire for change of German laborers.[18] Seymour Lipset reports on the subversion or "cooptation" of radical populists in Saskatchewan by conservative administrators who used their power to frustrate changes initiated by the radical government.[19]

---

[12] Bell, *op. cit.*, p. 15.
[13] C. Wright Mills, *White Collar* (New York: Oxford University Press, 1956), pp. 224-238.
[14] Robert Presthus, *The Organizational Society* (New York: Alfred A. Knopf, 1962).
[15] *Ibid.*, p. 258.
[16] Robert K. Merton, *Social Theory and Social Structure* (Glencoe, Ill.: Free Press, 1949), p. 155.
[17] Phillip Selznick, *T. V. A. and the Grass Roots* (Berkeley: University of California Press, 1956).
[18] Robert Michels, *Political Parties: A Sociological Study of the Oligarchical Tendencies in Modern Democracy* (Glencoe, Ill.: Free Press, 1959) Michels' findings do not confirm the idea that unions must inevitably become elitist. For contrary evidence, see Seymour Lipset and others, *Union Democracy* (Glencoe, Ill.: Free Press, 1956).
[19] Seymour Lipset, *Agrarian Socialism* (Berkeley: University of California Press, 1950).

Bureaucrats wield power, and it is not unlikely that they wield it in line with what they perceive are their best interests. This is what Karl Mannheim calls "bureaucratic conservatism," the tendency to resist innovations in a social system that constantly requires innovation to deal with the changes created by rampant technological advance.

BUREAUCRATIC HIERARCHIES—CONCENTRATION OF POWER. It may seem more than a little paradoxical that both student intellectuals on the American Left and George Wallace on the Right had as their chief targets of criticism, bureaucrats (who, in the matchless phraseology of Wallace, "were point-y heads who didn't even know how to park their bicycles straight"). In another sense, however, the paradox is only superficial, for both the Wallacites and the students perceived of bureaucracies as systems of power—systems of power that were inimical to the perceived interests of both groups.

We have discussed at some length the internal effects of the bureaucratic social order (such as alienation), but what of its effects on those it controls in an external sense? The question we are posing here is: can individuals outside the bureaucratic echelons of power have any sense of control over their own lives? The reason that we are forced to ask this question is that bureaucracies, especially those in control of vast economic resources, seem to develop a life of their own, external to the needs of those around them.

Consider here the growing concentration of economic power in conglomerates and corporate bureaucracies in America. In 1943, Robert Brady[20] described trade associations such as the National Association of Manufacturers as a mass of bureaucratic power threatening American democracy. The trend Brady feared has not abated in recent times in the United States. Williard Mueller, a former chief economist of the Federal Trade Commission, spoke of this power in 1969:

> You may recall that I testified before this committee in 1965, should post war trends in aggregate concentration continue, by 1975 the two hundred largest manufacturing corporations would control two-thirds of all manufacturing assets. Unhappily, we have reached this level ahead of schedule. Today the top two hundred manufacturing corporations already control two-thirds of all assets held by corporations engaged primarily in manufacturing.[21]

The power of corporate elites in foreign affairs has been documented by Domhoff[22] and many others. The military-industrial complex, a blur of private and military bureaucracies, accounted for more than 20% of the manufacturing jobs in fourteen of the fifty American states.[23] The question of the amounts and varieties of military spending is a political one which need not be resolved here. The essential problem seems to be that of accountability; how are the military or industrial or university bureaucracies subject to control by those whose lives they so deeply affect? It is the feeling of some that bureaucracies are unguided missiles, with potentially deadly effect and no clear aim.

We should make it clear that bureaucratic nightmares are not the monopoly (no pun intended) of capitalism. Milovan Djilas has graphically outlined the bureaucratization and institutionalization of privilege in the U. S. S. R. In his view, bureaucrats, managers, and intellectuals have become the functional equivalents to the capitalist robber barons in contemporary Russia.

Bureaucracies can become unbelievably powerful instruments for change or for guarding the status quo. In either case, the functionally rational world of the bureaucrat is subject to attack by those who would resist his control.

[20] Robert A. Brady, *Business as a System of Power* (New York: Columbia University Press, 1943).

[21] Hearings Before the Subcommittee on Antitrust and Monopoly of the Committee on the Judiciary, United States Senate, Ninety-first Congress, November, 1969.
[22] G. William Domhoff, *Who Rules America* (Englewood Cliffs, New Jersey: Prentice-Hall, Inc., 1967).
[23] Fred J. Cook, *The Warfare State* (New York: Collier Books, 1964), p. 188.

ANTIBUREAUCRATIC MOVEMENTS

STUDENT MOVEMENTS EAST AND WEST

The conspiratorial theory of history and the outside agitator theory, both the bêtes noires of the conservative, received a healthy revival in 1967 and 1968. For it seemed that wherever one looked, campuses were ablaze (sometimes quite literally) with radical activity. Fear of the young by the old was rampant. Many older citizens of Kent, Ohio, cheered when four students were killed by National Guardsmen in a campus disturbance in 1970. Typical explanations for the student protests in the United States revolved around such clichés as communist influence, not enough discipline by their parents, or moral degeneration.

In 1965 on the Memphis State University campus, violence broke out as students protested the relatively new war in Vietnam. Rumors were circulated at the time that a helicopter of Russian design had dropped outside agitators into Memphis to, of course, agitate. Fortunately for international relations, no helicopter with Russian license plates was ever found on the Memphis State campus. One can only imagine that equally colorful explanations for student dissent in Poland and Czechoslovakia must have circulated among the Iron Curtain conservatives.

In the United States, the student movement gave a foretaste of things to come, when, in late 1964, Berkeley students organized the prototype for later groups with the Free Speech movement. The movement began in an attempt to expand the rights of students to pamphleteer and raise money for political causes on the University of California campus. Hal Draper comments:

> To some it is a mystery that the Berkeley revolt should have broken out against the "liberal"

"I don't think it's anything intellectual, dear—they're from the university."

An antistudent cartoon. (© *Punch,* March 22, 1967, London.)

administration of President Clark Kerr. . . . In his 1960 book *Industrialism and Industrial Man,* Kerr intimates quite clearly that he has been going through a process of changing his original convictions, but this does not necessarily involve any conscious abandonment of liberalism as the framework for his rhetoric. What he has been super-imposing on this framework is a newly embraced concept of bureaucratic managerialism as the social model to be accepted.[24]

We cannot examine the tortuous maze of happenings at Berkeley in the following year. They included the rise and demise of student heroes such as Mario Savio, the dirty speech movement (an unintentional parody of the Free Speech movement), political repression, violence, sit-ins, and continuing turmoil. As the student leaders perceived it, the enemy was the faceless bureaucrat, motivated only by his desire for order and power. Many other pressures were beginning to be felt on campuses at this time, including the very real fear of fighting in a war few American students supported wholeheartedly. The Selective Service, another bureaucratic apparatus, interfered with students' lives. It, like the university, was seen as an inflexible bureaucratic nightmare created as a tool *against* the young.

It is true that most students at Berkeley did not take an active role in the protest activities, although 10,000 signed a petition supporting the aims of the Free Speech movement. Nonetheless, the minority which did participate was an interesting group in more areas than its radicalism.

In a survey of Free Speech movement students who were arrested in a sit-in in December, it was found that:

> Most are earnest students of considerably better than average academic standing. . . . Of the undergraduates arrested, nearly half had better than "B" averages. . . . Twenty were Phi Beta Kappas; eight were Woodrow Wilson fellows; twenty have published articles in scholarly journals; 53 were National Merit Scholarship win-

ners or finalists, and 260 have received other academic awards.[25]

The fact that many of the students were inordinately bright does not guarantee the correctness of their political attitudes (whatever correctness may mean). What it does indicate is that highly intelligent and thoughtful students may be more aware, in an ideological sense, of bureaucratic contradictions in their lives. They are probably quicker to turn personal problems into political issues.

The rhetoric of the Port Huron Statement, the working papers for the Students for a Democratic Society (S.D.S.) in 1961, expresses the alienation of leftists in America.

> We would replace power rooted in possession, privilege, or circumstance by power and uniqueness rooted in love, reflectiveness, reason and creativity. As a social system we seek the establishment of a democracy of individual participation, governed by two central aims: that the individual share in those social decisions determining the quality and direction of his life; that society be organized to encourage independence in men and provide the media for their common participation.[26]

The idealistic humanism of S.D.S. was not to survive sectarian fights, repression, and tactical ineffectiveness. By 1969, one faction of the fragmented organization wrote of the change occurring in the increasingly embittered student radicals.

> This summer produced a different kind of energy. After a year of moving, kids were more pissed than ever . . . action has generally been short and tight. . . . It's been a time to tighten up, hang into groups, feel that tension mounting inside. . . . In Chicago the war is coming home . . . over 2000 people rallied outside the Federal Building, marched to Grant Park . . . storefronts and pig wagons were stoned. In the resulting fights fifteen people were hospitalized, ten of the pigs, eighteen people were busted, thirteen of whom are S.D.S. people who have been organizing in Chicago for the National Action.[27]

---

[24] Hal Draper, *Berkeley: The New Student Revolt* (New York: Grove Press, 1965), p. 16.

[25] *Ibid.,* p. 14.

[26] From the pamphlet: "Port Huron Statement" (prepared for the most part by Tom Hayden), 1961.

[27] *New Left Notes* (October 2, 1969), p. 1.

In their anger at the bureaucratic structures of American society (the military, the government, and huge corporations), some S.D.S. youth moved from nondogmatic and nonviolent positions to the mindless "trashing" of store-windows in Chicago. By 1970, S.D.S. was no longer an important force in the American student movement.

S.D.S. had perhaps reached the pinnacle of success in the 1968 Columbia University student strike. Columbia, an academically superior school, was not noted for its political activism. Yet by the spring of 1968, it was to symbolize the conflicts between student and establishment. Two events provided a catalyst for the student uprising in the Ivy League school. The first was the exposure by some students of clandestine ties between the University and the military arm of the federal government. The Columbia *Spectator* reported that the university was and had been affiliated with the Institute for Defense Analysis and that secret military research was being carried on by the Institute on such topics as "Chemical Control of Vegetation in Relation to Military Needs." A later report by Columbia graduate students indicated that 46% of Columbia's total budget came from government contracts and that about one fourth of this consisted of classified defense contracts. This indicated to the students that Columbia was clearly not an institution free of political interference. Goal displacement had occurred. (Students were prone toward stronger language.) Many began to associate their university's efforts with the hated war in Vietnam. Trouble was imminent as demonstrations concerning the issue began to take place. To compound the situation, Columbia students became aware that the university wished to construct a new gym in a city park used primarily by residents of Harlem. Both black and white radicals saw this as exploitation of the black community.

"*Us they call 'The Fuzz.'*"

A middle-class view of the student movement. (© *Punch,* October 28, 1968, London.)

Direct actions began to take place, some of which were rather zany. In March, students who were attending a lecture on "The Student and the Draft" carried toy guns around the room and sang military tunes. The Colonel addressing the students was suddenly hit in the face with a lemon meringue pie (a sweet "blow for freedom" for the student dissidents).

More important actions were also occurring at Columbia. A dean was held captive in his office when he refused to negotiate student demands; black students occupied Hamilton Hall; the Low Library was "liberated" by whites; and right-wing counter protesters surrounded the occupied buildings to prevent food and supplies from reaching the activists.

> It wasn't all grimness and torment of course. In Fayerwether (another occupied hall), a couple got married during the occupation. For the Low occupiers, it was funny enough just to be living in Grayson Kirk's inner sanctum. The same hardened revolutionaries who had smashed the doors to enter Low, at first hesitated to move his furniture—they might scratch it![28]

Finally, after several days of fruitless negotiation, the police broke into the occupied buildings and arrested more than seven hundred students, many of whom were bloodied in the dragging-out process. The police invasion of the campus radicalized many of the liberal and moderate students. A highly successful student strike was called, and for the remaining school year, Columbia was essentially closed.

James Kunen, who kept a diary of his participation in the Columbia affair, expresses here a mixture of confusion, fatalism, commitment, and resentment.

> Monday, July 8, Back at Columbia I went to a class at the Strike Committee's Summer Liberation School. . . . There was one oldish man in the class who features "hierarchial" society and manages to talk about it no matter what the subject is supposed to be. . . . Two good ideas of his:

do away with "post no bills" signs so people could put up their ideas on walls, and likewise make a page in every newspaper available for anybody to write anything he wants, not subject to the selection of the editors.[29]

> Tuesday, July 9, It makes me feel quite sad. I mean, I'm an American, and look at what my country is doing. And I can't seem to do a thing about it, or anybody else. We've gone into the streets, and we've gone to Washington, to the Pentagon, and what good does it do? You work in politics and you win the people to your side, and what good does that do? I'm about ready to give up.[30]

By Friday, July 19, Kunen's anger had overwhelmed his fatalism and he was warning the establishment:

> Think twice before you pour your stinking bloody money into more weapons because people are hungry and we won't let you. We need good schools and houses for people to live in and it could be done and we're going to make this country do it. We've had it up to here with you and you don't have much time left, man. . . . You're playing with fire and fire burns baby. I mean this. I mean it well. Hear me: you're going to get human or your stinking bodies are going up against the wall. I don't get mad easily but I'm mad now and I'm going to stay mad until things change.[31]

Kunen's diary ends ambiguously, as did the Columbia strike. Some compromises were struck; the institution stayed intact, and it continued to be a bureaucracy among bureaucracies in modern America.[32]

WEST EUROPEAN STUDENT REVOLTS

Perhaps the most significant of all the student uprisings in 1968 took place not in America,

[28] Barbara and John Ehrenreich, *Long March, Short Spring: The Student Uprising at Home and Abroad* (New York: Modern Reader, 1969), p. 136.

[29] James Simon Kunen, *The Strawberry Statement: Notes of a College Revolutionary,* Copyright by Random House, Inc., New York, pp. 93-94.
[30] *Ibid.,* pp. 94-95.
[31] *Ibid.,* p. 111.
[32] Columbia students did a great deal of research on the power structure of the university, showing relationships between administrators and trustees of the university and large corporations. This was printed as a pamphlet, "Who Rules Columbia?" It tended to reinforce the radicals' contention that the university was only a bureaucratic adjunct to a national power elite.

A French student cartoon celebrating liberation for the young, the homosexual, and women.

but in France. It was the Sorbonne, the international symbol of academic excellence which triggered a crisis that for a time threatened to topple the government of General de Gaulle. Tension had been rising in the student community for some time, and if American students were frustrated by insensitive bureaucratic universities, the French had even more cause for frustration. From 1960 to 1964, the number of students attending the university increased by

64

60% with no increase in faculty staffing.[33] The overcrowded classrooms were packed, many with professors merely reading their own textbooks to the students. Some students bought copies of the professor's lectures and stayed home.

Then, too, students at the Sorbonne are among the most politically active in the world, with Maoist, Castroite, Trotskyist, and Anarchist philosophies competing for dominance. Small student organizations (les groupuscules) that organized to protest the examinations, which were administered impersonally, set the destiny of the students' careers. External issues such as the Vietnam War and the economic system further frustrated the students, but the examinations were the focal point of the protest.

> Exams [the activists argued] were the mainstay of the University's oppression and manipulation of the student. Exams give the student their number, their price tag for the outside world. Exams force students to regurgitate the ideological nonsense their professors have pumped into them. With exams, they said, the University undertakes its primary act of violence against the autonomy of the student's existence.[34]

By April and May of 1968, student action had escalated to confrontations with the "flics," the Parisian police. Stephen Spender witnessed the preparation for the conflicts.

> The street battles which took place near the Sorbonne in mid-May between students and police were ritualistic. In late afternoon, while it was still daylight, the students started building barricades. Those I saw on Friday were particularly elaborate. First they tore up paving stones and piled them up as though they were rebuilding memories of 1789, 1848, 1870. . . . Then they scattered over the paving stones and among the leaves, boxes, wood, trash. . . . Lastly . . . they tugged, pulled with much rumbling, neighbouring parked cars . . . and placed them on their sides, like trophies of smashed automobiles by the

sculptor Cesar, on top of the paving stones among the branches.[35]

Real violence came on May 10, the "night of the barricades," as hundreds of students were bloodied in confrontations with the police. The police regarded any young person in the Latin Quarter as an enemy and beat and arrested the young without discrimination. It was at this point that many powerful leftist labor unions began to support the demands of the students. Unlike the American scene where students and workers had viewed each other as aliens and enemies, the French worker and student did communicate in May and found several areas of agreement. The one word that symbolized an attractive goal for both student and worker was the idea of *autogestion,* which translates roughly into English as direct self-government. Workers' councils would control factories; student organizations would administer universities.

Of course, many differences in life-style did separate student and worker. While workers wanted more material goods ("Le Communisme, c'est le luxe pour tous"),[36] students tended to regard materialism as a moral corruption. Revolution was to be spontaneity, communication, love, and personal freedom. Nevertheless, while the students were occupying the Sorbonne and Nanterre, workers seized the Sud-Aviation plant near Nantes; moreover, workers at two Renault factories seized their buildings.

A pamphlet distributed by the National Union of Higher Education put forth the radical students' hopeful views:

> The University struggle and the mass political struggle that has been grafted on to it have strongly promoted . . . the aspiration for an entirely new society. . . . In such a society, the surplus wealth derived from social production would be devoted not to the consumption of new commodities that only differ from the old ones in nature and not in function, but to social investments: health, edu-

---

[33] Ehrenreich, *op. cit.,* p. 75.
[34] *Ibid.,* p. 79.

[35] Stephen Spender, *The Year of the Young Rebels,* Copyright by Random House, Inc., New York, 1968, p. 39.
[36] "Communism means luxury for everyone."

cation, and art are among the most important of these. The necessity for specialization in work will be replaced by the possibility of learning and exercising several trades in one lifetime, and not just in terms of economic needs but by the free choice of the individual.[37]

Even as intense conflicts between students, workers, and government continued, many observers reported that students were not totally embittered by the struggle. When one student was asked what his political philosophy was, he replied, "Je suis Marxiste, tendance Groucho!"[38]

The student-worker dreams of *autogestion* were not to come to fruition. The powerful Communist party of France, which had originally supported the students, withdrew its support to allay further violence, and squabbles between student factions lessened their momentary unity. Most importantly, de Gaulle promised some university and economic reforms and united the bourgeoisie behind him as he won a smashing victory in new general elections.

The German student movement began to ferment at about the same time as the French and American. Most of the radical activities centered around the Free University of Berlin, a new institution created after World War II. The university was to be an experiment in faculty-student cooperation, but as time progressed the faculty became less attuned to student suggestions; concurrently, the student body was becoming radicalized. Some leftist speakers were banned from speaking at the campus, which generated demonstrations. Of course, German students were attuned to world events and protested their government's relationships (indirect though they were) with the Vietnam War and apartheid in South Africa. Coincidentally, the vanguard of the German student movement was the S.D.S. (Sozialisticher Deutscher Studentenbund); it had no ties to the American organization of the same initials.

In Germany in 1967, the S.D.S. and other leftist student organizations organized massive protests (20,000 strong) against the war in Vietnam and against the visit of the Shah of Iran. At a reception for the Shah, eggs and tomatoes were thrown. The police were called in, and one student was killed—shot in the head. Of course, students throughout Germany were outraged, and massive protests followed. The next year, on April 11, Rudi Dutschke was shot in the head and nearly killed by a rightist assassin. Dutschke, or Red Rudi as he was called, was the most famous of the New Left leaders in the country. The activist students' rage was directed toward the rightist newspapers of publisher Axel Springer. In 1968, Springer controlled nearly half the newspaper circulation in West Germany.[39] The antistudent biases of his news accounts had always touched a raw nerve with university people. As students occupied buildings in the manner of their French or American confreres, others began burning Springer newspapers and overturning delivery trucks. Political repression of the students was not long in coming, for the students were widely disliked by their middle-aged countrymen who were shocked at their flamboyant life-style. Also, since the students had little support from organized labor, they were increasingly isolated in their position.

EAST EUROPEAN STUDENT REVOLTS

In postwar Poland, the students began to mirror the Western students. The issues, of course, were different and the social structure quite unlike that which Western students fought against. In 1956, Polish students and workers had stood shoulder to shoulder in their confrontation with Soviet Russians in a futile attempt to increase their country's autonomy. In the early 1960's, the Gomulka regime, a hard line foe of liberalizers, began to use repression to quiet intellectuals who had demanded more freedom of

---

[37] Quoted in Herve Bourges, *The French Student Revolt: The Leaders Speak,* B. R. Brewster, translator (New York: Hill and Wang, 1968), pp. 94-95.
[38] "I'm a Marxist in the manner of Groucho."

[39] Ehrenreich, *op. cit.,* p. 40.

expression on political, aesthetic, and philosophical matters. One of the dissidents, a young philosophy professor named Leseck Kolakowski, was dismissed from the Communist Party for his outspoken defense of other dissenters. Several students at the university who had signed petitions and open letters against the curtailment of freedom of speech were expelled in 1967.

Adam Michnik, one of the students, was a powerful figure in the official Communist Youth Organization. His expulsion triggered mass activity:

> The big student demonstrations began March 8, when 1,500 assembled in the University of Warsaw courtyard to protest the arrest of Adam Michnik and Henryk Szlajfer for having led the demonstrations against the banning of *Dziady* [a liberal publication]. The students demanded the release and reinstatement of their two comrades and shouted "Long live the writers!" and "Long live Czechoslovakia."
> These demonstrations were at first orderly. Then the regime organized groups of club-carrying civilians, later described as "Party Activists," to break up the demonstrations.[40]

Finally special militia units were sent onto the campus. George Weissman comments:

> As has been the case in country after country, the savagery of the specialists in police brutality infuriated the whole student body and brought tens of thousands of students into the fighting, which erupted onto the streets and spread throughout the city.... Rapidly, solidarity actions by students spread throughout the country. Protest meetings were held in Lublin, Gliwice . . . and Wroclaw. In Pozman, Gracow and Katowice, demonstrators clashed with police.[41]

At the polytechnic school in Warsaw, the students held an American style sit-in. In the end, of course, the students could not hold on to their occupied buildings. More repression was in store for demonstration leaders, many of whom were accused of having Trotskyist or even

Zionist leanings. What did the students of Poland really desire? Basically what Western students wanted—an end to bureaucratic elitism not of the capitalist, but of the socialist variety.

Jacek Kuron, one of the student leaders, criticized his society in this way:

> The decisions of the elite are sovereign and made without consulting the workers or the rest of society. Neither the workers nor the mass of the party members can influence these decisions.... We shall call this autocratic, party-state ruling elite, which on its own makes all key decisions of national importance and all political and economic decisions, the central political bureaucracy.... Disorganized though ordinary party members may be for any attempt to sway the decisions of the bureaucracy, they are well organized by party discipline for carrying out the tasks assigned to them. Anyone who balks is expelled.[42]

Students in Poland were not alone in their desire for change. In October of 1967, students in Prague protested when a series of electrical failures (nearly nightly) interfered with their studies. Their protest was stopped with the official violence of the police. This, of course, served to focus the students' attention on the injustices of their society. Stephen Spender interviewed a number of Czech students:

> The story they told was of the growing dissatisfaction of the more critical minded members of the University with the governmental organization for Czechoslovak Youth (CSM) . . . later on it became simply the youth branch of the centralized party bureaucracy transmitting the orders and propaganda of the party.... Resistance to the CSM and to the party showed in the emergence of various organizations in the University.[43]
> . . . when we talked they were modest about the role of the students in the liberalizing movement. They said that they had acted in defense of their positions as students, and not aggressively. It was censorship, bureaucracy, centralization and sheer boredom with the CSM which had finally brought them to the position where they found they were criticizing the regime.[44]

---

[40] George L. Weissman, editor, *Revolutionary Students in Poland Speak Out 1964-1968*, Copyright © 1968 by Merit Publishers, reprinted by permission of Pathfinder Press, Inc., p. 5.
[41] *Ibid.*

---

[42] *Ibid.*, p. 18.
[43] Spender, *op. cit.*, p. 68.
[44] *Ibid.*, p. 71.

As we have seen, students on both sides of the imaginary iron curtain have reacted in remarkably similar ways to bureaucratic domination. In a strategic sense the student movements ended, temporarily at least, in defeat. Russian tanks ended the Czech rebellion, and the National Guard has ended several student revolts in America. It would seem that youthful idealism and bureaucracy are not compatible paths. It would seem that the two forces will be in dialectical conflict for the forseeable future.

THE CHINESE CULTURAL REVOLUTION

In 1966, events in Communist China perplexed Western observers. A massive upheaval was in process and the nature of that turmoil was not clear. The Cultural Revolution, which had its most violent period from 1966 to 1968, was a complex phenomenon not easily disposed to analysis. Isaac Deutscher saw the revolution as a pathological outpouring of xenophobic chauvinism mixed with a purge like the one that followed Stalin's take-over of postrevolutionary Russia. The Red Guard, which led the Cultural Revolution, was described by Deutscher in this way:

> . . . they have acted . . . in a hooligan-like manner, stopping any debate, and muzzling any criticism of the Maoist line. This has led to a senseless attack and humiliation not only of the party cadres but also of the old revolutionary intelligensia. . . . In the name of Marxism—Leninism, Shakespeare, Beethoven, Balzac are denounced as a specimen of bourgeois degeneration.[45]

Deutscher is correct that antiforeign ideologies did prevail in many quarters during the revolution. This is only a minor effect of the turmoil, nonetheless. To understand the cultural Revolution we must understand first, that it, like the other movements described in this chapter is youth-oriented and antibureaucratic in char-

acter. However, it differs from other student movements in two crucial ways. First, it did have massive consequences in changing the power structure of the society, and second, it was supported by the dominant political force in society, Chairman Mao Tse-Tung himself.

John Lewis sees the revolution in this way:

> Clearly the view held in Peking . . . is a mixture of a Maoist emphasis on mass spontaneity and ideological uniformity combined with enforced order and organizational control. . . . Mao wished to destroy a party linking a well defined structure, the principle of working-class leadership and the role of technical expertise and replace it with a revolution of the poor and blank. . . . By attaining even partial success he has broken the concentration of power at the top and in the hands of bureaucratically oriented cadres.[46]

Joan Robinson sees the conflict in 1966, as between rightists and those who wished for permanent revolution. Who were the rightists? Those who, in postrevolutionary China insisted

> . . . on the need for organization and authority [according to their argument]. Every army and every industry in the world is run on the basis of a chain of command from the top downwards. That those in a higher grade in the hierarchy should have a more comfortable standard of life than those below is . . . desirable since it adds prestige to authority. The workers need tutelage; obedience and diligence are required of them; they are none the better for having their heads full of political wind. The task of industrialization must be carried out fast. It is nonsense to wait till the mass of the population are educated. We must build up a corps of managers and civil servants; that means we must draw upon the old lettered class, even if they were landlords or reactionaries in the past.[47]

In a word, the rightists were bureaucrats who worked to quell revolutionary fervor and get down to the business of organizing Chinese

---

[45] Isaac Deutscher, *On the Chinese Cultural Revolution* (London: Bertrand Russell Peace Foundation, 1967), p. 16.

[46] John Wilson Lewis, *Party Leadership and Revolution in China* (London: Cambridge University Press, 1970), p. 27.

[47] From Joan Robinson, *The Cultural Revolution in China* (Baltimore: Pelican Books, 1969), p. 16. Reprinted by permission of Penguin Books, Ltd.

society along the lines of postrevolutionary Russia.

It was at Peking University where the Cultural Revolution first became a dramatic reality. For on June 1, 1966, a poster was put up attacking the rightist tendencies of the head of Peking University. The movement quickly spread to several other educational institutions as well as factories, where leaders were criticized via poster. University administrators at one university cut off electricity and shut down the students' canteen. Within a month, however, the principal of Peking University had been dismissed.

More important, or course, was Mao's reaction to the events. On August 8, he put up his own poster entitled "Bombard the Headquarters" which stated in part: ". . . some leading comrades from the central down to the local levels . . . have . . . [adopted] the reactionary stand of the bourgeoisie, they have a bourgeois dictatorship and struck down the surging movement of the Great Cultural Revolution of the proletariat. . . ."[48]

At Peking University, the genesis of the movement, round the clock discussions by students involved such issues as getting rid of elitism and bureaucracy. Some of the proposals of the revolutionary students were as follows:

. . . a certain amount of time each year should be devoted to taking part in factory or farm work, military drill and class struggle in society.

In teaching methods, the stress should be on self-education and discussion. Teachers should give adequate tutoring, practice the democratic method of teaching, follow the mass line, and resolutely abolish the cramming method of teaching. . . .

From now on, the colleges should enroll new students from among young people who have tempered themselves in the . . . great revolutionary movements . . . and not necessarily just from these who have been through middle school. This will enable great numbers of outstanding workers, former poor and lower-middle peasants,

and demobilized army men to be admitted to college.[49]

More than two million of the Chinese young involved themselves in the Red Guard movement, which dedicated itself to weeding out rightists and bureaucrats from power. Armed with Mao's words "Rebellion is justified" (surely the only time in history such words have been emitted from the absolute ruler of a country), the young invaded factories, offices of civil servants, and schools with their revolutionary messages. Sometimes violence broke out, as in the summer of 1967 in Shanghai. There also was an occasional disruption of production. Yet Robinson reports a 10% increase in agricultural production from 1966 to 1967.

The symbol of bureaucratic conservatism, Liu Shao-Ch'i, was officially President of China and second in command to Mao. He was constantly held up to scorn by the Red Guard and in 1967 was under house arrest. Liu was called what the Red Guard felt was the ultimate insult —"the Chinese Khrushchev."

The position of the Peoples' Liberation Army is of some interest to us because the military is usually the ultimate in hierarchical and bureaucratic organization. Peng Teh-Huai, the Minister of Defense until 1959, attempted to model the Chinese army after the Soviet model with an orthodox chain of command. Lin Piao changed the character of the military radically:

. . . there are no badges and no permanent ranks. . . . All eat, sleep, and study the thought of Mao Tse-Tung together. . . . The soldiers run farms to feed themselves and go out to help the commune members when they are short-handed. The old guerrilla tradition, that the Army are fish swimming in the waters of the people, is cherished more than ever.[50]

Robinson relates the story of a young man who enlisted in the Peoples' Liberation Army with the expectation of learning important skills

[48] Ibid., p. 80.

[49] Quoted in Victor Nee, The Cultural Revolution at Peking University (New York: Monthly Review Press, 1969), p. 69.
[50] Robinson, op. cit., p. 32.

since he was literate. He was instead, to his shame, placed on a pork farm to raise pigs for the army's needs.

> The political officer got him to read "Serve the People" and talked it over with him. He learned to feel that there is no low or high in service. He came to love his pigs; he saved the life of one that was sick by nursing it day and night. When his girl friend came to visit him, the first thing she asked was what work he was doing. Putting on a solemn air, he said: My work is very onorous and very honorable; I am serving the people by minding pigs. She laughed: Why are you so pompous? Why don't you say simply that you are working in the piggery? I don't believe that you have read "Serve the People."[51]

The Peoples' Liberation Army supported Mao and his young revolutionists in their struggle to restructure society for permanent revolution. In the main, the Red Guard was successful in challenging the basic framework of Chinese institutions. It is true that wild episodes such as the burning of the British Chancellory in Peking in a burst of anti-foreign frenzy did occur on occasion. Yet most dispassionate observers do not now look upon the Cultural Revolution as an outbreak of collective violence.

What is to be learned from the events in China? Perhaps most importantly, that revolutions do not automatically end bureaucracy as Marx had predicted.

Beyond this, the Cultural Revolution forces us to confront the basic issue of whether continued bureaucratization is an inexorable law of history. As we have suggested before, most Western sociologists from Durkheim and Weber to the present have argued that bureaucracy and increasing specialization in a chain of command is the wave of the future. The Chinese advocates of the Cultural Revolution argue that this does not have to be. Professors can spend mornings doing stoop labor, lecture in the afternoon, and attend political or militia meetings in the evening. Common laborers can philosophize

concerning Mao's *Little Red Book,* do farm work, and learn to administer political cadres. Thus the lines are clearly drawn, and since this book has no pretense at futurology, we will not predict either the early decline of bureaucracy or its timeless existence.

"ECO-FREAKS" AND SPACESHIP EARTH

As we have stated earlier, the bureaucratic organization is probably man's greatest weapon for controlling or manipulating people or other natural resources. As man has learned, the ecological balances of nature are infinitely complex and fragile. With industrial development, balances of nature have been ripped apart, with sometimes disastrous consequences. We cannot list the effects of smog, air, and water pollution, and depletion of resources here. The question is sometimes posed as to whether the ecology problem is an aesthetic one (Don't be a litterbug) or one dealing with the basic issue of man's survival. It is, of course, both. The villain in the ecological dilemma is sometimes seen as the egocentric individual, sometimes the economic system such as capitalism or technology itself. The fact is, as John Kenneth Galbraith has noted in his *The New Industrial State,* that socialist countries can do more adequate social planning because of their centralized control of the economy. Yet economic institutions in Russia, as in the United States, often develop goals that are not always best for the society as a whole. In Russia, Galbraith maintains

> Full social authority over the large enterprise is proclaimed. Like that of the stockholder and the Board of Directors in the United States, it is celebrated in all public ritual. The people and the party are paramount. But in practice, large and increasing autonomy is accorded to the enterprise.[52]

Galbraith is telling us that productive enterprises, even in socialist countries, develop goals

---

[51] *Ibid.,* p. 34.

[52] John Kenneth Galbraith, *The New Industrial State* (Boston: Houghton Mifflin, 1967), p. 107.

such as increased efficiency, production quotas and so forth; often they, like the huge capitalistic conglomerations, fail to take note of the ecological consequences of their activities. Murray Bookchin argues:

> From the standpoint of ecology, man is dangerously over-simplifying his environment. The modern city represents a regressive encroachment of the synthetic on the natural, of the inorganic (concrete, metals, and glass) on the organic, of crude, elemental stimuli on variegated, wide ranging ones. . . . The simplification process is carried still further by an exaggerated regional (indeed, national) division of labor. Immense areas of the planet are increasingly reserved for specific industrial tasks or reduced to depots for raw materials. Others are turned into centers of urban population. . . . The point is that man is undoing the work of organic evolution. By creating vast urban agglomerations of concrete, metal, and glass, by overriding and undermining the subtly organized ecosystems that constitute local differences in the natural world . . . man is disassembling the biotic pyramid that supported humanity for countless millennia.[53]

Bookchin is telling us that bureaucratic concentrations of economic power, in whatever form, are a threat to life on the planet. This, of course, is a highly controversial point of view. Yet when a steel company finds it more efficient to dump wastes in a river, or a foundry finds it more profitable to polute the air than to filter it, there can be no doubt that concentrations of economic power (with their massive political influence) do represent a real threat to continued human existence of the planet.

Implicit in all our discussions of social movements thus far is that a social movement represents a group of people acting in what they believe are their best interests to change power relations in a given society. It is perhaps obvious to a peasant who sees hunger, disease, and exploitation all around him to organize against these problems. Yet the problems associated with the destruction of the environment are usually of a more subtle nature, unless a major catastrophe occurs such as the floods in West Virginia in 1972 caused, in large part, by strip mining.

Most people are content to, in the words of Voltaire, "cultivate one's own garden" with little concern about destruction of the biosphere. Some groups, however, are an exception to this rule: scientists, conservationists, and other concerned citizens have formed movements in the United States to combat despoliation of the environment.

Groups such as the Sierra Club, Friends of the Earth, the Environmental Defense League, and the Environmental Action Committee fought industrial interests in the United States. The fight was an uphill one at best, since corporate lobbyists contribute the lion's share of financing to many influential politicians. Of course, war increases ecological disasters. In South Vietnam, the defoliant Agent Orange, together with napalm and strafing, has left nearly one fourth of the land barren.[54]

Thus, the problem of creating a livable environment would seem to be a huge one, for the movements do not at present have mass support. In addition, cleanup of the environment interferes with profits. In 1971, *Fortune* magazine, a spokesman for a large segment of the business community, was led to say with some degree of relief, "Some of the hysteria about ecology has died down."[55]

This may have been more in the nature of wishful thinking by *Fortune*'s editors, since "eco-freaks" were busily plotting schemes to control the increasingly polluted environs of the United States. The tactics of the conservationists and ecologists were threefold: (1) educational, (2) political, and (3) direct action. Those concerned with preventing ecological destruction were further divided along ideological lines. In the United States, radicals argued for an abolition of capitalism as requisite to a habitable

---

[53] Reprinted from Murray Bookchin, *Post Scarcity Anarchism* (Berkeley: The Ramparts Press, 1971), pp. 65, 67.

[54] John Lewallen, "Ecocide: Clawmarks on the Yellow Face," *Earth* (April, 1972), pp. 37-43.
[55] *Fortune Magazine* (November, 1971), p. 62.

earth. Far more numerous were reformist groups who depended on pressure group tactics to fight on an issue by issue basis. Finally, there were those who dropped out of the technological society to live in a primitive, almost tribal communal setting. Bill Wheeler, guru of a large communal group in Northern California, discusses the communard's faith in individual morality by reorganizing society on a subsistance-level communal basis:

> Voluntary primitivism could only evolve within an economy of abundance, such as the United States today. . . . It proposes a synthesis of the technologically sophisticated life style with a voluntary return to the ancient tested ways—living close to God's nature and in harmony with the elements.[56]

It is common knowledge that most Americans would never cut their technological advantages to the point of the young communalists. For the ecology-minded, the most promising routes to curb earth-pollution seemed to be political and reformist. In California in 1972, a referendum was placed on the ballot by nearly 500,000 signatures. If passed, it would have created: ". . . a swift phaseout of all lead in gas, a ban on any new state leases for off-shore oil drilling, a five year moratorium on nuclear power plant development . . . a ban on the use of any persistent chlorinated hydrocarbon, such as DDT."[57]

The People's Lobby pushing the referendum in California faced the state Chamber of Commerce which poured several million dollars into a blitz media campaign to dissuade Californians from voting against corporate interests. Still, the People's Lobby planned to continue their tactics to "get the facts before the people."

Moreover, the political reformers were not without their victories. The American Super-sonic Transport plane (S.S.T.) was defeated in the Congress in 1970 due in large part to the efforts of the ecology-minded groups who had argued and lobbied against the environmental effects of the proposed project.

Beyond the respectable ecology activists, individual terrorists attacked rampant technological progress with a vengence. Some put pebbles, sand, and epoxy in the air conditioning units of new and (by the activists) unwanted shopping centers. Some put liquid metal in parking meters. And in a semi-tongue-in-cheek ceremony in Washington, D. C., an "ecotage" contest was held by those engaged in a relentless attack on rampant progress and despoliation of the environment. Winners of the contest, who wore black masks, were the "eco-commandos" of Miami Beach, Florida.

> Among other things, they had staged a raid on six sewage treatment plants and two motels in the Miami vicinity, dropping "bombs" of harmless, but long lasting yellow dye at the plant and motel discharge points to show where Miami's sewage really goes.[58]

The struggle goes on. Seemingly it is a struggle involving man against machine, but in reality it is a struggle of the unorganized to become organized and to confront the unresponsive institutions called bureaucracies.

We cannot judge here whether bureaucracies deserve the attacks made on them by students, politicos, communards, and conservationists. We can only say that bureaucracies will continue to exert dominance over the lives of individuals and that the internal "needs" of bureaucracies, such as growth and expanded use of resources, often conflict with the very people they are to serve. We can feel safe in saying, as did Max Weber a half century ago, that the future will be a dialectic of increasing bureaucratic control and increasing movements to resist that control.

---

[56] Quoted in Ron E. Roberts, *The New Communes: Coming Together in America* (Englewood Cliffs, N. J.: Prentice-Hall, Inc., 1971), p. 51. An analysis of other communal groups' relationships to the technological society is given here also.

[57] John Lewallen, "Grand Mix Meets American Pie," *Clear Creek* (April, 1972), p. 53.

[58] Karin Sheldon, "Eco-Commandos Win Golden Fox," *Clear Creek* (April, 1972), p. 17.

ON THE POSSIBILITIES OF HUMANIZING BUREAUCRACIES: AD-HOCRACIES AND WORKERS' COUNCILS

It would be wrong to leave the study of bureaucratic trends and antibureaucratic movements without asking a final utopian question: How is it possible to humanize bureaucratic structures and to make them responsive to human needs rather than elite's fiats?

First, it is necessary to point out that some of the antibureaucratic movements described in this book (especially the student movements) have failed because they were never able to convince the public that there are satisfactory ways of meeting human needs without bureaucratic institutions and planning. It has been said that, given the choice between tyranny and anarchy, most individuals would opt for the safe but oppressive form of tyranny.

Yet, given the opportunity to choose between working and functioning in alienating, dehumanizing bureaucratic forms and in yet unborn alternatives to the system, who can say that workable alternatives would not be chosen? What, then, could we consider a human alternative to the bureaucratic forms discussed in this book?

First, our hypothetical institution would accept, as does bureaucracy, the need for planning and rationality. Mysticism and a feeling of awe for the universe may indeed have value but not in organizing mankind to destroy the most unholy demons of war, poverty, racism, and sexism. Movements or organizations that reject planning reject the possibilities of their own success. It goes without saying that planning itself is as often used for destruction and oppression as for the aid of the oppressed. Yet we would argue that human progress in its more obvious forms cannot be implemented by any alternative to planning. Again, planning is not enough. Our utopian form would involve a nonmanipulating form of planning, quite unlike that extant in much of the world today. J. B. Priestly cites the

kind of mass manipulation our yet unborn institutions would avoid.

> To succeed in mass communications you must flatter the customer and never disturb him. And that, of course, is what is happening on a gigantic scale in America, and on an increasing scale here and elsewhere. . . . Everything must be falsified, science distorted, religion sentimentalized, human relations hopelessly over-simplified, so that nobody is challenged, disturbed, asked to reflect or feel deeply.[59]

How do we lessen this tendency toward manipulation in our bureaucratic society? Christian Bay in his seminal work *The Structure of Freedom* cites two possibilities.

> Local autonomy or decentralization in as many areas as is practicable is one way toward diminishing somewhat the huge inequality in manipulative power in modern mass societies. . . . Another social structure variable affecting potential freedom is the degree of vertical mobility in a society, and notably the degree to which it is possible for individuals to make great gains or losses in wealth and power. If the stakes are great, people come to feel justified in using ruthless means. The cruder kinds of coercion are barred by our legal institutions, but there are few laws that prevent even the most ruthless manipulation. . . .[60]

Decentralization and egalitarian change are necessary, then, to rid an institution of manipulation. The paradox here is that manipulation is often used by institutional elites to retain control and to frustrate meaningful change.

"Manipulation," C. Wright Mills argues, "becomes a problem whenever men have power that is concentrated and willful but do not have authority. . . ."[61] The question then becomes, how does one gain legitimate authority? The idealistic answer would be that authority must be born of the rational collective will of group participants. Yet as we have pointed out, substantive rationality becomes increasingly diffi-

[59] J. B. Priestly, *Thoughts in the Wilderness* (New York: Harper and Row, 1957), p. 11.
[60] Christian Bay, *The Structure of Freedom* (New York: Atheneum, 1965), p. 325.
[61] C. Wright Mills, *The Power Elite* (New York: Oxford University Press, 1957), p. 71.

cult with the specialization demanded by the division of labor. That is to say that the bureaucratic mentality breeds a kind of narrowness of view that blinds one to the larger social picture and a larger view of self-interests. What we are suggesting here is that an end to manipulation and alienation would necessitate a radical transformation of the division of labor. The resultant reduction in specialization coupled with broad humanistic educational forms could buffer bureaucratic elitism.

As we have stressed, both capitalism and the state socialism of Eastern Europe have been increasingly afflicted with bureaucratic structures. Even more interesting is the fact that both capitalists and socialists have called for similar changes in bureaucratic structure.

First, let us examine some of the changes proposed by two scholars in the United States: Warren G. Bennis and Alvin Toffler.

Bennis declares that "Bureaucracy, with its 'surplus repression,' was a monumental discovery for harnessing muscle power via guilt and instinctual renunciation. In today's world, it is a lifeless crutch that is no longer useful."[62]

---

[62] Warren Bennis, "Beyond Bureaucracy" in Irving Louis Horowitz and Mary Symons Strong, editors, *Sociological Realities* (New York: Harper and Row, 1971), p. 147.

"Shall we celebrate?"

(The paper the worker is holding is marked "award." The suggestion is that when production goes up the managers get the champagne, while the worker just gets a certificate.)

USSR—I. Sychev (*Krokodil*)

The situation of the Russian worker. (From *Krokodil,* USSR.)

How will this less than useful organization be supplanted? In the future, Bennis believes:

> The key word will be "temporary"; there will be adaptive, rapidly changing *temporary systems*. These will be "task forces" organized around problems to be solved. The problems will be solved by groups of relative strangers who represent a set of diverse professional skills. . . . The "executive" thus becomes a co-ordinator or "linking pin" between various task forces . . . people will be differentiated not vertically, according to rank and role, but flexibly and functionally according to skill and professional training.[63]

Alvin Toffler follows Bennis' ideas in his best-selling *Future Shock*. The concept that will replace bureaucratic organizations is the "Ad-hocracy." Besides being an interesting play on words, the Ad-hocracy represents an idea much like the one Bennis expresses. Men will perform tasks that involve planning, as does the bureaucracy. Yet the "super industrial" man described by Toffler will occupy no clearly defined slot, will perform no mindless repetitive tasks. This will be accomplished by automated machines according to Toffler.

> The embryonic Ad-hocracies of today demand a radically different constellation of human characteristics. In place of permanence, we find transience—high mobility between organization, never ending reorganizations within them, and a constant generation and decay of temporary work groupings. Not surprisingly, we witness a decline in old fashioned "loyalty" to the organization and its sub-structures.[64]

Thus Toffler sees an end to the inflexible and seemingly irreversible processes of bureaucratization. Toffler is, of course, a former editor of *Fortune* magazine and is by no means a socialist. It is interesting in this light to compare his ideas to those of East European socialists concerning bureaucracy.

The idea of workers' control of industrial

management is not a new one.[65] It appeared in Paris in 1871, Russia in 1917, Bavaria in 1919, Spain in 1936, and finally in Hungary and Yugoslavia in the 1950's. Yugoslavia is the most recent and quite likely the most permanent example of the workers' council.

In 1950, Yugoslavia began to plan for the creation of workers' councils that would share in the creation and management of industrial endeavors. Jiri Kolaja describes the philosophy of the councils.

> In several Yugoslav publications issued since 1950, the Marxist theme of the withering away of the state has been stressed and skillfully employed. It is stated that the primary unit of self-government is the territorial unit of the community called the commune. . . . To underline the decreasing role of the state, enterprises are defined not as state property but as social property. On the other hand workers in the enterprise are entitled to "manage" it but not to own it.[66]

The workers' councils are composed of between 15 and 120 members. Workers are elected by their peers each two years, and no worker

[63] *Ibid.*, pp. 146-147.
[64] Alvin Toffler, *Future Shock* (New York: Bantam Books, 1970), p. 146.

[65] See the brief history of workers' councils in Thomas R. Brooks, *Tool and Trouble: A History of American Labor* (New York: Delacorte Press, 1971), pp. 26-27.
"Over the long run, Jacksonian economic policy (protective tariffs, the bank, veto and paper money), as Professor Arthur Schlesinger, Jr. ruefully concedes in the *Age of Jackson,* cleared the way for the subsequent growth of giant corporations and for the lobbying of special privilege. More importantly, the Jackson revolution also overturned Jeffersonian federalism—with its emphasis on decentralism and encouragement of 'the art of association together' within a federal framework. In this context, the workingmen's political movements of the 1830's were Jeffersonian rather than Jacksonian, for structurally, these parties were *worker's councils* [italics added], an economic or industrial equivalent of the town meeting. This form of organization has recurred many times in the history of labor, in widely separated places—the Paris commune of 1871, the American Knights of Labor in the 1830's, the Russian Soviets of 1905 and 1917 (before the Bolshevik subversion of the idea), the CIO in the auto and rubber cities of the 1930's, and in Hungary during the revolution of 1957. All these were expressions of rebellion by working people against the centralizing tendencies of their respective times."
[66] Jiri Kolaja, *Workers Councils: The Yugoslav Experience* (New York: Frederick A. Praeger, 1966), p. 2.

may serve two consecutive terms. The elections are not merely formalistic since most seats in the council are contested.[67] Moreover, an elected member of the council cannot be fired or transferred during his tenure in office, but he can be recalled from office.

The workers' council discusses topics such as investment plans, production costs, quality and marketing problems, problems of wage scales and so forth.

The worker's income is composed of two parts. First, his normal wage, 60% of which is guaranteed by the community, and, secondly, a share of the institution's profits.

Jiri Kolaja's study of Yugoslav workers' councils found a high degree of worker apathy toward the functions of the council. Yet other researchers have found opposite results.[68] The fact is that workers' councils sometimes live up to their ideological commitments, sometimes fail. At their best, however, the workers' councils promote what we have called substantive rationality.

To the extent that workers' management is successful, it enables—or rather compels—the worker to see beyond the narrow horizons of his minute task and to take on a greater perspective which encompasses his economic unit, his department, his factory, his industry, and in fact, the entire economy.[69]

We have considered Ad-hocracies and workers' councils[70] as alternatives to bureaucratic social organization. In another sense they may be seen as syntheses between bureaucratic trends and antibureaucratic movements. We would not, of course, offer these options as ultimate forms of social organization. They, too, may be outmoded or ineffective in fulfilling human needs in the future. When that day comes, one can be sure the genesis of further social movements will be near.

---

[67] Paul Blumberg supports this contention in *Industrial Democracy* (New York: Schocken Books, 1969), p. 2.

[68] *Ibid.*, pp. 228-230.

[69] *Ibid.*, p. 233.

[70] For other sources on workers participation in management see the following: Jaroslav Vanek, *The Participatory Economy* (Ithaca: Cornell University Press, 1971); Nabagopal Das, *Experiments in Industrial Democracy* (New York: Asia Publishing House, 1964); *Workers Management in Yugoslavia* (Geneva: International Labour Office, 1962); Herbert J. Spiro, *The Politics of German Codetermination* (Cambridge: Harvard University Press, 1958).

CHAPTER 6 CULTURAL IMPERIALISM: NATIVISTIC AND NATIONALISTIC MOVEMENTS

In the colonial world, the emotional sensitivity of the native is kept on the surface of his skin like an open sore which flinches from the caustic agent.

Franz Fanon

CULTURAL IMPERIALISM AS A SOCIAL TREND

To many of the European elites, the uncharted world of the nineteenth century must have appeared as a large apple ripe for the plucking. The so-called colored peoples of the southern hemisphere found themselves inundated with white settlers and traders who often violated native folkways while "civilizing" the savages. It is said that one African leader of the nineteenth century remarked that "the white men took our land as he gave us his Bible." In one sense, both acts—the taking of land and the exportation of the white man's religion—are separate aspects of what has been called imperialism.

The word imperialism is vague and not without unfortunate connotations. It is, in the minds of many, simply a rhetorical device designed by "vulgar Marxists" to attack modern capitalism. In one sense, of course, imperialism predates

capitalism by more than a millennium. The Roman Empire (Imperium Romanum) provides us with an early form of the expansion and colonization we have come to associate with imperialism. George Lichtheim has pointed out that in modern times, the term imperialism has come to have four separate meanings:

> [First] national oppression of the sort practiced in the old dynamic East European empires before 1914-18; (2) colonialism of the Anglo-Indian type during and after the mercantilist era; (3) "liberal imperialism" classically represented by the British and foreign markets open to western capital; (4) the transfer of surplus value from the poor countries to the rich through trade relations which in practice discriminate against undeveloped economics.[1]

Whichever definition one accepts (and it is possible to accept all of the above), imperialism does imply the hegemony of one nation-state

---

[1] George Lichtheim, *Imperialism* (New York: Praeger Publishers, 1971), p. 134.

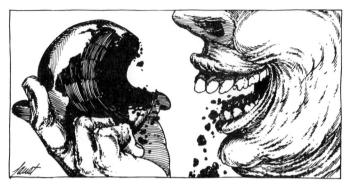

THE NATION / *April 19, 1971*

A portrayal of imperialism. (From *The Nation*, April 19, 1971, New York.)

over another. Robert Blauner views this imperialist or colonialist dominance in four ways. First, Blauner maintains,

> . . . colonialization begins with a forced, involuntary entry. Second there is an impact on the culture and social organization of the colonized people which is more than just a result of such "natural" processes as contact and acculturation. The colonizing carries out a policy which constrains, transforms, or destroys individual values, orientations, and ways of life.[2]

Blauner goes on to add the elements of colonial or external administration along with racism as necessary components of a colonialist system. While racism, the use of force, and external administration are indeed necessary components of colonialism, the concept of value destruction is of most interest to us at this point.

Usually Europeans, engaged in colonial or imperialistic ventures, have confronted a social system where the village is the basic unit of social life. The traditional village is often filled with the pain of extreme poverty and disease. Yet it would be wrong to suppose that the tribal or agrarian village is nothing but fear and misery. As William McCord explains in his *The Springtime of Freedom*, the village represents a sense of continuity and meaning for the individual. Moreover the village represents cooperation:

Each villager becomes closely involved with his neighbors, he is truly their "brother," even though symbolically they may divide by caste or religious differences. Everyone knows the other members of the village, their vices, virtues, and eccentricities. Regardless of his temperament, even the most misanthropic villager must engage in cooperative enterprises with his fellows, for the preservation of them all depends upon mutual aid.[3]

Village life in underdeveloped countries is, in fact, a total way of life. It is an economic system, of course, based on reciprocal barter and subsistence-level farming. More than this, the village is a series of rituals marking birth, marriage, death, and natural events.

Again, the village gives to its inhabitants a unified world view. For as Gerth and Mills point out

> In the village the various situations in which men play roles are not so widely different from one another and are transparent to all. . . . The variety of roles which any given person plays is not very wide, and each is translatable into the other. In such a society a single vocabulary of motives may be used by a person for all his roles, or at least he will use the same motives in speaking of some conduct pattern to his wife and to his neighbor, to his working mates, and to the village head.[4]

[2] Robert Blauner, "Internal Colonialism and Ghetto Revolt," *Social Problems* 16 (Spring, 1969), pp. 393-408.

[3] William McCord, *The Springtime of Freedom: The Evolution of Developing Societies* (New York: Oxford University Press, 1965), p. 23.

[4] Hans Gerth and C. Wright Mills, *Character and Social Structure: The Psychology of Social Institutions* (New York: Harcourt, Brace & World, 1953), p. 121.

BRADLEY, in Chicago Daily News

The Uplift

Cultural imperialism and civilization. (From *Cartoons Magazine*, vol. 7, no. 2, February, 1915. H. H. Windsor, editor and publisher, Chicago.)

The first contacts between European and non-European in the underdeveloped world usually have revolved around barter and trade. Nevertheless, "we find that the economic relationship which began as barter often ended in a system of compulsory labor or slavery."[5] The forced labor systems developed by the Spanish, Dutch, English, or French were seldom benign. The plantation system, developed to exploit the colony of its material and human resources, had two essential effects on the native population.

First and most obvious, it was destructive to human life. In the Belgian Congo, at the turn of the twentieth century, vast profits were accumulated by King Leopold with his state-controlled rubber plantations:

Each village was ordered by the authorities to collect and bring in a certain amount of rubber— as much as the men could collect and bring in by neglecting all works for their own maintenance. If they failed to bring in the required amount, their women were taken away and kept as hostages in compounds or in the harems of government employees. If this method failed, native troops, many of them cannibals, were sent into the village to spread terror, if necessary by killing some of the men; but in order to prevent a waste of cartridges they were ordered to bring in one right hand for every cartridge used. If they missed, or used cartridges on big game, they cut off the hands of living people to make up the necessary number.[6]

Sir H. H. Johnston estimates that within 15 years the native populations in the Congo were reduced from twenty million to less than nine million.[7] Similar, though perhaps less grisly, stories could be told of much of the colonized

---

[5] E. Franklin Frazier, *Race and Culture Contacts in the Modern World* (Boston: Beacon Press, 1957), p. 108.

[6] Bertrand Russell, *Freedom Versus Organization: The Pattern of Political Changes in Nineteenth Century European History* (New York: W. W. Norton and Company, 1962), p. 401.

[7] Sir H. H. Johnston, *The Colonization of Africa*, Cambridge: Historical Series (no date given), p. 352.

world of Africa, Southeast Asia, as well as North and South America.

Beyond the fact that European expansionism destroyed peoples (the entire native population of Tasmania was wiped out, for example), it tended to destroy the cultural heritage of the native population. Unlike European profiteering, the destruction of native cultures did not always occur by design. More subtle changes in village life began to take place. A monetary economic system changed the elaborate barter system. New tools came into use, forcing older craftsmen to change their vocations. Old lines of authority were challenged by men who had influence with the white man. And of course, of key importance is the fact that old religious systems and magical rites were challenged both by the white man's religion and his technologic prowess.

It is easy to see results of rapid conversion from a barter economy to one based on monetary exchange when one looks at the South Vietnam of the late 1960's and early 1970's. Saturation bombing, defoliation, and forced relocations caused South Vietnamese peasantry to move to areas like Saigon en masse. The rationale for this "American sponsored urban revolution" (as Samuel Huntington, professor of government at Harvard, calls it) was to remove the Viet Cong infrastructure from the countryside where it had always thrived. ("The use of customary village patterns and symbols allowed the Viet Minh to build a bridge between past and present, rather than servering its links to the past," writes anthropologist Eric Wolf.)[8]

The urban population of the small country increased from a mere 15% in 1965 to 60% in 1971. The result of this rapid social change has been in many ways catastrophic for the peasantry. Saigon, the quaint little Indo-Chinese city with French ambiance, had its streets flooded with refugees as its population increased tenfold. It was not long before the influx of tall, white, and comparatively wealthy foreigners had

A view of Russian imperialism. (© *Punch*, April 16, 1969, London.)

created a great impact on the city. Peasant women, separated from the land, began in some cases to practice prostitution as a means of survival. Their husbands or fathers often dealt in the black market, stolen goods, or perhaps drugs. What had happened was that the need for survival had overpowered the old folkways of the village. Moreover, survival in the city also brought with it a destruction of ancient religious forms that were tied to ancestor worship in the local village. By the early 1970's, American servicemen found resentment from the Vietnamese —noncommunist as well as communist.

This then is the essence of cultural imperialism—*the forceful impingement of one value structure on another*. It is, of course, frequently associated with economic exploitation, but this is not always true. What is certain is that the village structure of peasant society provides a kind of psychological security for its inhabitants. When this security is shattered by economic

---

[8] Quoted in "The Strange Economics of the Vietnam War," *Ramparts* (November, 1971), p. 36.

change or invasion by foreigners, the peasantry is likely to react because the value structure is threatened. This does not necessarily mean that it will rise in open revolt. Contrary to certain Maoist thinkers' views, the peasantry is not easily given to revolt. Yet many have been pushed into extreme situations—their economies threatened, their religions challenged, and the very authority structure of their societies obviated. Many peasants reach a point where they can no longer tolerate the changes imposed upon them by an alien culture. Thus paradoxically, Eric Wolf maintains, ". . . it is the very attempt of the middle and free peasant to remain traditional that makes him revolutionary."[9]

The dominance of one people over another is sometimes economic, sometimes political or military, but on the psychological level it frequently produces a common commodity—hatred. That is, hatred for the oppressor and hatred for oneself. As Franz Fanon, the black psychiatrist and revolutionary advocate, argued,[10] the oppressed begin to define themselves (sometimes unconsciously) in the same way as their masters. When the native is subjugated to the European, he begins to use European standards to judge himself. By those standards he is usually found wanting. The peasant or native is most often without education, social status, or technological skills, and if he uses these things as a benchmark for his self-esteem he is in psychological trouble. The answer to his problem may be the joining of a nativistic religious group or a revolutionary nationalistic movement that promises to expel the foreigners and restore the world to its former simplicity and security.

Black Americans have been uprooted both from their African culture and, in some cases, from their rural southern background in America. Has this resulted in self-hatred for some black Americans who have defined themselves by the standards of white society? Many black leaders have testified to this fact. Martin Luther King chastized American blacks for their "slave mentality" as well as whites for their paternalism or racism. The black Americans on the bottom of the social heap do find it difficult to develop a sense of self-worth. In large northern cities in the United States, the Black Muslims have reached many of the "lumpen" black people who have been ignored by more respectable religious or civil rights organizations. The Honorable Elijah Muhammad, leader of the Muslims, speaks to the problem of black self-esteem in this way:

> Did you say that you are ugly? Your ugliness is not permanent. You were not created ugly, that is why God promises to you in the Bible and the Holy Quran that you will be restored to your ancient beauty and to your ancient self. You are far from being yourself. . . . The most beautiful people of the earth are the Black people when they are in their natural self. . . . It is ashamed in this day, and time, that one million Black people here on the South Side of Chicago, Illinois are not doing something for self. We the Black people should be sane, truthful, and loving toward one another and run the South Side of Chicago, Illinois, ourself. But since you do not have this love for self and without the knowledge of self someone else must rule you.[11]

We can see then, that cultural imperialism has a number of effects on the native culture, many of which are unfortunate. Hence, it is not surprising to witness social movements which have as their aim the restoration of pride and self-esteem in the native or peasant populace.

REVITALIZATION MOVEMENTS AND CULTURAL IMPERIALISM

It is often maintained that Christianity, the religion of most white Europeans, has an essen-

---

[9] Eric Wolf, "Peasant Rebellion and Revolution" in Norman Miller and Roderick Aya, editors: *National Liberation: Revolution in the Third World* (New York: Free Press, 1971), p. 57.

[10] Franz Fanon, *Black Skin White Masks* (New York: Grove Press, 1967).

[11] Honorable Elijah Muhammad, "Be Yourself!" *Muhammad Speaks* 10, no. 8 (November 6, 1970), p. 16.

tially conservative effect on its believers. Many Marxists or anarchists have pointed to Christianity as a kind of ideological support for the ruling elites of a given society. Certainly the conservative side of Christianity ("render unto Caesar that which is Caesars") is a powerful one. Nevertheless, given the proper historical circumstances, Christianity has proved a powerful catalyst to radical social movements. The Judeo-Christian idea of the return of the Messiah, for example, is quite compatible with many revolutionary ideologies. For when the Messiah returns, social justice shall prevail. In many parts of the world, justice for the so-called colored population is nonexistent. Thus, the far-off day of the return of the Messiah is often mixed with powerful revolutionary appeals. As we shall see later, the blend of nativism and Christianity is often an explosive one.

The latter half of the nineteenth century saw the peak of exploitative colonialism on a worldwide scale. Africa had been carved into administrative districts by the English, the Germans, the French, the Belgians, and others. On the American continent black Africans were in near-slavery or the slavery of the plantation system. Genocidal wars against the Indians in North, South, and Central America had drastically reduced their numbers. India was under the domination of the English, and China had her door forcibly opened to settlement and trade by a combination of European powers.

The peasant population of the underdeveloped world saw their children learning European languages, European religions, and European fashions. In short, they saw their own culture subject to imminent destruction. In a culture where a series of guideposts are missing or blurred, individuals sometimes suffer severe emotional problems.

Anthony F. C. Wallace conceives of culture as a series of these guideposts, which he calls "cognitive mazeways." Cognitive mazeways are threatened or destroyed by some forms of cultural imperialism. This produces tension within the individual. Wallace states the case in this way:

> Whenever an individual who is under chronic, psychologically measurable stress receives repeated information which indicates that his mazeway does not lead to action which reduces the level of stress, he must choose between maintaining his present mazeway and tolerating stress, or changing the mazeway in an attempt to reduce the stress.[12]

Wallace goes on to point out that these attempts to reduce stress by changing one's cultural guideposts or cognitive mazeways often become collective efforts. Collective efforts toward change are most likely to occur when the native culture has been severely threatened by foreign dominance. The native culture becomes "internally distorted" with symptoms of individual malaise such as "alcoholism, extreme passivity and indolence . . . intragroup violence, disregard of kinship and sexual mores, irresponsibility in public officials, states of depression and self-reproach and probably a variety of psychosomatic and neurotic disorders."[13]

It is at this point in the destruction of the native culture when a figure or group arises offering hope and a more satisfying life-style, according to Wallace. The individual is likely to be perceived as a prophet by those who accept him.

> A supernatural being appears to the prophet-to-be, explains his own and his society's troubles as being entirely or partly a result of the violation of certain rules, and promises individual and social revitalization if the injunctions are followed and the rituals practiced.[14]

Many of the revitalization movements cited by Wallace and others contain mixtures of the prophetic tradition of the Judeo-Christian faith combined with traditional nativistic beliefs. In the three revitalization movements described

---

[12] Reproduced by permission of the American Anthropological Association from *The American Anthropologist* 58, no. 2, 1956, p. 266.
[13] *Ibid.*, p. 269.
[14] *Ibid.*, p. 270.

below, varying mixtures of Christianity, traditionalism, and cultural imperialism have formed movements that have challenged the white or European dominance of the native world.

THE GHOST DANCE AND THE PLAINS INDIANS

By the late 1800's, the Plains Indians of North America had reached their lowest ebb. They had been driven into the most barren wastelands imaginable as reservations; the white man had killed many of their finest warriors (occasionally along with women and children). Alcoholism, venereal disease, and tuberculosis diminished the population. Near starvation was commonplace.

In 1870, a prophet appeared to the Paiute Indians of Nevada. He called himself Wovoka, the messiah. Wovoka had been raised by a Mormon family after his father, Tavibo, died. Mormonism, of course, is one of the most messianic of all Christian sects, and it is likely the young boy was highly influenced by Morman theology. When he was 20 years old, the sun went into eclipse and Wovoka (whose name in English means the Cutter) fell asleep and was taken into the spirit world.

> After showing him all, God told him he must go back and tell his people they must be good and love one another, have no quarreling, and live in peace with the whites; that they must work, and not lie or steal . . . that if they faithfully obeyed his instructions they would at last be reunited with their friends in this other world, where there would be no more death or sickness or old age. He was then given the dance which he was commanded to bring back to his people. By performing this dance at intervals, for five consecutive days each time, they would secure this happiness to themselves and hasten the event.[15]

Wovoka's ethical teachings mirrored those of the founder of Christianity. "You must not fight. Do no harm to anyone. Do right always."[16]

Justice would triumph in the end, and the Indian would ascend to his rightful place in his own land. The time of shame would end. The white man and his destructive way would disappear. How was this to occur? As the Ghost Dance spread from tribe to tribe, different answers were given to this question. Among the Arapaho, it was believed that a wall of fire would drive the white man off the earth, while Indians would survive by means of sacred feathers that would help them ascend to the promised land. The Cheyenne and Kiowa believed that a new earth would come forth, sledding over the old, covering the white man and all his works. The Paiutes of California believed a great flood would drown all whites. Among the Sioux it was believed that

> . . . the white man's gunpowder would no longer have power to drive a bullet through the skin of an Indian. The whites themselves would soon be overwhelmed and smothered under a deep landslide, held down by sod and timber, and the few who might escape would become small fishes in the rivers.[17]

It was among the Sioux that a version of the Ghost Dance made its greatest impact. It was also among the Sioux that the legend of the invincible Ghost Shirt took root. No white man's bullet could pierce the sacred material according the the Sioux myth. Indeed, the Sioux in the 1880's had need of myths. After a series of bloody battles with Federal troops, they had been confined to barren reservations such as the Rosebud in South Dakota.

One of the worst tragedies of Indian-white relations occurred on December 29, 1890, when a group of Sioux appeared to surrender to white troops at Wounded Knee, South Dakota. As the Indians were surrendering their weapons to the Federal troops, a great deal of tension arose in the camp as the soldiers overturned tepees, beds, and furniture in their search for guns. Yellow Bird, a medicine man, walked among the warriors telling them that the whites would be helpless against the Ghost Shirts and to resist the

---

[15] James Mooney, *The Ghost-Dance Religion and the Sioux Outbreak of 1890* (Chicago: University of Chicago Press, 1965), p. 14.
[16] *Ibid.*, p. 19.

[17] *Ibid.*, p. 29.

troops. A shot was fired at the soldiers. A volley from the white troops tore into Indian braves as well as women and children. When the shooting stopped, over 350 bodies of men, women, and children were scattered for 2 miles in the snow.

In a sense, the Wounded Knee massacre destroyed a movement as well as a large number of human lives. Most of the Plains Indians began to reject the entire idea of the Ghost Dance.

> When one of the women shot in . . . the massacre was approached as she lay in the church and told that she must let them remove her Ghost Shirt in order the better to get at her wound, she replied: "Yes, take it off. They told me a bullet would not go through. Now I don't want it anymore."[18]

It was at this point that large numbers of the Plains Indians turned to the use of peyote, a carrot-shaped cactus which produces visual and auditory hallucinations. The visions and perceptual changes created by ingesting the plant are given great spiritual significance by members of the peyote cult. The use of the drug predates the coming of the white man. (It has not been shown to be harmful in a physiological sense for those who participate in the cult.[19]) The Plains Indians who formed the cult later incorporated it as the Native American Church. It too has generous portions of Christianity mixed with traditional ritual.

It was, of course, no accident that the popularity of the peyote cult followed the demise of the Ghost Dance. As Vittorio Lanternari explains in his *Religions of the Oppressed:*

> The Ghost Dance promised redemption and liberation at a time when the Indians were ready for rebellion, and provided the motivating force for uprising such as that of the Sioux; the peyote cult emerged when the Ghost Dance was being snuffed out and the Indians were forced to admit defeat, but when, however, the white man had

changed his attitude and substituted assimilation in place of destruction.[20]

THE CARGO CULT IN MELANESIA

New Guinea has long been the source of many anthropological studies. One of the reasons for the great interest anthropologists have given the area is the proliferation of nativistic movements in the islands. The Taro Cult, the "Vailala Madness," and the Cargo Cult were all studied thoroughly by social scientists[21] for it was believed that all of the aforementioned movements represented a response to the coming of the white man to the islands.

The Taro Cult began in about 1914 when a native prophet, Buninia emerged from a trance in which he had been visited by a Taro[22] or food spirit. The "Taro Men" developed dances, singing, and community eating rituals that were followed by trances, seizures, and ecstatic experiences. Believers in the cult were assured that their ancestors would bring them much food as well as European garments, textiles, and tools. The native people of the area were, of course, reacting to the relative wealth of their new white neighbors. The Taro Cult was able to offer them what they had little of, that is, hope for material improvement.

Whites had come into the area in about 1895 with gold on their minds. Gold fields were established with the aid of native labor. But as Peter Worsley points out:

> Heavy loads had to be carried for long stages, there was no provision against epidemics, and the chilly mountain nights were death to natives accustomed to the temperature of the coast.

---

[18] *Ibid.*, p. 34.

[19] See for example W. La Barre, D. P. McAllester, J. S. Slotkin, O. C. Steward, S. Tax, "Statement of Peyote," *Science* 104 (1951), pp. 582-583.

[20] Vittorio Lanternari, *The Religions of the Oppressed: A Study of Modern Messianic Cults* (New York: Mentor Books, 1965).

[21] See E. W. F. Chinnery and A. C. Hadden, "Five New Religious Cults in British New Guinea," *Hibbert Journal* 4 (1917), p. 339.

[22] The taro, a kind of sweet potato, is the staple diet for the islanders.

The death rate was 21 percent in 1903-04 . . . in 1906, it was still 17.7 percent. . . .[23]

It is not difficult to surmise that under these conditions hostility toward the white man would develop. Many of the beliefs of the Taro men were thinly disguised in their antiwhite content. More than this, however, cult members stressed friendliness and amity toward traditionally antagonistic tribes. By the 1930's the Taro movement began to decline in importance. It was, of course, frowned upon by the British administrators as an antiwhite, antigovernment organization. It was not perceived as a great enough threat to the colonial system to be harshly suppressed. In summation:

> The Taro Cult, though focused upon traditional and still-vital interests, crop fertility, the curing of sickness and the cult of the ancestors . . . exhibited many features which call for its consideration with millenarian[24] movements proper.[25]

The so-called Vailala Madness was supposedly initiated by an old man named Evara. Evara went into a trance at the death of his father and awoke giving forth prophesies.

> He prophesied the coming of a steamer carrying the spirits of dead ancestors on board, who would bring with them the "cargo." . . . The spirits had revealed that all the flour, rice, tobacco and other "trade" belonged to the Papuans, not the whites. The latter would pass into the hands of its rightful owners, the natives. To obtain these goods it was necessary to drive out the whites.[26]

Adherents of the Vailala Madness often went into trances speaking in strange tongues. To communicate with the forthcoming ancestor spirits, the natives constructed temples that contained a strange mixture of tradition and western customs. Special flagpoles were hoisted to act as "radio aerials" to communicate with the spirit ships that were hopefully approaching.

At numerous times, British administrators became enraged as the natives gave up both work and trade to wait for their ancestor spirits.

By the end of World War II, when the Japanese ended their occupation of the islands, the many varieties of the Cargo Cult had begun to decline. Nevertheless, it had accomplished a number of important goals for its followers. First, it had destroyed many of the traditional religious systems of people. More importantly, however, the cults had broken down the tribal insularity of the islands.

In 1946, a movement appeared on the islands that was essentially political rather than religious. Paliau, a native leader of the Manus district, formulated an organization whose ethical system was predicated on Roman Catholicism and traditionalism. "He called for economic cooperation, communal organization and the concentration of population in a way which would wipe out the distinctions between former separate communities."[27] Although Paliau's program was spoken of in religious terms (a Garden of Eden would result from following his teachings), it was in fact a political formula for nationalism.[28] Paliau was arrested in 1951 for subversion. Upon his release, members of his movement began to join the political establishment, and in the end the power structure simply "absorbed" or canalized the essentially radical ideas of the movement.

Peter Worsley sums up the current situation in the Melanesian Islands.

> It would be early yet to say just what cultural and social groupings are going to emerge from this highly fluid situation. We are, in fact, witnessing the early stages of formation of national groupings in Melanesia. . . . After the post-war efflorescence of Cargo ideas, largely conditional by the hardships of reconstruction, there ap-

[23] Reprinted by permission of Schocken Books Inc. from *The Trumpet Shall Sound: A Study of the "Cargo" Cults in Melanesia* by Peter Worsley. Copyright © 1968 by Peter Worsley.
[24] Millenarian movements are those which stress the imminent end of the world with a period of social justice following.
[25] Worsley, *op. cit.*, p. 74.
[26] *Ibid.*, p. 81.

[27] *Ibid.*, p. 187.
[28] For an account of the Paliau movement see Margaret Mead, *New Lives For Old* (New York: William Morrow, 1956), Chapters 7 and 8.

pears to have been a considerable slackening of enthusiasm, with the persistence of a period of high world prices for local products and plentiful employment.... Though the movements in Melanesia have had a radical, anti-white and even communistic flavour in the past, they will probably follow the path of similar movements in the history of other regions and become passive sect in the future.[29]

REVITALIZATION MOVEMENTS IN AFRICA

The African experience with cultural and economic colonialism parallels that of the North American Indian and the Malanesian in many ways. It is not surprising then, to find similarities in their reactions to European dominance. David Diop's "Africa" expressed poetically the views of many Black Africans:

> Africa, my Africa . . .
> Your beautiful black blood spilled
> through the fields
> the blood of your sweat
> the sweat of your labor
> the labor of your slavery
> The slavery of your children
> Oh tell me, Africa
> Is this really you, the back bent
> And laid low by the weight of your meekness
> This trembling, red-striped back
> Which says yes to the whip on the noonday
> roads[30]

The mood of many Black African intellectuals toward European colonialism became an ideology—"negritude." In its essence, negritude represents a desire for a return to the non-European view of life. Beyond the antiwhite implications of the ideology, it represents an incentive for being, in Jean-Paul Sartre's phrase, "in love with all the forms of life," that is, all the traditional forms of life rejected by European culture. Negritude resulted in a revival of African art forms among many intellectuals, but

for the masses of certain colonial areas it took the form of a revitalization movement.

In the Congo, for example, a powerful native prophet, Simon Kimbangu, arose in the year 1921. Kimbangu, who had been trained in a British Baptist mission, received what he believed was a call to regenerate his people. His teachings consisted basically of Old Testament morality mixed with a kind of negritude. Biblical tales of David and Goliath were cited by Kimbangu as symbolic of black-white relations in the Congo.

It was said of Kimbangu that he performed many miracles, including the raising of the dead. In time, his followers were calling Kimbangu God of the Black man. "Kimbangu prophesied the imminent ousting of the foreign rulers, a new way of life for the Africans, the return of the dead and the coming of a Golden age to be awaited in the arms of the native church."[31] Kimbangu was, in the end, arrested for preaching his subversive doctrines. He died in prison in 1950. New prophets, however, had arisen to carry the fires of the nativistic movement. Andre Matswa, a Congolese convert to the Kimbanguist movement, began to be regarded as a coequal in the nativist movement. When Matswa died in 1942, he had been conferred with the title of Jesus Matswa or the Black Christ. Kimbangu and Matswa were not pacifists, nonetheless. One prophecy circulated in 1930 proclaimed:

> The time of red blood is come. . . . Those who rise up shall enter into the glory of the victorious kingdom. . . . The whites do not know that they shall find death and destruction in a foreign land. The buffalo and the elephant are powerful animals which can do any labor because of the size of their bodies. They are as strong as Goliath. But they lack the intelligence to make ready the paths and roads of their departure. The death of the elephant and the buffalo is at hand. The liberation will be final.[32]

---

[29] Worsley, *op. cit.*, pp. 254-256.
[30] David Diop, *Coups de Pilon*, Wilfred Carty, translator (Paris: Presence Africaine, 1956), p. 21.

[31] Lanternari, *op. cit.*, p. 26.
[32] Georges Balandier, *Ambiguous Africa: Cultures in Collision* (New York: Pantheon Books, 1966), p. 211.

Interestingly enough, many of those associated with Simon Kimbangu's movement saw a real kinship between themselves and the British Salvation Army who arrived in the Congo in 1935. Salvation Army personnel came to the area with a good deal more humility than did most Christian missionaries. Moreover, they were service-oriented in their approach to the native peoples. Many of the Congolese regarded the Salvation Army whites as simply different members of the Kimbangu sect. They pointed to the large red S on the Salvation Army uniforms as further proof of this connection between Simon Kimbangu and the Salvation Army.

The Kimbangu movement left its imprint on many other nativistic cults springing from Christianity. In the French colonies, for example, new prophets began to come forth preaching the doctrines of Kimbanguism combined with their personal interpretations of the black man's Christianity.

In South Africa where the Dutch preached their Calvinism mixed with large helpings of European racial superiority, it was only natural that nativistic movements would arise. Most of the movements, such as the Zulu Congregational Church (founded in 1896), the African Congregational Church (1917), and the Native Primitive Church (1940), were offshoots of European churches that preached Christianity while at the same time injecting subtle feelings of inferiority into the black South African. In 1954, it was estimated that 1,286 native churches with 761,000 members existed in South Africa.[33]

Why did these revitalization movements take the shape they did? Georges Balandier gives us a partial answer in his *The Sociology of Black Africa*. Those groups represented a native movement that

> . . . reacted on the plane where it felt itself to be most directly threatened—that of its beliefs and attitudes; on the only plane, that is to say, where it could take the initiative, since elsewhere it could only submit more or less passively to the

economic and political imperatives of the colonial powers. This transference of political activity to the plane of religious activity, moreover, occurs frequently in a situation of dependence, for to some extent the latter serves to conceal the former.[34]

Further, Balandier explains,

> . . . the new movements sought to restore . . . broken ties and rebuild the community. They brought people together, unified them, tried to establish a more broadly based fraternity than that of the old clans, which had almost broken down. In this way, an entire ethnic group began to discover a sense of unity and become conscious of its position.[35]

AN EVALUATION OF REVITALIZATION MOVEMENTS

We have surveyed briefly some of the movements designed to resist cultural imperialism. There are many more. In the 1950's in Kenya the Mau Mau, a secret society, was formed among the Kikuyu to drive the British out of East Africa.[36] The Mau Mau, a religious movement in New Zealand, was founded in 1826 to drive the British out of lands occupied by the Maori tribesmen. It later sparked war in the area. In the United States, both the Black Muslims and the Ku Klux Klan exhibit some features of revitalization movements. Both exhibit religious and magic features, and both see themselves as an oppressed nationality. Moreover, both see their former culture threatened or destroyed by external forces.

What do revitalization movements really accomplish? Are they typically successful in restoring the old ways to a people whose lifestyle has been challenged? In most, if not all cases, the answer seems to be no. Most of the movements, as we have seen, borrow elements

[33] Quoted in Lanternari, *op. cit.*, p. 41.

[34] Georges Balandier, *The Sociology of Black Africa*, Douglas Garman, translator (New York: Praeger Publishers, 1970), p. 463.
[35] *Ibid.*, p. 464.
[36] For an excellent analysis of the Mau Mau see Norman Mackenzie, *Secret Societies* (New York: Collier Books, 1967), Chapter 2.

of religious beliefs from the very individuals who oppress them. Moreover, it is impossible to go back to the life-style of the isolated village after contact with the larger world. Does this mean that revitalization movements are all doomed to failure? Not in the least, for one of the most evident facts about their existence on a worldwide scale is that they provide (or attempt to provide) unity and hope to a people who are on the verge of losing both. Hope is a humanizing quality. It is the ability to plan and to look forward, to progress. When it is lost, concern for oneself as well as one's fellow man is often lost as well.

As for the idea of unity, it is clear that it is a necessary prelude to true independence. One of the advantages Europeans possessed in their struggle to subdue the underdeveloped world was the disunity of the native populace. It is important to perceive revitalization movements as a real attempt to find ethnic unity through common symbols and rituals.[37] It is no accident that the white supremacist government of South Africa has worked to retribalize the Bantu population of that area. A unified front of black Africans comprising 80% of the population would be a formidable opponent in any form of conflict.

In reality, it is important to view revitalization movements as fulfilling personal needs of the individual while at the same time preparing the native population for future political action. In this sense, we can call these movements prepolitical because they often set the stage for nationalistic movements of the future.

MOVEMENTS OF "NATIONAL LIBERATION"

When we speak of social trends and social movements, we are speaking of an abstraction that may or may not convey a sense of reality to the reader. Nevertheless, movements and trends do make their mark on individual lives. Occasionally the life of one individual reflects a micro-

cosmic mirror image of social tendencies. The life of Malcolm X in twentieth century America is a case in point.[38]

The Autobiography of Malcolm X spells out clearly the degradation of a strong and sensitive personality. Malcolm, or Detroit Red as he was called, had operated in the fringes of society as a petty thief, pimp, pusher, and addict. While in federal prison, he discovered the Black Muslim movement.[39] Preaching black superiority and an end to domination by the "blue-eyed white devils," the Muslims represented a true revitalization movement. Malcolm explained:

> The religion of Islam, had reached down into the mud to lift me up, to save me from being what I inevitably would have been: a dead criminal in a grave or, if still alive, a flint-hard, bitter, thirty-seven-year-old convict in some penitentiary, or insane asylum. Or, at best, I would have been an old Detroit Red, hustling, stealing enough for food and narcotics, and myself being stalked as prey by cruelly ambitious younger hustlers such as Detroit Red had been.[40]

Yet Malcolm X soon found himself in conflict with the Honorable Elijah Muhammad. Part of the conflict was personal, but by 1963, the differences between the two men were ideological as well. According to Malcolm, the Black Muslim movement had gone "as far as it can" because it was too narrowly sectarian and too inhibited. "I am prepared," Malcolm said, "to cooperate in local civil rights actions in the South and elsewhere and shall do so because every campaign for specific objectives can only heighten the political consciousness of the Negroes." Malcolm said Elijah Muhammad had prevented him from participating in civil rights struggles in the South although he had many opportunities to do so. "It is going to be different now, . . . I'm going to join in the fight wherever Negroes ask

---

[37] See Lanternari, *op. cit.,* pp. 200-210.

[38] Malcolm X, *The Autobiography of Malcolm X* (New York: Grove Press, 1965).
[39] An excellent analysis of the dynamics of the movement is found in C. Eric Lincoln's *The Black Muslims in America* (Boston: Beacon Press, 1961).
[40] Malcolm X, *op. cit.,* pp. 290-291.

for my help, and I suspect my activities will be on a greater and more intensive scale than in the past."[41]

Malcolm's analysis of the enemy of black people changed also. From the mystical anti-white ideology of the Muslims, Malcolm found a new enemy—the socioeconomic system.

> It's impossible for a white person to believe in capitalism and not believe in racism. And if you find one . . . and they have a philosophy that makes you sure they don't have their racism in their outlook, usually they're socialists or their political philosophy is socialism.[42]

Here we can see that Malcolm had left the religious rationale for his fight against the oppression of black Americans. Malcolm's own group, The Organization of Afro-American Unity, was founded in June of 1964. It died with its founder on February 21, 1965. In many ways, Malcolm X did not have a consistent ideology to offer those who followed him. Yet he had come to the conclusion that a secular revolutionary nationalist movement was preferable to the religious separatism of the Muslim movement.[43]

We are not arguing here that all revitalization movements prepare the way for nationalistic political movements. It is also obvious that this transformation would occur in the lives of only a few individuals. Yet, it may be that in some cases revitalization movements are necessary forerunners to the secular and political movements of nationalism. Men fight what they feel is oppression with the weapons at hand. If the society has powerful religious symbols of unity, they may likely be used to further the aims of the oppressed. On the other hand, essentially secular ideologies such as liberalism, anarchism, socialism, or communism may afford ideological

comfort for the oppressed in more technologically developed societies.

In the 1970's, nationalistic movements existed within the developed as well as the underdeveloped world. French separatists caused the Canadian government many crises. Northern Ireland was convulsed with a nationalistic-religious-economic civil war. Even General de Gaulle and his successors were threatened by "Celtic" nationalism within France itself. Nation-states have grown in size and power but not without creating many problems of social mixture. When minorities in any nation are slighted, nationalistic movements become an attractive option.

It is in the underdeveloped or third world where nationalistic movements have gained most power. Many nationalistic leaders in the southern hemisphere countries have concluded that the poverty and misdevelopment of their society is due to Western capitalistic expropriation of human and natural resources. This is true insofar as the larger nations have selfishly manipulated the cheap labor markets and raw materials of third world countries. Nevertheless, other factors besides colonialist exploitation are at work in keeping the poor nations poor. These are facts such as peasant conservatism, a high birth rate, and the difficulty of diversifying the economic system.

At any rate, socialism and nationalism make for a potent revolutionary mixture in Latin America, Southeast Asia, or Africa. This is interesting in light of Marx's assertion that nationalism is ultimately a conservative ideology designed to trick the working class into giving up its solidarity. It has been said that European socialism was destroyed (or nearly so) by World War I. This was a war in which French and German workers were asked to refuse to fight a war created, their leaders told them, for the benefit of capitalism. Nationalism proved a stronger motivating factor than working class solidarity as German, English, and French workers died in the trenches for the glory of their respective countries.

It is also interesting that Marx believed that

[41] M. S. Handler, "Malcolm X Splits with Muhammad," *New York Times* (March 9, 1964).

[42] Malcolm X, *Malcolm X Speaks* (New York: Merit Publishers, 1965), p. 69.

[43] An extended analysis of Malcolm's ideological transformation is found in George Breitman's *The Last Year of Malcolm X* (New York: Schocken Books, 1968).

peasants had little revolutionary value because of their concern for tradition and their lack of ability to communicate with other peasants a few villages distant.

Barrington Moore has pointed to the real revolutionary potential of the world's peasantry:

Because peasant discontent has frequently expressed itself in reactionary forms, Marxist thinkers often regard peasant radicalism with a mixture of contempt and suspicion or, at best, with patronizing condescension . . . to point out that Marxist successes have come out of peasant revolutions . . . is to conceal more significant issues. . . . First, the utopian radical conceptions of one phase become the accepted institutions and philosophical platitudes of the next. Secondly, the chief social basis of radicalism has been the peasants and the smaller artisans in the towns. From these facts one may conclude that the wellsprings of human freedom lie not only where Marx saw them, in the aspirations of classes about to take power (i.e., the proletariat) but perhaps even more, in the dying wail of a class over whom the wave of progress is about to roll (the peasantry). . . .[44]

The peasantry, then, is a potentially powerful force in nationalistic movements if it is aroused —and it has been aroused in areas such as Southeast Asia with Vietnam's National Liberation Front, Laos' Pathet Lao, as well as other groups such as the Huks in the Philippines.

REFORMIST NATIONALISM

Can the poor nations resist dominance by the large and powerful without massive bloodshed or guerilla war? The answer is that this has occurred in a number of cases—usually those where colonial powers were unwilling or unable to risk bloodshed in containing the nationalistic

[44] Barrington Moore, *Social Origins of Dictatorship and Democracy: Lord and Peasant in the Making of the Modern World* (Boston: Beacon Press, 1966).

TH. HEINE, in Simplicissimus   Copyright, International Copyright Bureau

JOHN BULL IN TROUBLE
"Wonder how long I can keep this position."

John Bull in trouble. (From *Cartoons Magazine*, vol. 7, no. 2, February, 1915. H. H. Windsor, editor and publisher, Chicago.)

movement. The British were forced to make compromises with the Indian nationalist movements when World War II began. Moreover, the British were willing to leave several of their African colonies with little struggle when the winds of change blew over North Central Africa. Nevertheless, in Nigeria and on the Gold Coast, nationalistic movements had the support of an educated middle-class group of Africans. Kwame Nkrumah, an African who had taken postgraduate work in England, rapidly ascended to power in the Gold Coast Convention Peoples Party. Even though he had been imprisoned by the British government, he was finally empowered by that same government to form a responsible and constitutional form of government in the Gold Coast.

In India it was Gandhi, an English-trained lawyer, who took charge of the movement for independence. Gandhi led a mass movement that involved Indian intellectuals, merchants, and peasants. While Gandhi did envision national liberation, the governmental system he proposed was essentially patterned after the British Constitution. He did wish to facilitate more economic cooperation[45] than he found in the Western

world, but tragically, his life was cut short before he could confront the massive economic problems of his new nation.

In another sense, we can see the creation of the United States of America as a kind of reformist nationalism. The movement of 1776 was led not by peasants but by an aristocracy and the merchant class. Even after the Americans had found themselves at war with the mother country, they patterned their institutions on those of the English system. This, then, is the essence of reformist nationalist movements—the participation of the middle and upper classes in the fight for independence.

In a more recent and subtle case of resistance to social and cultural imperialism, Salvador Allende, the legally elected Marxist president of Chile, attempted in 1971 to form a coalition with the Chilean middle classes and the poor. From the middle classes and intellectuals, he asked for support on the basis of ridding the country of North American cultural and economic domination. From the peasants, he appealed for support on the basis of land reform. The United States government placed severe pressure on the Chilean economy while wooing the military. In September 1973 Allende was killed in a bloody military coup. Within a week the U. S. government recognized the military dictatorship.

[45] See Jawaharlal Nehru, *The Discovery of India* (New York: The John Day Co., 1946).

Vadillo, Siempre (Mexico)

A Latin view of American cultural imperialism. (Vadillo—Siempre, Mexico.)

REVOLUTIONARY NATIONALISM—
GUERILLA MOVEMENTS

If nationalist reformist movements are likely to have the active participation of the upper and middle classes, the reverse is likely to be true with revolutionary nationalistic movements.

As we shall see, revolutionary movements are likely to occur in poor nations with a very weakly developed middle class. It is important here to note the difference between a poor nation and an underdeveloped one. John Gerassi's description of Latin America points to the difference between that continent and the less wealthy nations of Western Europe.

> A country can be poor, yet its potential can be fully and equitably exploited. If so, it is developed. Switzerland, Denmark, Austria, New Zealand are poor countries, especially in comparison to the United States. . . . But the former are well balanced. There are few beggars. There are no deaths from starvation and there is enough distributed wealth so that competition can allow social mobility. Small farms in Denmark are solvent because there are not so many huge ones as to be able to crush all others. Nor is Denmark . . . (unlike Latin America) owned 40% by corporations from just one foreign power and 51% by corporations of three allied foreign powers.[46]

As we look at the foreign domination of the underdeveloped world, we can find two forms of domination, direct and covert. As for direct domination, the United Fruit Company, an American

---

[46] John Gerassi, *The Great Fear in Latin America* (London: Collier-Macmillan Ltd., 1963), p. 392.

"You Mean We're All CIA Agents?"

San Francisco Chronicle

American dominance in the third world. (From *The San Francisco Chronicle* © Chronicle Publishing Co. 1969).

firm, controlled 35% of all exports from Honduras, 69% of Panama's exports, and 41% of Costa Rica's exports in the year 1955. Its gross profits for the same year were three times as high as the total governmental budgets of Costa Rica, Guatemala, and Panama.[47] It is obvious that a cheap labor force and backward, often corrupt, governments are an asset to those concerned only with profit. Because it is without capital and the skills to exploit its natural resources, the plight of the underdeveloped country is a series of crises. Ronald Segal underscores the tragedy: "What is finally terrifying is not so much that the gap between the rich and the poor is so wide already but that it is widening yet farther all the time."[48]

Beyond the crucial questions of economics, many Latin Americans are angered at the fact that North American clothes, television programs, and foods are supplanting Latin customs. Latin American students, for example, are notoriously anti-gringo. Proud of their own heritage, they see (rightly or wrongly) the leviathan to the north infecting all their institutions.

These are the conditions under which revolutionary nationalistic movements are likely to grow—poverty in the extreme and the presence of a hated foreigner who symbolizes exploitation.

Unlike reformist organizations, revolutionary nationalists are forced into clandestine activities. Often this amounts to guerilla warfare. The guerilla movement may take its ideals from a Maoist, Castroist, or home-grown revolutionary philosophy (such as the Tupamaros of Uruguay). In any case, such movements are not easy to organize. Ché Guevara failed, for example, in his attempt to organize Bolivian peasants. The Huks in the Philippines were nearly destroyed after World War II. Other examples of failure could be cited as well. Nevertheless, it would seem that revolutionaries are not driven by the idea of

probable success but by a lack of other alternatives. It amounts, quite literally in some cases, to asking a man if he wishes to die by gunfire or watch his family and friends die by starvation or disease. Obsessive hatred is often a powerful motivating factor as well.

Francois Sully has listed serially the goals and strategies of guerilla operations. They are as follows:

1. Strategic planning . . .
2. Setting in place the clandestine political infrastructure of the movement: recruiting of couriers, messengers, etc.
3. Psychological operations to dramatize the cause of the guerrillas at home and abroad . . .
4. Selective terrorism to eliminate potential opponents of the insurgency in the countryside.
5. Sabotage of lines of communication to isolate the territorial base areas of the guerrilla.
6. Creation of safe areas and strongholds to shelter command headquarters—usually in sparse mountain areas.
7. Development of liberated areas in populated rural regions to be administered by the guerrillas.
8. Proselytization among the enemy to entice defectors and ruin his morale.
9. Gradual strangulation of cities by the rural areas under guerrilla control, organization of the urban population for civil disobedience.
10. A general offensive carried out by a liberation army to knock out the last vestiges of government presence.
11. Negotiations to formalize the transfer of power to the political forces born from the guerrilla movement.[49]

These, then, are strategies used by most of guerilla organizations in Southern Africa, Latin America, or Asia. As we pointed out previously, guerilla movements fail more often than they succeed. Nevertheless, when the guerilla idea takes hold and when the guerilla movement gains support in the countryside, it is nearly impossible to eradicate, as both the French and Americans found out in the tragic 25-year period following World War II in Vietnam.

[47] S. May and George Plaza, *The United Fruit Company in Latin America* (Washington: National Planning Association, 1958), pp. 15-16.
[48] Ronald Segal, *The Race War* (New York: Bantam Books, 1966), p. 395.

[49] Francois Sully, *Age of the Guerrilla* (New York: Avon Books, 1968), pp. 215-216.

REVOLT OF THE NEGROES IN SAN DOMINGO.

An early anti-imperialist revolt.

One need not be a prophet to predict continuing guerilla warfare in Southeast Asia, South America, and Southern Africa. A case in point is the Portuguese territory in Africa.

Ironically, the Portuguese, who have the lowest literacy rate and highest infant mortality rate in Europe, are the most tenacious in holding on to their African colonies—Angola and Mozambique. Gulf Oil and the American-owned Sunray Mozambique Oil Companies have a monopoly on gas and oil rights in the two colonies. Needless to say, this benefits the masses of the native populace very little. In 1959, 97% of the African population was illiterate in Mozambique. (In 1964, the government spent only 4% of its total budget on education.) These and other facts (such as the minimum wage for African workers, which is one fourth that of European laborers) point to the classic colonialist situation.

In June of 1962, the Mozambique Liberation Front was formed, and in 1967 it was estimated that nearly 8,000 trained and equipped guerillas fought authorities in the countryside.[50] Here again, the recurring pattern of poverty, foreign domination, and a recalcitrant colonial elite have brought about the chronic violence we call guerilla warfare.

EXPERIMENT IN DECOLONIALIZATION— THE UJAMAA VILLAGE IN TANZANIA

As we have seen, the path of anticolonial movements is not a smooth one. Violence, ter-

---

[50] Eduardo C. Mondlane, *Mozambique: A Country at War* (London: Harold Darton and Associates, 1968), p. 8.

rorism, and disorder are as often as not, part and parcel of the drive for independence. Yet even at the point of formal independence, former colonies face problems of the greatest magnitude. When the hated foreigners have been driven from the shores of the homeland, tribalism, economic dependence, and political instability still remain to frustrate the aspiration of the newly "freed" masses.

Franz Fanon was not optimistic about the future of new nations. "The national middle class which takes over power at the end of the colonial regime is an underdeveloped middle class. It has practically no economic power. . . ."[51] Moreover

> . . . the national economy of the period of independence is not set on a new footing. It is still concerned with the groundnut harvest, with the cocoa crop and the olive yield. In the same way there is no change in the marketing of basic products, and not a single industry is set up in the country. We go on sending out raw materials; we go on being Europe's small farmers, who specialize in unfinished products.[52]

Fanon believed that in most cases the national bourgeoisie, educated to European tastes and desires, would betray the goals of national liberation. When the inevitable economic crises would occur in the new country, an ethnic or tribal scapegoat would be found. Asian shopkeepers would be pointed to as saboteurs of economic growth. Again, tribal jealousies, such as those manifest in Kenya or Nigeria, are covertly encouraged by politicians hoping to cover their own economic incompetence. Again, Fanon states:

> The colonial power increases its demands, accumulates concessions and guarantees and takes fewer pains to mask the hold it has over the national government. The people stagnate deplorably in unbearable poverty; slowly they awaken to the unutterable treason of their leaders.[53]

Fanon's prophecies have been born out in many African countries where the movements for national liberation have failed to significantly improve the lot of the peasantry or to mobilize the masses for political and economic development. Yet for all his dismal utterances, Fanon was not a man without hope. A decade after his death in 1961, events occurring in East Africa held the possibility of proving his prophecies wrong and his hopes correct.

Tanzania, the largest country in East Africa, received its independence when Tanganyika and Zanzibar, former British colonies, united in 1963. Tanzania, a one-party state, was committed from its beginnings to African socialism. Julius Nyerere, a former secondary school teacher, became Tanzania's first president. It was his desire to keep the revolutionary fires burning in East Africa after the British had formally left. Nyerere's concept of socialism, unlike Marx's, did not see capitalism as a natural phase of economic development. Nyerere wrote in 1962:

> African socialism . . . did not have the "benefit" of the Agrarian Revolution or the Industrial Revolution. It did not start from the existence of conflicting "classes" in society. Indeed I doubt if the equivalent for the word "class" exists in any indigenous African language. . . . The foundation and the objective of African socialism, is the extended family. The true African socialist does not look on one class of men as his brethren and another as his natural enemies. . . . He rather regards all men as his brethren—as members of his ever extending family. . . . "Ujamaa," then or "familyhood," describes our socialism. It is opposed to capitalism, which seeks to build a happy society on the basis of the exploitation of man by man; and it is equally opposed to doctrinaire socialism which seeks to build its happy society on a philosophy of inevitable conflict between man and man.[54]

T.A.N.U. (Tanganyika African National Union) under Nyerere's leadership was com-

---

[51] Franz Fanon, *The Wretched of the Earth* (New York: Grove Press, 1968), p. 149.
[52] *Ibid.*, p. 151.
[53] *Ibid.*, p. 167.

[54] Reproduced by permission of President Mwalimu, Julius K. Nyerere, from *Ujamaa: Essays on Socialism* (Nairobi: Oxford University Press, 1968), pp. 11, 12. Copyright by Julius K. Nyerere.

mitted to egalitarianism and economic development. Some[55] have argued that these goals are mutually incompatible. It was the position of the African socialists, nonetheless, that an underdeveloped (or misdeveloped) country's greatest resource is her people rather than her industrial potential.

In 1967, the T.A.N.U. party met in northern Tanzania and produced the Arusha Declaration, a manifesto "for socialism and self-reliance." Under the declaration, banking firms, import-export houses, and grainmilling organizations were all nationalized in a classic socialist manner. With the aid of the Swedes, the East Germans, and the Chinese, cooperatives were established in cotton ginneries, maize and rice mills, and coffee curing works.

If, however, T.A.N.U. was to continue the decolonializing process after independence, it was necessary to change not only economic institutions but the mentality of the common people as well. This was necessary because, as the principal of Kivukoni College (in Dar Es Salaam) told the author:

> Colonial education attempted to mystify native students to preserve its power. For example, we were told by the British that textile mills must be located in temperate climates to be successful. This was written in all our texts and fortunately for the British, we believed this for a long time. The chief duty of an anti-colonialist education is demystification.[56]

Educational change was given key emphasis in the decolonialist movement in Tanzania. The elitist notions of the English educational system were to be replaced with an egalitarian method.

Nyerere's plan is that

> ... schools must in fact, become communities—and communities which practice the precept of self-reliance. ... This means that all schools, but

especially secondary schools and other forms of higher education, must contribute to their own upkeep; they must be economic communities as well as social and educational communities. Each school should have, as an integral part of it, a form or workshop which provides the food eaten by the community, and makes some contribution to the total national income.[57]

Tanzanian education has begun to fulfill its promise. Many schools, including Kivukoni College, the training school for T.A.N.U. party members, have forms in which students, faculty, and staff work together a portion of the day to produce their own foodstuffs, as well as to perform janitorial duties. This is in stark contrast to a number of African countries that have, in spite of their anticolonialist rhetoric, adapted in full the educational system of the English, French, or Germans.

Basic to the concept of African socialism is, nevertheless, control of economic institutions. For many African leaders, such as Kwame Nkrumah, late president of Ghana, African socialism means public ownership of the means of production, basic industrialization, socialist education, and national planning.[58]

The Tanzanian leadership has, of course, opted for these programs; more importantly, however, it has introduced a concept foreign to western socialism—that of the Ujamaa village. The word Ujamaa is Kiswahili and can be translated roughly as a sense of familyhood. It is, in fact, a traditional African term laden with ethical and social import. Nyerere argues:

> The traditional African family lived according to the basic principles of Ujamaa. Its members did this unconsciously, and without any conception of what they were doing in political terms. The family members thought of themselves as one, and all their language and behavior emphasized

---

[55] See for example Raymond Aron, *Progress and Disillusion: The Dialectics of Modern Society* (New York: Mentor Books, 1968). Aron argues that technological progress (hence economic progress) necessitates hierarchical relations.

[56] Personal conversation, July 1972.

[57] Julius K. Nyerere, *Education for Self-Reliance* (pamphlet), Government printer, Dar Es Salaam, Tanzania, 1968.

[58] See Kwame Nkrumah, "The Basic Needs of African Socialism" *Pan Africa* (April 19, 1963).

their unity. The basic goods of life were "our food," "our land," "our cattle."[59]

The traditional village is not completely romanticized by Nyerere; it was (and is) poverty stricken. Also the position of women has been, as Nyerere puts it, "to some extent inferior. It is impossible to deny that the women did, and still do, more than their fair share of the work in the fields and in the homes. By virtue of their sex they suffered from inequalities which had nothing to do with their contribution to the family welfare."[60] Another weakness of the traditional village (although Nyerere does not mention it) is that village cooperation was often limited to fellow clan members. If development of the nation is to occur, clan ties must not weaken regional and national cooperation.

The T.A.N.U. party had supported the development of Ujamaa villages in nearly all areas of the nation. Government publications such as the *Dar Es Salaam Daily News* report daily on the successes of Ujamaa experiments. For example, on July 26, 1972 the *News* cites the Matendo village as an ideal in African socialism.

> Two lively projects have been undertaken by the villagers. Their first aim is to build 249 houses. They have also undertaken the task of harvesting cotton on their 16 hectares farm. . . . Mr. Kibungu told me that four days of each week are allotted to the collective projects and the rest of the days are spent on the members' individual occupations. . . . One thing that impresses an outsider is the seriousness shown by the peasants "service before self," and that really would make us go Ujamaa and indeed, socialists.[61]

Despite the official optimism of the government press, many problems are associated with the Ujamaa experiment, and they are not inconsequential. At one Ujamaa village in the West

Lake region, Rumazi, production was low, and socialist cooperation almost nonexistent. A check into the situation by T.A.N.U. authorities showed why:

> Out of the forty-two settlers I interviewed at Rugazi, thirty-six said they had been forced to the village and eight out of these added that they had been intimidated. Two of them went further and said that they had been put in the lock-up by a Divisional Executive Officer. When they were released they were told to go to Rugazi and if not worse things would happen to them.[62]

This technique of forceable resettlement violated both the spirit and the law of the Arusha declaration. Nevertheless, overzealous administrators have often been guilty of sabotaging Ujamaa principles.

Another major source of frustration for the advocates of Ujamaa is tribalism and localism. Often a new village will combine peoples of several tribes, clans, and localities (usually landless peasants). When a village is begun, hardships are many; government assistance is often insufficient or spasmodic. This means that the villagers must sacrifice for each other in order to survive. Experience has shown that many residents of the new Ujamaa will share food and shelter only with members of their own clan or locality. This presents difficult problems for the village. B. B. Bakula, a Senior Education Officer, believes that Ujamaa villages should, in fact, utilize clan similarities in creating new social structures. He describes one successful Ujamaa village, the Omurunazi, as follows:

> It is my contention that traditionalism does exist in the new settlement. The clan heads helped in the registration of the recruits especially when they held the post of cell leader. Their role in mobilizing men for the scheme was important. Ninety per cent of those in my interview sample were motivated to join the scheme basically by a desire for economic improvement. An essential ingredient of traditional resettlement practices

---

[59] Julius K. Nyerere, *Socialism and Rural Development* (pamphlet), Government printer, Dar Es Salaam, Tanzania, 1967.

[60] *Ibid.*

[61] Shamlal Puri, "Matendo Village: A Model in the Making," *Dar Es Salaam Daily News* (July 26, 1972), p. 7.

[62] I. K. S. Musoke, "Building Socialism in Bukoba: The Establishment of Rugazi Ujamaa Village," *University of Dar Es Salaam: Studies in Political Science* 2, pp. 1-14.

was that the settlers were motivated by this same desire. In the new settlement, there was a general tendency for the people from the same village to stay together. At Omurunazi communalism was evident as the settlers interacted with each other. Cooperation centered mostly on a clan basis and there was even greater cooperation in the smaller structures of lineages which formed the clan. Furthermore, leadership was exercised by the recognized clan heads in most cases.[63]

Some of the problems of the Ujamaa experiment are quite easy to define, such as a scarcity of land. Some are more ambiguous, such as the difficulty of politicizing an agrarian people. Will the Ujamaa experiment work? That will be an open question for some time to come. Not only does this experiment in African socialism face internal problems, it also faces an outside world with infinitely more wealth and political power. The decolonialization movement in Tanzania, like any other movement in a small country, can be frustrated or even extinguished by a larger more conservative social system.

As we review the Ujamaa experiments in Tanzania, it would be well to try to understand it in terms of the three worldwide social trends that are shaping the modern world—industrialization, bureaucratization, and cultural imperialism. First industrialization: The Ujamaa leaders such as Nyerere are aware that industrialization, such as one can see in the developed world, has produced economic surplus. This is a requi-

site for human growth and development. Yet rapid industrialization has often carried with it a rampant destruction of tradition and a creation of predatory class relations with a resultant increase in human misery. The ideal of the Ujamaa is to avoid the pitfalls of industrialization while maintaining the desired economic growth. Tanzania has made significant economic gains in the last decade. Yet it, like all other underdeveloped countries, is a David in a world of Goliaths.

Bureaucratization: The building of a nation-state with humane values necessitates planning, one of the cornerstones of bureaucracy. At its best, the Ujamaa promises planning at the grassroots level. Insofar as it is able to carry this out, it can avoid the alienation and goal displacement so characteristic of most modern bureaucracies.

Cultural imperialism: The Ujamaa experiment is clearly a negation of many of the values of imperialism—racism, foreign domination, and economic injustice. Yet one aspect of imperialism has not been entirely harmful to the Tanzanian people. This derives from the fact that imperialism produces a common oppression of colonial peoples that in turn can lead national consciousness rather than the tribal mentality. The enlargement of social scale can produce more universal cooperation, which is necessary in combating poverty, ecological suicide, and perhaps even war.

The Ujamaa village experiment is, like most other human endeavors, unclear in its outcome. Nevertheless, its aims are humane, and it is out of such experimentation that human progress becomes a possibility.

---

[63] B. B. Bakula, "The Effect of Traditionalism of Rural Development: The Omurunazi Ujamaa Village, Bukoba," *University of Dar Es Salaam: Studies in Political Science* 2, pp. 15-33.

CHAPTER 7   THE INDUSTRIAL TREND: OLIGARCHY AND EGALITARIAN SOCIAL MOVEMENTS

There'll be a union label in Berlin
When those union boys in uniform march in;
And rolling in the ranks there'll be UAW tanks:
Roll Hitler out and roll the union in.

UAW-CIO Labor Song

The historic process of rationalization, according to Max Weber, is the dominant tendency of our time. This process deals with the organization of life through a division and coordination of activities on the basis of an exact study of men's relations with each other, with their tools and their environment for the purpose of achieving greater efficiency and productivity.[1] But it is more than this; it is also a disenchantment with the world: "The extent and direction of 'rationalization' is thus measured negatively in terms of the degree to which magical elements of thought are displaced, or positively by the extent to which ideas gain in systematic coherence and naturalistic consistency."[2] Two historical trends that point up this process are the Commercial and Industrial Revolutions, as well as the egalitarian

movements born within them. The Commercial Revolution of the sixteenth to eighteenth centuries began the radical transformation of feudalism, and the Industrial Revolution in the eighteenth century began the radical transformation of capitalism. Toynbee, who studied nineteenth century Great Britain, coined the phrase "Industrial Revolution" when Britain became the "workshop of the world." In retrospect, the revolutionary rhetoric may have been an overstatement since many of the characteristics attributed to it—introduction of machines, new sources of power, the factory system of production, and new businessmen willing to risk capital—occurred before this period, if at all, in many places.[3]

Nonetheless, there is general agreement that

---

[1] Julian Freund, *Max Weber* (New York: Vintage Books, 1969), p. 18.

[2] Hans Gerth and C. Wright Mills, *From Max Weber: Essays in Sociology* (New York: Oxford University Press, 1946), p. 51.

[3] Arnold Toynbee, *The Industrial Revolution* (Boston: The Beacon Press, 1956). See also John Bowditch and Clement Ramsland, *Voices of the Industrial Revolution* (Ann Arbor: University of Michigan Press, 1968), p. iii.

the trend in the last two centuries toward the mechanization and industrialization of the world, sometimes labeled industrialism, constitutes a *radical* transformation from the pre-industrial context. It is moving the world from a nexus of villages and towns to sprawling cities and from cottage industries to multinational corporations, creating spreading middle classes as well as new groups in poverty and relative deprivation. Equality becomes an idea to be grounded in reality.

The industrial trend, or industrialism, has three aspects to consider: (1) the revolutionary technological changes in the method of manufacturing, in the modes of transportation, and in the facilities for the exchange of information; (2) the rise of the factory system as a new method for the organization of industry and the discipline and application of labor; and (3) the general economic, political, social, and cultural results of the new technology and the factory system.[4] We are concerned with the third aspect as it affects the rise of *oligarchy* and *egalitarian* social movements, recalling that we stated previously that industrialization has within it the necessity for oligarchy and the ideal of egalitarianism (p. 59). Moreover, industrialization now means either nationalism or internationalization.

THE OLIGARCHIC TENDENCIES

To trace the general effects of the industrial trend, a digression on the previous Commercial Revolution is necessary because it marks the origin of the nation-state and the tendency of "oligarchization."[5] In the words of Becker and Barnes:

The chief impulse that the Commercial Revolu-

tion brought to the growth of national states came from the rise of the middle class and their alliance with the monarchs in the attempts to destroy the anarchy and decentralization of the feudal system . . . a loyal officialdom, opposed to the feudal aristocracy, appeared in the new *noblesse de la robe*—the middle class merchants and lawyers who filled the royal offices. Through the intervention of capital, through the flood of wealth streaming into the royal treasuries from the national share in the profits of the new commercial and industrial enterprises, the kings were provided with the indispensible financial power to hire their own administrators and to support a national army independent of the feudal lords.[6]

Political centralization and mercantilism continued and the European middle classes gained in power. The English Revolution of the seventeenth century and the American and French Revolutions of the eighteenth century were bourgeois revolutions with political doctrines based on the natural rights of life, liberty, property, revolution, and popular sovereignty.[7] In England, where the Commercial and Industrial Revolutions seemed to have the most immediate impact, intellectuals reacted. Pope, Burke, Adam Smith, Robert Wallace, Paley, Locke, Bentham, Spence, Olgilvie, Paine, Godwin, and others began to examine rights of all kinds, and questioned the emergence and role of government and private property.[8] For example, Adam Smith's *An Inquiry into the Nature and Causes of the Wealth of Nations* (which appeared in the same year as the American Declaration of Independence) relates the wealth of nations to the changes in the division of labor. The division of labor greatly increases the quantity of work but:

Every man is rich or poor according to the degree in which he can afford to enjoy the necessaries, conveniences, and amusements of human life. But after the division of labour has once thoroughly taken place, it is but a very small part of these with which a man's own labour can supply him. The far greater part of them he must derive from the labour of other people, and he must be

---

[4] Howard Becker and Harry Elmer Barnes, *Social Thought from Lore to Science* (New York: Dover Publications, 1961), Vol. 2, p. 595.

[5] An awkward term recently used by Roberta Ash, *Social Movements in America* (Chicago: Markham Publishing Company 1972), p. 24.

[6] Becker and Barnes, *op. cit.,* Vol. 1, p. 371.

[7] *Ibid.,* pp. 370-405.

[8] Harry W. Laidler, *History of Socialism* (New York: Thomas Y. Crowell Company, 1968), pp. 71-81.

rich or poor according to the quantity of that labour which he can command, or which he can afford to purchase.[9]

This rationalization, this increase in the division of labor as a result of the Commercial and Industrial Revolutions led to the so-called bourgeois revolutions and governments where the smug elites from the old regimes had to settle for a few or none of past privileges. Slavery and wage-slavery now existed side-by-side. But these social changes in the stratification of Europe and the new world resulted in unrest, stirring, disenchantment, and discontent with intellectuals and the newly created working classes and peasantry. The humanitarian movement was in motion:

> The Industrial Revolution was one of the most severe social crises which has thus far taken place in the history of human society. It tangled and tore the whole web of social life in the Western world, and forced extensive readjustments to meet the new conditions of living. The misery and suffering which resulted led to a large number and variety of proposals for social and economic reconstruction. Nothing which has previously taken place gave so tremendous an impulse to the humanitarian movement.[10]

This dialectical impulse toward humanitarianism took several forms. Historically, there were many blueprints and experiments for reform and reconstruction—many that stressed equality as inequality became more visible. There were utopian and intellectual experiments and some government action in England, as an example, ranged from the Elizabethan Poor Law of 1601 to the Reform Bill of 1832.

The ruling classes and elites adopted a minimum number of reforms from 1600 to the middle of the nineteenth century while refining industrial techniques. From all this came the working man's interest in various socialist ideas being articulated by the intellectuals of the period.

Early attempts at reform and reconstruction by elites and reformers were more to save the old order than to prepare the new one and were not

reaching the workers. In France, for example, when a revolution had been waged for liberty, equality, and fraternity, the workers lost out to the commercial and manufacturing classes. Anticombination laws were soon passed. Gatherings of artisans were declared riotous: "An 1803 statute declared that those involved in coalitions to cease work were punishable by imprisonment of from one to three months, and that the leaders of such coalitions were subject to terms from three to five years."[11] Thousands of testimonies are available as to the radical nature of the transformation; testimonies from the "voices of the industrial revolution"—Quesnay, Smith, Bentham, Malthus, Ricardo, Carlyle, Saint-Simon, Owen, Cabet, Marx and Engels, and the poets Tennyson, Clough, Pottier, and Hood[12] to Marcuse, Bell, and Harrington:

> But with the Industrial Revolution, history turned a corner. For the first time ever, the production of genuine abundance was within the technical competence of man. As a result, there was a material basis for decency. And with the appearance of the modern working class, driven to economic and political organization by the necessities of daily life, a social force had come into being that would be impelled toward the theory and practice of justice.[13]

In general, there is agreement that the Industrial Revolution has produced both oligarchic as well as egalitarian tendencies in society; such tendencies are reflected in the competing ideologies and groups caught up in the industrialization process.

OLIGARCHY, IDEOLOGY, AND THE RISE OF POLITICAL PARTIES

Political parties are an integral part of the rise and continuation of industrialization. They represent the oligarchic tendencies and the embodi-

---

[9] Bowditch and Ramsland, *op. cit.,* p. 19.
[10] Becker and Barnes, *op. cit.,* Vol. 2, p. 598.

[11] Laidler, *op. cit.,* pp. 277-278.
[12] Bowditch and Ramsland, *op. cit.,* pp. iii-xvii.
[13] Michael Harrington, *The Accidental Century* (Baltimore: Penguin Books, Inc., 1965), p. 38.

ment of ideology in industrial societies. They are the more organized aspects of social movements and reflect social trends as well. The relationship of political parties to social movements (including ideology) has been well demonstrated by Heberle. (They may even represent the more organized, even "class interests" of a given movement.) He says there are four basic types of empirical relations between movements and parties:

> 1. A party may be part of a broader social movement, as is the British Labor Party, which forms one of the three branches of a labor movement.
> 2. The party may be independent of any particular social movement and embody in its membership all or part of several social movements; this has been the tendency in the major American parties.
> 3. The same social movement may be represented in several political parties: for example, the socialist movement in various socialist parties, the labor movement in socialistic, communistic and other parties.
> 4. Finally, a social movement may reject on principle the affiliation with any political party, as for example did the anarcho-syndicalistic movement of the I.W.W.[14]

He says further that it is not easy to define the above relationships because of oligarchic tendencies such as bureaucracy within parties and movements, and whether or not officers and workers work merely for honor of office or for pay.[15] Definition is further complicated by the fact that movements and parties can be of one or another type of authority, namely institutional or charismatic. Allegiance in the first is because of legality of office, and in the second because of what an individual ordains to be so. The consequences for staff structure follow from the type of authority. In the case of administrative authority, administrative functionaries get legitimacy from basic statutes. In the case of charismatic authority, followers get bestowed upon

them the offices. But, Heberle says, "In most parties and in most organized cores of social movements, the two principles of staff structure are mixed."[16]

The necessity for oligarchy, or leaders and followers, in the application of industrial techniques goes without saying. Division of labor is necessary to get the job done. Bureaucracy is inevitable as rationalization of production proceeds. But is this also the case for egalitarian social movements? Yes, we would say, all movements need organization to bring about change. Whether this necessity for organization must take the form of a political party is moot. Nonetheless, we have seen in the last few hundred years political parties arising within the industrial trend—some for maintaining certain groups in power, and others to change that power. Perhaps the most incisive commentator on this is Robert Michels. For example:

> The life of political parties, whether they are concerned chiefly with national or with local politics, must, in theory, necessarily exhibit an even stronger tendency towards democracy than that which is manifested by the state. The political party is founded in most cases on the principle of the majority, and is founded always on the principle of the mass.[17]

Elites with either a class, status, or power base have formed political parties with ideologies of direct appeal to the masses, to the so-called majority, and to democracy. More will be said about this in our chapter on the "Negation of the Negation" or how elites in social control, in various ways, keep egalitarian social movements from emerging and succeeding. On the other hand, the masses, the disenfranchised, the peasants, and the working classes also have formed political parties with democratic ideology. We would call these the more organized aspects of egalitarian social movements. In both cases,

---

[14] Rudolf Herberle, *Social Movements: An Introduction to Political Sociology* (New York: Appleton-Century-Crofts, 1951), pp. 179-180.
[15] *Ibid.,* pp. 280-284.

[16] *Ibid.,* pp. 287-290.
[17] Robert Michels, *Political Parties: A Sociological Study of the Oligarchical Tendencies in Modern Democracy* (New York: Hearst's International Library Company, 1915), pp. 2-3.

there are oligarchic tendencies within democratic ideology. Again in the words of Michels:

> ... in modern party life aristocracy gladly
> presents itself in democratic guise, whilst the
> substance of democracy is permeated with
> aristocratic elements. On the one side we have
> aristocracy in a democratic form, and on the other
> democracy with an aristocratic content. The
> democratic external form which characterized
> the life of political parties may readily veil from
> superficial observers the tendency towards aris-
> tocracy, or rather towards oligarchy, which is
> inherent in all party organization.[18]

Michels says such oligarchic tendency is almost
spontaneous with the aristocratic-type elites, but
oligarchic tendencies are to be questioned in
revolutionary parties whose aims are to negate
such a thing and have arisen almost dialectically
to struggle against this tendency.[19]

POVERTY, INCREASING DEPRIVATION, AND EGALITARIAN MOVEMENTS

The industrial trend yielded a necessary but
repressive division of labor and created a class
of laborers dependent on wages in an urbanized
environment. Antithetically, however, these
laborers, and the intellectuals beginning to speak
for them, thought that industrialization should
lead to more equality and not more inequality. As
thousands came to the industrial towns and
cities over the decades to become wage earners,
the necessity for organization became apparent.
Unemployment, taxation, and indebtedness—
scourges for millennia—increased.

We saw previously that the egalitarian promises of the French Revolution were scuttled as
far as industrial workers were concerned. Despite the codes and penalties for organizing to
improve working conditions and general welfare,
however, the workers created labor organizations
in the form of cooperatives. The socialist utopians
of France (Babeuf, Cabet, Saint-Simon, En-

fantin, Fourier, Blanc, and Proudhon) kept alive
the idea of progress and equality as the bourgeoisie took over the power formerly in the hands
of the nobility. The revolution of July, 1830, and
the revolution of 1848 resulted in much labor
unrest as well as enthusiasm for organization;
some three hundred producers' cooperatives
were formed in Paris during the 1830's and
1840's.[20]

In England, workers were extremely oppressed by creeping industrialism, and they and
intellectuals looked to the French Revolution for
ideas. Yet there was no comparable revolution.
The bourgeoisie had had firm control since the
revolution of 1688. Whereas there was a backward aristocracy in France that had to be over-
thrown by the middle class, such was not the
case in England. "The nobility took part in the
business enterprises of the bourgeoisie, led the
political parties of the bourgeoisie, and were, so
to speak, at the head of bourgeoisie society. In
England after 1688 a democratic mass movement could not direct itself against the king or
the aristocracy alone."[21] (Historically, in mid-
seventeenth century England there were the
Levellers who influenced proposals such as
equal electoral districts, frequent parliaments,
specific limitations on the executive power, and
universal suffrage,[22] but they had little actual
effect.) Even though Parliament in 1769 made
the destruction of machines a capital offense,[23]
in the early nineteenth century the Luddites or
machine smashers wanted to return to the good
old days of the past. They were acting against the
dominant substructural transformation of industrialization and merely brought on more repressive legislation and the hanging of workers, but

---

[18] *Ibid.*, pp. 10-11.
[19] *Ibid.*, p. 11.

[20] Laidler, *op. cit.*, pp. 44-70, 277-278.
[21] Arthur Rosenberg, *Democracy and Socialism: A Contribution to the Political History of the Past 150 Years* (Boston: Beacon Press, 1965), pp. 49-50.
[22] Will and Ariel Durant, *Rousseau and Revolution,* Vol. 10 in *The Story of Civilization* (New York: Simon and Schuster, 1967), p. 679.
[23] Crane Brinton, *The Anatomy of Revolution* (New York: Random House, 1965), p. 165.

103

they did point to the agony of the workers in the city factories.

The Commercial and Industrial Revolutions as trends expanded and involved the New World in dramatic ways. Population began to increase. The land grabs and black and white enslavements of Europeans and Africans from the sixteenth century onward led to one of the greatest forced migrations in world history. Monarchs of the old world paid off their aristocrats with land and favors. Commercial adventurers of all types, with the help of the ruling class, enslaved hundreds of thousands of blacks and whites in the conquest and settlement of America. European imperialism led to world colonialism, and these trends are the basis for the success of these two dramatic revolutions. The shift from agrarian to industrial capitalism in America brought into existence many new groups and social movements.

The continuation of the Commercial Revolution in America began with the development of northern towns and of plantations and farms. England, Spain, France, Holland, and other countries carved up and settled the country as fast as they could. Of course, thousands of warm bodies of any kind were required. Aristocrats and adventurers began to round up the unemployed vagabonds and the imprisoned of Europe, and they enslaved or indentured thousands. Others went to the New World because of streets and hills that were lined with gold, El Dorado, the get-rich-quick myth. Thousands of black slaves were shipped in after 1819 to work in the fields of the Atlantic seaboard. Many resident old world aristocratic elites made great profits, and those elites who migrated lived fine lives because of the advantages provided by these new workers:

> The only difference between these white slaves, sold in American ports, and the blacks was that the slavery of the whites was limited and the blacks were slaves for life. . . . It may be said with truth that both black and white slaves formed the basis of the landed aristocracy of the colonies before and long after the revolution. . . . With the resources of life in their hands and whites and blacks held in servitude, the ruling classes had

all the advantages that the masters of any age might wish.[24]

They exercised great social control over the workers brought in. Branding, maiming, imprisoning was not uncommon for the whites, while working blacks to death was considered profitable. Generally, white slaves, after being manumitted or released from servitude, remained in poverty; many of them formed the historical sources of the "poor whites."[25]

The nature of poverty has changed in the last two centuries. Religious sanctions of the necessity for the poor to "stay in their place" have been increasingly challenged. The rise in population as well as the dramatic national and international migration patterns make millions of people instantly aware of social, political, and economic differences. Also the rise of mass media (pamphlets and newspapers in the eighteenth century, mass distribution of books in the nineteenth century, and radio and television in the twentieth century) has made it possible for many of the world's poor to see themselves with new eyes. "Poverty is safe when it is aware and alone."[26] A culmination of this awareness in the United States was Harrington's book *The Other America*,[27] which is said to have led to reforms like the War on Poverty. It would be stretching things to say it led to riots among blacks, but it certainly was part of the revolution of rising expectations.

Poverty has changed in many areas of the world from the benign paternalism of peasant life to the dynamically intensified poverty of the uprooted urban areas. This change is largely because of the form that industrial capitalism has taken since the French and Industrial Revolutions began. Table 2 deals with this shift in thought about the poor in terms of the social

---

[24] James O'Neal, *The Workers in American History* (New York: The Rand School of Social Science, 1921), p. 40.
[25] *Ibid.*, pp. 45-54.
[26] Ronald Segal, *The Race War* (New York: Bantam Press, 1966), p. 11.
[27] Michael Harrington, *The Other America* (Baltimore: Penguin Books, Inc., 1963).

TABLE 2. SUMMARY OF SHIFTS IN SOCIAL THOUGHT CONCERNING THE "POOR" IN THE NINETEENTH CENTURY

	THE PAST: *Pre-French and Industrial Revolution*	THE PRESENT: *Post-French and Industrial Revolution*
SOCIAL RELATIONS	Status Gemeinschaft Particularistic	Contract Gesellschaft Universalistic
PREVAILING CONCEPTUAL ATTITUDE	Subjective Nonproblematic Legitimate Sacred Unrecognized "Paupers" Inegalitarian order	Objective (subjective) Problematic Illegitimate Secular Recognized (consciousness) "Poverty" Egalitarian forces
RESPONSIBILITY (CAUSES)	Individual Local community Fate Natural	Individual-social The State The society Functional
CURES	Partial Private Charity, doles None Pessimistic	Total Public (private) Assistance, welfare Socialism Optimistic

relations, attitudes, responsibility, and cures for poverty. We might say that technological factors often increase the intensity of poverty by constantly destroying possibilities for hand labor. This applies not only to the mechanical ditch digger in cities but also to the mechanical cotton picker in Mississippi. Urbanization around the world also has changed the nature of poverty— whether it be the unorganized urbanization of the last few hundred years or the organized urbanization sponsored by the American government in South Vietnam in the 1960's. Furthermore, poverty is both *absolute* (in the developing nations half of the children die before the age of ten) and *relative* (students and women in the U. S. complain they do not have a sense of control over their destiny).

Poverty, once defended as a holy state of being,[28] is of historical and immediate concern. It is of historical concern because poverty is a label referring to a condition of millions of people of the past and present. Various theories of poverty form an extremely important part of social, political, and economic thought in the world today. More immediate concern is related to the application of these theories into movements. The current international ideology or social policy is

---

[28] I. M. Rubinow, "Poverty," in R. A. Seligman and Alvin Johnson, editors, *Encyclopedia of the Social Sciences* (New York: The Macmillan Co., 1937), Vol. 12, p. 289. See also "Vows (Christian)" by A. J. Grieve, in James Hastings, editor, *Encyclopedia of Religion and Ethics* (New York: Charles Scribner, 1925), Vol. 12, p. 650.

for developed countries to assist underdeveloped countries; for example, the Alliance for Progress of the United States and the Aswan High Dam Project of the Soviet Union. In addition, almost all countries have domestic policies that include programs to raise the level of living of their own peoples, for example, the Russian Five-Year Plans, French "Planification," British Welfare State Programming, and the United States "War on Poverty" as part of "The Great Society." One sociologist has referred to this *social planning* as a special case of the phenomena that make up "social movements."[29]

George Simmel's *Soziologie*[30] offers an important statement on how the concept of poverty relates to social relations in general. Insofar as man is a social being, says Simmel, he has both rights and corresponding obligations[31]; therefore, the "poor" also have rights and obligations within this larger framework of social relations. His major concern is with assistance to the poor;

the right to assistance belongs in the same category as the right to work and the right to life.[32] Simmel believes the rights of the poor to be a priority but also says it is unclear to whom the rights of the poor ought to be addressed. The solution of this question reveals very deep sociological differences. Whereas assistance to the poor was ascribed to smaller social circles (like the local community) in the past, says Simmel, the tendency is to consider assistance to the poor as a matter pertaining to the widest political circle, the State.[33]

The change from handling the poor at local levels to doing so by the State takes poverty as misery in its immediate sensate form to the abstract, according to Simmel.[34] This shift is summed up in the statement: private assistance is subjective and helps the *poor;* the State assists objectively the condition known as *poverty.* This leads Simmel to consider the relative character of poverty in the form of *individual* versus *social* poverty:

> The poor, as a sociological category, are not those who suffer specific deficiencies and deprivations, but those who receive assistance or should receive it according to social norms. Consequently, in this sense, poverty cannot be defined in itself as a quantitative state, but only in terms of the social reaction resulting from a specific situation: it is analogous to the way crime, the substantive definition of which offers such difficulties, is defined as "an action punished by public sanctions." Thus today some do not determine the essence of morality on the basis of the inner state of the subject but from the result of his action; his subjective intention is considered valuable only insofar as it normally produces a certain socially useful effect . . . the individual state, in itself, no longer determines the concept, but social teleology does so; the individual is determined by the way in which the totality that surrounds him acts towards him.[35]

Simmel says that when this action on the part of the totality occurs, we arrive at a *social* meaning

Text continued on p. 111.

---

[29] Alvin Boskoff, "Social Change: Major Problems in the Emergence of Theoretical and Research Foci," in Howard Becker and Alvin Boskoff, editors, *Modern Sociological Theory in Continuity and Change* (New York: The Dryden Press, 1957), pp. 279-280.

[30] George Simmel, "The Poor," *Social Problems* 13, no. 2 (1965), pp. 118-140. We are aware of the possible implications of resting the case of poverty as a sociological phenomenon on the theoretical position of Simmel. In the words of Rudolf Heberle, this is a functionalist approach where social types like the poor are complexes of relationships. "Society is, for Simmel, essentially psychic interaction between human beings both as individuals and as human beings. Society is really not a substance but a process, a happening (*Geschehen*), or 'something functional,' something that human beings do and experience." See Rudolf Heberle, "The Sociology of George Simmel: The Forms of Social Interaction," in Harry Elmer Barnes, editor, *An Introduction to the History of Sociology* (Chicago: The University of Chicago Press, 1948), pp. 255-257. As such, criticisms of Simmel apply to this thesis. A most devastating criticism is Pitirim A. Sorokin, "Sociologistic School: The Formal School and a Systematics of Social Relationship," in his *Contemporary Sociological Theories* (New York: Harper and Row, Publishers, Inc., 1928), pp. 489-513. Yet, taking the criticisms as they come, we know of no better framework upon which the case for poverty as a consideration of social stratification and as a stratum may rest.

[31] Simmel, *op. cit.*, p. 118.

[32] *Ibid.*, p. 120.

[33] *Ibid.*, p. 129.

[34] *Ibid.*, p. 129.

[35] *Ibid.*, p. 138.

1916 Spanish views of war and peace. (From *Cartoons Magazine,* vol. 7, no. 2, February, 1915. H. H. Windsor, editor and publisher, Chicago.)

A Thousand Victims a Day   **A Thousand and One**

In this cartoon Death is shown in the guise of Typhoid and Tuberculosis, claiming more victims than the scientific engine of war.

War Makes for a Certain Equality   **Peace Knows No Such Thing**

For legend see p. 107.

An Incident of War Time   An Accident in Times of Peace

Intoxication of Blood   Intoxication of Alcohol

For legend see p. 107.

Evacuation   Dispossessment

Companions of War   Companions of Peace

For legend see p. 107.

of the poor. Having established that poverty is determined by social teleology, Simmel turns to the social *meaning* of the poor man.

THE SOCIAL MEANING OF THE POOR MAN

Simmel's reasoning leads him to say that the *social* meaning of the poor man in contrast to the *individual* meaning makes the poor into a kind of "estate" or unitary stratum in society. Now, this stratum is categorical, not united by interaction among its members but by the collective attitude that society as a whole adopts toward it.[36] The tendency towards interaction ("socialism") was not always lacking however, says Simmel. In the fourteenth century, there were unions of the poor, but growing differentiation of society made such unions impossible:

> The class of the poor, especially in modern society, is a unique sociological synthesis. It possesses a great homogeneity insofar as its meaning and location in the social body is concerned; but it lacks it completely insofar as the individual qualification of its elements are concerned. It is the common end of the most diverse destinies, an ocean into which lives derived from the most diverse social strata flow together. No change, development, polarization, or breakdown of social life occurs without leaving its residuum in the stratum of poverty.[37]

This condition of the stratum of the poor, says Simmel, does not give rise to sociologically unifying forces:

> In this way, poverty is a unique sociological phenomenon: a number of individuals who, out of a purely individual fate, occupy a specific organic *position* [italics provided] within the whole; but this position is not determined by this fate and condition, but rather by the fact that others—individuals, associations, communities—attempt to correct this condition.[38]

Simmel's discussion on the *social* meaning of the poor man brings out several aspects that have been ignored in recent discussions of what poverty means. First, it is a sociological fact that the poor are an estate or stratum; and, second, their position can have "sociation" or not. Both points relate to the ways we conceptualize stratification within a society. The first asks the question of *who* determines various social positions and the second seeks the degree of social relatedness or consciousness within these social positions. For Simmel, it is obvious that people other than the poor determine the poor's *position* and that the degree of sociation has gone through a shift from more sociation to lesser sociation among the poor in modern society because of increased differentiation.[39] (Both aspects are very much related to how broadly or narrowly one wants to conceptualize poverty and how to get rid of the condition.)

Simmel shows the concept of poverty as a *social* fact because it is defined in terms of some social reaction. Poverty, as such, came about when assistance to the poor became the defined responsibility of the widest political circle, the State. Also, in times before the nineteenth century, according to Simmel, there were degrees of social interaction among the poor, but this was no longer the case in the nineteenth century. State responsibility and lessening "sociation" came about as a result of the increasing differentiation of society. It should be noted that Simmel is not very specific as to just what he means by differentiation in his discussion on the poor. Possibly he would say that there was an increased division of labor and, because of certain shifts, interdependence replaced interaction.

George Simmel has been updated, so to speak, by Lewis Coser, who reiterates Simmel's basic points in a more current style:

> Historically, the poor emerge when society elects to recognize poverty as a special status and assigns specific persons to that category. The fact that some people may privately consider themselves poor is sociologically irrelevant. What *is* sociologically relevant is poverty as a socially recognized condition, as a social status [sic].

---

[36] *Ibid.*, p. 139.
[37] *Ibid.*, p. 139.
[38] *Ibid.*, p. 140.

[39] *Ibid.*, p. 139.

We are concerned with poverty as a property of the social structure.[40]

The poor are recognized as having a special "status" by society. It is negatively determined by what the status holders do *not* have. There is no expectation of social contribution from them. They have low social visibility but have no legitimate mechanism to shield their behavior from observability, as nearly all other status groups have. In short, they have no privacy according to Coser.[41] This paraphrase of Coser contains a contradiction because, on the one hand, the poor have low social visibility, and on the other, they have no privacy. Coser is not very complete in his discussion on this apparent contradiction. He says that the poor are physically, and possibly morally, kept out of sight by other members of society. He then says that the poor must open their lives to public investigators. This apparent contradiction is insightful because the poor are more or less invisible to *all but* social workers and agencies.[42]

It had been mentioned earlier that both Simmel and Coser refer to those in poverty as a stratum determined by what these people do *not* have. Oscar Lewis reacts to this idea of the poor. He says we must distinguish between poverty and the culture of poverty. Admitting that the culture of poverty is a catchy phrase, Lewis says it is *not* a term signifying the absence of something. This term for him signifies a culture in the traditional anthropological sense:

> . . . it provides human beings with a design for living, with a ready-made set of solutions for human problems, and so serves a significant adaptive function. The style of life transcends

national boundaries and regional and rural-urban differences within nations. Wherever it occurs, its practitioners exhibit remarkable similarity in the structure of their families, in interpersonal relations, in spending habits, in their value systems and in their orientation in time.[43]

Note that Lewis' concept implies a kind of social interaction much like Simmel's (that some poor of the past had "sociation").

A thorough treatment of poverty by I. M. Rubinow settles the question of where one might begin the general discussion on the nature of poverty:

> Fundamentally poverty is a negative term denoting absence or lack of material wealth. Such absence, however, is seldom absolute and the term is usually employed to describe the much more frequent situation of insufficiency either in the possession of wealth or in the flow of income. . . . There can scarcely be a satisfactory answer to the question as to how much is enough without some arbitrary agreement as to the objective.[44]

He says that the determination of the state of poverty must rest upon some distinction between legitimate and excessive desires, and upon some underlying theory as to the purpose of human existence; moreover, an appraisal of individual deviations from a prevailing economic well-being depends upon a particular theory of the historic destiny of human society.[45]

In summary, industrialization and all that it implies was most likely responsible for the first attempts to estimate poverty. Rubinow says that *the earliest and most comprehensive attempts to estimate poverty were made in England because agricultural and industrial changes created a more acute and widespread problem of relieved and unrelieved poverty.*[46] The surveys of Arthur Young, Sir Frederick Eden, Charles Booth, and B. Seebohn Roundtree led to an early consciousness of the extent of poverty in England. Attempts were also being made in other coun-

---

[40] Lewis Coser, "The Sociology of Poverty," *Social Problems*, 13, no. 2 (1965), p. 141.
[41] *Ibid.*, pp. 142-145.
[42] This observation about invisibility is in accord with our experiences as social caseworkers. It is also in accord with the whole thrust of a recent book on poverty by Michael Harrington, who says that it is invisibility which characterizes the modern poor. See Michael Harrington, *The Other America* (Baltimore: Penguin Books, Inc., 1963), pp. 9-24. Unfortunately Harrington does not bring out the lack of privacy in their lives.

[43] Oscar Lewis, "The Culture of Poverty," *Scientific American*, 245 (October, 1966), p. 19.
[44] Rubinow, *op. cit.*, p. 284.
[45] *Ibid.*, p. 284.
[46] *Ibid.*, p. 286.

tries to estimate the extent of poverty. In France and elsewhere in Europe, poverty estimates were simultaneous with the development of revolutionary and utopian ideas. The German experience was somewhat different because of the introduction of social insurance at an early stage of development, says Rubinow. In the United States, Robert Hunter and Maurice Parmalee, among others, gave estimates that were sensational at the time.[47]

SHIFTS REGARDING RESPONSIBILITY FOR POVERTY

Related to poverty estimates is the question of *who* or *what* is responsible. The primary way of analyzing responsibility is the *individual* versus the *social*. Rubinow says:

Although it is by no means easy to draw a definite line of demarcation between misconduct and misfortune, personal and social factors, individual and social responsibility or responsibility and a blind sequence of events, these two types of explanation have been regarded as mutually exclusive and have provoked much controversy in the literature.[48]

The controversy that Rubinow points out here is more or less still with us. This dichotomy of individual versus social responsibility also sustains Simmel's observations cited earlier. The State begins to assume responsibility in some way as soon as it views poverty in an objective sense. Yet even though society labels the people as being in the state of poverty, the poor are there because of their own misfortune. For Simmel, the responsibility of the State is simply to maintain *some* minimum for *some* people in *some* form of assistance.[49]

---

[47] *Ibid.*, p. 286. For a broader perspective on the points brought out in this section, see the historical treatment by Howard Becker and Harry Elmer Barnes, "The Quest for Secular Salvation: Social Reform in Relation to the Sociological Impulse," in Becker and Barnes, *op. cit.*, Vol. 2, pp. 595-636.

---

[48] Rubinow, *op. cit.*, p. 288.

[49] Simmel does not state it quite as succinctly as this, but it is implied in the work cited previously.

A radical view of capitalism. (Reprinted courtesy Sawyer Press, Los Angeles, Calif. 90046 U. S. A.)

Thus far in our general statement on poverty, we have more or less limited the discussion to the fact that poverty is related to some kind of conscious comparison on the part of some strata within the society. Differences in social conditions, and objective estimates of them, paralleled the various transformations such as bureaucratization and cultural imperialism that occurred in the nineteenth century and before. Explicit in our discussion has been the fact that the Industrial Revolution led to greater social differences and as a result poverty was born. Another revolution is the idea of *democratization*.

The impact of egalitarian ideas cannot be overlooked in our discussion of poverty. Inequities in the society range from food to justice. Rights and obligations, in the sense that Simmel brought them out, refer to citizenship as well as assistance. A digression into democratization is necessary as we try to see how the concept of poverty relates to changes in social stratifications and the emergence of egalitarian movements.

Bendix, in his book *Nation-Building and Citizenship*,[50] cites John Stuart Mill to give an example of *traditional* authority relationships. Mill says: ". . . the lot of the poor, in all things which affect them collectively, should be regulated *for* them, not *by* them."[51] The distribution of rights and obligations was based on hereditary privilege in medieval political life. In sum, says Bendix, medieval European societies excluded the majority of the people from the exercise of public rights.[52] Bendix then says a "great transformation" occurred in the seventeenth and eighteenth centuries, and Mill's statement no longer holds.

Tocqueville's famous studies of the French Revolution and American democracy form the basis for Bendix's comments.[53] Tocqueville observes that traditional authority relations de-

clined; the "masters" (aristocracy of the medieval period in this sense) retained their *rights* but evaded their *obligations* or responsibilities. During the early phase of the English industrialization, the responsibility of protecting the poor was explicitly rejected. For example, new interpretations of the causes of poverty were advanced like the Malthusian argument for the inevitability of poverty.[54] Tocqueville saw the revolutionary threat when: (1) the master continues to expect servility, but rejects responsibility, and (2) the servant claims equal rights and becomes intractable.[55] The various protests that grew out of this condition led to the "age of democratic revolution" which extends to the present, according to Bendix.[56] This consideration leads Bendix to distinguish and analyze the various rights that come under the push for "citizenship." Taking T. H. Marshall's typology of rights—civil, political, and social—Bendix shows that the establishment of equal rights under the law stands side by side with the fact of social and economic *inequality*:

> The juxtaposition of legal equality and social and economic inequalities inspired the great political debates which accompany the nation-building of the nineteenth century. These debates turn on the types of inequality or insecurity that should be considered intolerable and the methods that should be used to alleviate them.[57]

Needless to say, this active, conscious comparison of rights in the nineteenth century is related to the concept of poverty. The inequalities or

---

[50] Reinhard Bendix, *Nation-Building and Citizenship* (New York: John Wiley and Sons, Inc., 1964).
[51] *Ibid.*, p. 40.
[52] *Ibid.*, p. 43.
[53] *Ibid.*, pp. 40-104.

[54] *Ibid.*, pp. 58-59.
[55] *Ibid.*, p. 70.
[56] *Ibid.*, p. 72.
[57] *Ibid.*, p. 77. See also Stanislaw Ossowski, *Class Structure in the Social Consciousness* (New York: The Free Press of Glencoe, 1963), pp. 96-154. Ossowski says that the copresence of equality with hierarchical tendencies has a long tradition (p. 152): from equality among the Polish gentry, civic equality in Athens, universal equality of the French Revolution, the American creed, and the Soviet constitution. Demands for equality are not demands for equality in every respect. "Nonegalitarian classlessness" is the concept he advances to explain the existence of the demand for equality among the extensive ranges of social statuses and shares in the national income, p. 153.

inequities in the civil, political, and social *rights* of those in poverty led to a shift in nineteenth century social thought regarding this phenomenon. This shift can be summarized as the optimistic view toward poverty.

POVERTY CURES: THE SHIFT FROM PESSIMISM TO OPTIMISM

Various shifts in social thought have been noted. One was the idea that the society became conscious of itself in the nineteenth century. The identification of poverty as a social problem is related to a shift in social thought that is succinctly summed up by Rubinow:

> Social thought and popular opinion have gradually shifted from a fatalistic or apologetic to a critical or constructive point of view toward poverty, its meaning, its causes and effects. . . . The modification or dismissal of this pessimistic attitude among economists toward the problem of poverty has been the result not only of the industrial progress of the last century but of the attack on the Marxian school, which, taking conventional economics at its word, carried it to a logical conclusion by insisting that nothing short of the overthrow of the capitalistic system, under which poverty was considered to be inevitable, could eliminate it.[58]

These economists—the productivity school, the psychological school, and the ethical school—produced new theories, says Rubinow, related to the idea of *planned social effort:*

> In the first two decades of the twentieth century a large number of books on relief, abolition, or prevention of poverty appeared and at the same time much statistical evidence was brought together to break down the force of Marx' destructive criticisms. It was repeatedly declared by many writers that modern capitalism possessed the power to relieve, reduce, cure and entirely prevent real poverty.[59]

As it was in the first two decades of the century,

so it is now in the United States with its War on Poverty. The assumption that modern capitalism (or whatever we want to call the American economic style of life) can abolish poverty is one of the prevailing domestic ideologies.

The Marxian position maintains that poverty is a result of the way the capitalistic society is stratified. The only way to get rid of poverty is to bring about a restratification by revolutionary means. Consciousness (in Simmel's terms, "sociation") among the poor is a prerequisite. Russia, the country that claims to have utilized this perspective successfully, contends that a restratification has occurred in which inequality (and therefore poverty) is theoretically and practically impossible.

The capitalistic or non-Marxian position, as Rubinow pointed out, holds that poverty can be obliterated without a drastic alteration of existing stratification; rather, the obliteration can be brought about peacefully *in time*. No social interaction or consciousness on the part of the poor as a group is implied.

It is appropriate to carefully mention here the whole history of the rise of socialism in the more industrialized countries that were the objects of Marx's criticism. Socialism and the welfare state are intimately related to the success of capitalism in modifying itself. Rubinow, noting this, says that these two positions (Marxian and non-Marxian) are not mutually exclusive. They both vary in their positions on various social insurance programs that do not fit exactly into either scheme; he says furthermore:

> Certainly the question whether abolition of poverty does or does not require complete reorganization of the very fundamentals of modern industrial society remains and is likely to remain for many years the most challenging problem for economic theory and practice.[60]

The position that the abolition of poverty does *not* require the reorganization of the society bears the burden of the argument. It must opt for the cure that uses the concept of *social mo-*

---

[58] Rubinow, *op. cit.*, pp. 288-289. Perhaps the best summary of this attitude shift is in Becker and Barnes, *op. cit.*, Vol. 2, pp. 595-663.

[59] Rubinow, *op. cit.*, p. 289.

[60] *Ibid.*, pp. 291-292.

bility as a base of reasoning.[61] What this means is that the social layer occupied by those in poverty rises up and is assimilated into layers that are higher (those not in poverty). One writer has appropriately called this phenomenon *"guided mobility."* [62]

A shift in social thought in the nineteenth century led to the idea that something can be done to modify or abolish the poverty condition or stratum. This consciousness was largely in the mind of the middle class. Industrialism and democracy as ideas are said to have brought the shift about. As a result of these two influences, two opposing solutions grew to dominate the thinking about the way that poverty should be abolished. Within this thinking are the enabling factors for the *social reform movement* and socialism of the last one hundred years. The reader cannot fail to notice that no matter what the position, there is much optimism in the idea that man can, in fact, alter his *social* condition! The idea of progress and currently the idea of development or planned social change traces its grounding to these earlier ideas.

THE MIDDLE GROUND CALLED SOCIALISM

Both antagonists and protagonists of capitalism have been quite sensitive to Marxian predictions and point out where and when Marx is negated or sustained.[63] Counter to Marx's criticism of capitalism, modern capitalism has modified its structure in such a way that the revolution that Marx predicted never came, or at least has not come yet. The modifications in the capitalistic system sustain some of Marx's theory and refute some of it. The classic example of a refutation is the inability of Marx to predict the rise of the middle class. (Mills says that by their rise to numerical importance, the white collar people have upset the nineteenth century expectation that society would be divided between entrepreneurs and wage workers.) Whether the rise of the middle class in capitalistic countries constitutes social change in the stratification scheme of things or constitutes social mobility within the scheme is a moot point. The middle class do not seem to be either wage workers or entrepreneurs although they may suffer the alienation that Marx pointed out clearly.[64]

The rise of socialism, be the prefix "utopian," scientific, Christian, or Fabian, is central to the discussion. Needless to say, socialism has many formal denotations and pejorative connotations.[65] Its history is still as yet sketchy.[66] To

---

[61] Social mobility, its forms and fluctuations are treated extensively in Pitirim A. Sorokin, *Social and Cultural Mobility* (New York: The Free Press of Glencoe, 1959), pp. 133-163. Sorokin refers to two types of social mobility: vertical and horizontal. If his perspective is accepted, and if one views mobility and change as polar concepts, it may follow that there should also be spatial references to the notion of change; that is, *vertical* and *horizontal* social change. For the idea that a change in social stratification is social change, see Boskoff, *op. cit.*, pp. 272-275.

[62] Herbert J. Gans, "Social and Physical Planning for the Elimination of Urban Poverty," in Bernard Rosenberg, I. Gerver, and F. W. Howton, editors, *Mass Society in Crisis: Social Problems and Pathology* (New York: The Macmillan Company, 1964), p. 630. Saul D. Alinsky, "The War on Poverty—Political Pornography," *Journal of Social Issues*, 1 (January, 1965), pp. 41-47. S. M. Miller, "Poverty, Race and Politics," in Irving L. Horowitz, editor, *The New Sociology* (New York: Oxford University Press, 1965), pp. 290-312. T. H. Marshall, *Class, Citizenship and Social Development* (New York: Doubleday & Co., Anchor Books, 1965), p. 113. "The Dimensions of Poverty," in Ben B. Seligman, editor, *Poverty as a Public Issue* (New York: The Free Press, 1965), pp. 20-51.

[63] See Becker and Barnes, *op. cit.*, Vol. 2, pp. 658-663 for a summary. A recent analysis of Marx from a sociological point of view is Ralf Dohrendorf's *Class and Class Conflict in Industrial Society* (Stanford, Cal.: Stanford University Press, 1959).

[64] C. Wright Mills, *White Collar* (New York: Oxford University Press, 1956), p. ix. The notion of alienation is all through Mills' text. Although he rests much of his theoretical positioning on Marxian notions, he says they are inadequate, p. xx.

[65] A brief but relatively complete consideration of the term is given in R. N. Carew Hunt, "Socialism," in Julius Gould and William L. Kolb, editors, *A Dictionary of the Social Sciences* (New York: The Free Press of Glencoe, 1964), pp. 670-672. For the rise of it as a type of social movement see Heberle's *Social Movements, op. cit.*, pp. 63-90.

[66] This idea of the historical "sketchiness" of the development of socialism is this writer's opinion. Barnes

summarize the issue for purposes here, the scheme of the British sociologist T. H. Marshall is useful. For him there are two forms: Socialism A and Socialism B. Socialism A includes all schools of thought that set out to transform the social and economic system by abolishing capitalism either by violence or peaceful penetration. (This form includes the early Fabians.) Socialism B has a more mild and collectivist flavor that amounts to progressive welfare legislation.[67] (The transition of the concept of socialism to the current preoccupation with what is known as the welfare state has been handled more extensively by British sociologists because of England's unique history.[68])

The U. S. position has been one of accepting Socialism B or welfare stateism to keep its political and economic way of life intact.[69] For example, the issue of equality of opportunity is an American preoccupation at this time. Seymour Martin Lipset and Reinhard Bendix say that perhaps the American preoccupation with the slogan equality of opportunity is a reaction to the gradual purported idea that the system that

was once open is becoming closed. Lipset and Bendix say that to speak of equality of opportunity is to speak vaguely—yet the phrase has strong appeal for Americans.[70] "Ideological Equalitarianism," to use Lipset and Bendix's term, plays a large role in facilitating social mobility in the U. S.[71]

The two major questions that must be asked are the following: (1) To what extent is the force of democratization independent from or causally related to the force of industrialization? (2) To what extent is the force of industrialization related to the cause of poverty and the force of democratization related to the cure of poverty? These questions arise because poverty as a sociological phenomenon is the product of both the French and the Industrial Revolutions.

It logically follows from the previous discussion of poverty that any cure, or reduction of the stratum will be an attempt on someone's part—society as a whole or strata within the society such as the poor themselves—to shrink or reduce the inequalities of power and income manifested in the society. It has been shown that there are two ways of viewing the cure: one is to reduce *both* poverty and affluence; the other is to try to simply get rid of poverty. The first alternative is referred to as the social change cure. The second is referred to as the social mobility cure.

Poverty defined in terms of inequalities is very crucial to the development of how the concept of poverty fits into movements. This approach allows us to view cures of poverty in terms of the identification and reduction of these inequalities. In slightly different terms, poverty is reduced and cured to the extent that the poor in this stratum gain equality with others in the society. The labor movement is the classic case of egalitarian movement within the industrial trend and to this we can turn.

---

and Becker are more sure of certain types of socialism. For example, the liberally quoted Bertrand Russell points out the fact that Marx is associated with socialism as a power in Europe—especially the growth of "scientific socialism." See Becker and Barnes, *op. cit.*, Vol. 2, pp. 638-641.

[67] Marshall, *op. cit.*, pp. 284-287. For a consistent and unequivocal attack on socialism, socialists, and even sociology, see F. A. Hayek, *The Counter-Revolution of Science: Studies on the Abuses of Reason* (Glencoe, Ill.: The Free Press, 1952), parts 2 and 3.

[68] Marshall, *op. cit.*, p. 293. A whole chapter is devoted to this transition. The earlier involvement of Great Britain in social planning and experimentation became an important problem for British sociology before American sociology. The notable U. S. exception to this would be Lester F. Ward. See also Michael Young, *The Rise of the Meritocracy* (Baltimore: Penguin Books, Inc., 1951).

[69] Coser, *op. cit.*, p. 148, cites Simmel as observing that the notion of assistance was never aimed at the equalization of positions in society. He also cites Marshall as showing that these efforts were directed at abatement of poverty rather than the patterns of inequality. Coser implies that recent attempts by the U. S. are like those of the past. See also Young, *op. cit.*, p. 129.

[70] Seymour Martin Lipset and Reinhard Bendix, *Social Mobility in Industrial Society* (Berkeley: University of California Press, 1964), p. 81. See also: Lipset's *Political Man: The Social Bases of Politics* (New York: Doubleday & Company, Anchor Books, 1963), pp. 47-48.

[71] Lipset and Bendix, *op. cit.*, p. 78.

THE U. S. LABOR MOVEMENT FOR EQUALITY

The Industrial Revolution brought inequality and poverty out into the open with its bringing together of large groups of workers into small places. Workers, inspired by egalitarian and utopian ideas from intellectuals and by the awareness of their deplorable working conditions, struck upon the strategy of organization ranging from workingmen's associations to consumer cooperatives, to protective associations, to unions. This occurred almost simultaneously in England, France, Germany, America, and other industrializing countries. From the combination of egalitarian theory and concrete experience in the mines, mills, and factories came a cry for action that continues in our time.

The first actions were ones of desperation. Smash the things closest to them—the machines. As was pointed out previously, this action must have come early in the Industrial Revolution because the British Parliament passed a law in 1769 making this a capital offense. Workers' early attempts at organization reveal a history of failure. Employers did everything within their power to keep workers from organizing. But organize they did, secretly at first, and then openly. Heberle characterizes the backdrop of this labor movement as follows:

> The most important change in the structure of Western society which resulted from the rise of manufacturing industry was the growth of a legally free but economically dependent class of wage workers which makes up a very large proportion of the population in all industrialized countries and regions. In this class, the bourgeoisie created its antagonist.[72]

The workers in the mills, mines, and factories were not the owners of the means of production, and in this position they had no strong interest in the preservation of the capitalistic system. Their first efforts were to improve their condition within the system, but when their workers' organizations, trade unions, and consumer cooperatives were suppressed and destroyed, "the workers began to wonder whether an entirely different socio-economic order might not be needed in order to give the wage-earner full access to the accomplishments of Western civilization."[73]

Thus, there came into existence what we now know as the labor movement around the world. From the early industrial revolution, which needed inequality and oligarchy to function, arose this egalitarian labor movement in the last 150 years in a dialectical manner. Beginning in England, then the United States, then Europe, it has moved from local to national and international scale as the world continues to industrialize.

This complex historical development can be exemplified by the situation in the United States. The struggle against oppression and for equality in the American colonies began long before the Declaration of Independence and the Constitution came along. There were the antiproprietary revolts of the 1650's to the 1690's in Maryland and North and South Carolina, which had little or no effect on the existing colonial arrangements or the class structure. Bacon's rebellion of 1676 to 1677 against Indians, the governor, and the local oligarchy of Virginia was initially revolutionary but led only to reform. Leisler's revolt of 1689 to 1691 in New York was a militia mutiny against the monopolies and taxes of the time. Other agrarian class movements that erupted in the colonies in the 1740's through the 1760's included the Paxton Boys' revolt of 1764, which demanded lower prices, tax reform, and debt relief; the North Carolina Regulator movement of 1768 to 1771 calling for equity in the courts and tax resistance; and the 1766 uprising of the Hudson Valley tenants over the tenancy system. Ash says of these movements:

> These movements are important for several rea-

---

[72] Herberle, *Social Movements, op. cit.*, pp. 34-35.

[73] *Ibid.*, p. 35.

Coxey's Army. The forerunner of the Army of the Revolution.

An early uprising of the unemployed in America.

sons. First they are evidence of the extent of class hostilities; they are the spectacular peaks of an iceberg whose submerged portions are non-violent conflicts in the courts and assemblies and private dissatisfaction. This pervasive agrarian discontent was a necessary condition for the organization of militias and local revolutionary groups (Sons of Liberty, committees of correspondence and public safety, and others) that made the American revolution possible. Second, violent class conflict created an atmosphere in which armed challenges to authority were part of the everyday experience of many Americans. Again, the sense that British rulers and the American elite were vulnerable was a prerequisite for revolutionary mass action. Third, the movements are interesting and important because they show an extraordinarily clear understanding of class interests and of the ways in which political and legal institutions support the ruling class.[74]

The American Revolution as a social movement was aristocratic in its beginning and was carried out by rural country artisans, small farmers, and frontiersmen.[75] Few would deny that it led to independence and progress, "but that it was a spontaneous uprising of all the people, that it was a glorious vindication of the 'rights of man,' that it was waged by demigods having no sinister ends in view and no unworthy motives to conceal, all this is contradicted by the facts and especially by events that followed when peace was declared."[76]

That the revolution promised more than it delivered is a truism of our times. It did not abolish slavery or improve the plight of the growing working class in the colonies. The glaring example of some of the problems facing the "founding fathers" after the revolution was Shay's rebellion of 1786 to 1787. Bankruptcy and debt led large bodies of armed men to invade courts, and the new congress secretly raised money for troops in fear that a Federal arsenal would come under attack. Those who could not escape to the frontier began to feel the oppression

---

[74] Ash, *op. cit.*, pp. 67-68. This book contains excellent tables of the actions, perceived courses, and outcomes of the movements of the colonial era.

[75] Brinton, *op. cit.*, pp. 99-100.
[76] O'Neal, *op. cit.*, p. 122.

of the ever-increasing *industrial* might of the new nation in the last quarter of the eighteenth century.

As in England in the 1700's, America after the revolution faced the similar master historical trend of industrialization with its related necessity for oligarchy and consequent poverty and relative deprivation. O'Neal states:

> Attempts to organize and improve the conditions under which the workers had labored for centuries provoked retaliation from the master employers. *The first struggle of the working class was to win the right to struggle* [italics added]— the right to organize unmolested and acquire by their own efforts some measure of freedom which the revolution denied them.[77]

There is some uncertainty about when the first strike occurred in America. We could go back to 1677 when cartmen in New York refused to clean the streets and bakers of New York combined not to bake bread unless the price was right. Brooks says the first genuine labor strike was in 1766 when Philadelphia printers struck for a minimum wage of 6 dollars a week, and the first continuous organization of wage earners was the Philadelphia journeyman shoemakers, organized in 1792.[78] Wages in the new industrial operations were better than their counterparts in England of the 1790's, and this is offered as one of the reasons that there were no spontaneous strikes. Another reason is the fact that many of the first factory hands were women and children. Philadelphia, the "cradle of American unionism," says Brooks, was the place of the first organized walkout.[79] Even though there were many firsts during this period —the first wage scale, the first paid walking delegate, the first sympathetic strike, as well as the first general strike in 1809—individual bargaining rather than collective bargaining was the norm.[80]

Another strike in America was by sailors in New York in 1802 for 14 dollars a month instead of 10 dollars. Then came the Philadelphia struggle in 1806 when cordwainers (boot and shoemakers) were indicted for conspiracy for attempting to raise their wages. The American Revolution did not abolish the so-called conspiracy codes set up in England in the 1700's where labor associations to raise wages were forbidden. Nonetheless, the workingmen's movement was in motion as industrialism became the dominant tendency. The mechanics' associations of the revolutionary period led to workingmen's associations and parties.[81]

To go into an extended chronology of the workingmen's organizations between the Revolutionary War and the American Civil War would take us astray. But we must note that among the first demands was a system of free equal education and public schools as well as demands for the ten-hour day and better wages. An example of one of the workingmen's efforts was the rebellion of Philadelphia journeyman carpenters who struck in June, 1827, for the ten-hour day, an action giving birth to another first for workingmen to gain some measure of equality under creeping industrialism: the first city central labor organization, called the Mechanics' Union of Trade Associations. From this came, says Brooks, the first labor party in the world, the Working Men's Party.[82]

From the big depression of 1837 to the Civil War, wage slavery in the North was comparable to slavery in the South. Labor vacillated at first on the abolition of slavery because the abolitionists ignored the wage slavery of the North. But when the war started, entire unions enlisted for the cause of the North. Industrialization as a trend

---

[77] *Ibid.*, p. 159.
[78] Thomas R. Brooks, *Toil and Trouble: A History of American Labor* (New York: Dell Publishing Company, 1964), pp. 10-11.
[79] *Ibid.*, p. 17.
[80] *Ibid.*, p. 20.

---

[81] Ash, *op. cit.*, says two aspects of the worker's movement of this time are important: (1) members were pre-industrial, that is, they worked in small establishments; and (2) in goals and tactics, the associations were moderate and reformist organizing to make wage demands on employers and organize to work within existing party structure, pp. 86-87.
[82] Brooks, *op. cit.*, p. 23.

was accelerated by the Civil War. The workers' movement followed, too.

After the Civil War and before America's involvement in World War I, the workers continued to organize and federate at local, national, and international levels as well as by trade. It is the period when socialist ideas got linked up with the labor movement. The call for an eight-hour day was now heard on both sides of the Atlantic with the meeting of the First Congress of the First Socialist International in 1866 at Geneva, Switzerland. In addition to the maximum eight-hour day, resolutions called for international protective legislation for women and children and the abolition of night work for women.[83]

Since the Civil War, increased industrialism has been punctuated by periodic depression, and even though as a trend it has been able to absorb population increases by the tens of millions, wage slavery in the form of unemployment, horrible working conditions, insecurity, and poverty is ever-present. Labor organizations grew in idea, action, and spirit in hopes of sharing the increase in production and doing away with the depression and oppression. The workingmen's struggle in the labor movement is a complicated web of mostly defensive tactics—alliances, bands, factions, and federations to engage in boycotts, strikes, party formation, and manipulation.

A complete description of the structure and functions, social psychology, and strategy and tactics would be a long digression.[84] To tell the story, we can note three periods: (1) the "railroading" of the U.S. West, from just after the Civil War to the turn of the century, (2) the mill and mining period from the 1890's to World War II, and (3) the rise of white collar unions as the latest phase in the labor movement, from World War II to the present.

Railroad building as a phase in the industrialization of the United States (not to mention the world) put heavy demands on the political, economic, and labor organizations of the nation. Fantastic incentives and subsidies were given to adventurers, industrialists, and profiteers to lay the track as fast as possible. It took two centuries to get to the Mississippi from the Atlantic seaboard but only one half a century to annihilate the frontier of mountains and deserts. Hicks, in commenting on the impact of all this, says:

> Under railway leadership the population came in too rapidly to permit of thoughtful and deliberate readjustments. A society at once so new and so numerous was immediately confronted with problems it could not comprehend, much less hope to solve. Flight to a new frontier could no longer avail, for the era of free lands was over. The various agrarian movements, particularly the Alliance and Populist revolts, were but the inevitable attempts of a bewildered people to find relief from a state of economic distress made certain by the unprecedented size and suddenness of their assault upon the West and by the finality with which they had conquered it.[85]

The first great clash between capital and labor in the U. S., says Brooks, occurred "on" the railroad where 33,000 miles of railroad built between 1867 and 1873 led to "the first major combines in finance and business to come to the attention of the public; they were also the first to inspire near universal hatred."[86] This tendency led to the so-called Great Upheaval of 1877, which had at its base years of grievances and deprivations. On July 11, 1877, the Baltimore and Ohio Railway announced a wage cutback. Riots broke out all over the country, culminating in the Pennsy roundhouse riot where 20,000 enraged men and women confronted 1,000 Pennsylvania militia men from Philadelphia.

Frightened by the glare of flame-fed riots, civil

---

[83] Harry W. Laidler, *History of Socialism* (New York: Thomas Y. Crowell Company, 1968), pp. 762-763.
[84] See Heberle, *Social Movements, op. cit.,* for the categorical scheme to facilitate sociological study of a specific movement.

[85] John D. Hicks, *The Populist Revolt: A History of the Farmers' Alliance and the People's Party* (Lincoln: University of Nebraska Press, 1961), p. 2.
[86] Brooks, *op. cit.,* p. 50.

authorities reinforced the militia. The massive armories of our larger cities are monuments to that fear. The courts revived the old doctrine of conspiracy and applied it with renewed vigor to the unions.[87]

Meanwhile, the Knights of Labor formed a secret labor organization, beginning in 1869, and saw dramatic growth up until the gay nineties by opening its membership to both blue and white collar. On May 4, 1884, the Knights were able to bring the entire Union Pacific Railway system to a halt by protesting a wage reduction in Denver. They won. This led to the struggle in 1885 against the Gould system (Wabash, Missouri, Kansas, and Texas, and the Missouri Pacific Railways), and this was won, too. Labor, for the first time, met with an industrial giant "on equal footing"; membership mushroomed.[88] The optimism was temporary, however. The Chicago Haymarket Square bombing and shooting of May 3, 1886, ended the eight-hour day attempts and put the labor movement in doldrums over the issues of anarchy and violence. (Meanwhile, again, the American Federation of Labor [AFL] was formed around crafts in the 1880's, and under Samuel Gompers attempts were made at international alliance with groups like the British Trades Union Congress. On May 1, 1886, the Federation called for universal adoption of the eight-hour day. On this issue and on difference in organizational strategy—affiliate autonomy— the AFL took over when the Knights of Labor began to fail.)

One other social situation bears noting during the railroad period after the Civil War, that of the Debs rebellion against Pullman in 1894. Eugene V. Debs, in the industrial American Railway Union (ARU), gained a victory against Hill's Great Northern Railway. Cautiously, Debs approached Pullman of Chicago over grievances like wage cuts. Peaceful efforts failed. What followed is described as the Debs rebellion of

1894 with the ARU (125,000 boycotting railway workers) against the General Managers' Association (representing twenty-five railroads). Federal troops were called out, and on July 7, soldiers opened fire and killed some thirty persons.[89] Debs and his organization lost when starvation led to surrender. "Debs went to jail and on to socialism,"[90] which we shall have something to say about in the section to follow.

The mill and mining period of the labor struggle in the U. S. starts in 1892 with the struggle at the Homestead Works of Carnegie Steel Company in Pittsburgh, Pennsylvania. This time it was an attempt to destroy the union, in this case the Amalgamated Association of Iron and Steel Workers, an AFL craft union. Henry Clay Frick, "The Coke King," presided for the company, hired 300 private Pinkerton armed men, and called in the Pennsylvania state militia. Brooks notes a tendency in the labor movement evidenced in this strike.

> As the events at Homestead soon showed, craft unionism confronted by corporate power soon takes on the cast of industrial unionism. The Amalgamated was an AFL craft union, and there were only 800 skilled union men at Homestead. Confronted with an adamant Frick, the skilled men called a mass meeting of all the men, at which the 3,000 mechanics and common laborers decided to stand with the union men. An advisory committee—the kind of workers' council that is central to industrial unionism—was formed not only to direct the strike but to run the town itself.[91]

Violence followed. Ten persons lay dead; there was also an attempt on Frick's life by an anarchist. Many clashes in the mills and mines followed. Along with the railroads and steel, coal was becoming king. It was also at this time that we find the rise of the Industrial Workers of the World (IWW or Wobblies). They were preceded by the Western Federation of Miners (WFM), who during the last decades of the nineteenth century waged war against the owners of mines.

---

[87] *Ibid.*, p. 54.
[88] *Ibid.*, p. 65. Brooks refers to this as the Great Uprising of 1886, p. 97. (The Great Uprising of 1886 led to the Great Upheaval of 1887.)

---

[89] *Ibid.*, pp. 94-96.
[90] *Ibid.*, p. 97.
[91] *Ibid.*, p. 89.

The Wobblies began their organization in 1905, reached a peak in 1913, and still exist today. The IWW preamble states:

> It is the historic mission of the working class to do away with capitalism. The army of production must be organized, not only in the everyday struggle with the capitalists, but also to carry on production when capitalism shall have been overthrown. By organizing industrially, we are forming the structure of the new society within the shell of the old.[92]

Such an ideology demanded direct action and even violence, if needed, to win a strike. The Wobblies might be considered an example of militant unionism or a militant reform movement, because they operated in a twilight zone somewhere between sanctioned procedures of the craft unions and the revolutionary ideologies sweeping the world around the time of the Russian Revolution.[93] This singing union or "The Troubadors of Discontent" went from the migrant workers of the West to the textile workers of the East and won a great victory at Lawrence, Massachusetts, in 1912 by getting wage increases for the textile workers.[94]

There are many examples of the struggle for equality, and even a new economy, at this time. One is the Great Coalfield War in Colorado just before World War I.[95] The period between the wars is replete with attempts to make wage and working conditions better in the United States. The Great Depression of 1929 to 1939, as a phase in U. S. industrialization, saw union gains in membership and power, as exemplified by the activities of the United Mineworkers and John L. Lewis, its leader.

The third period of the United States labor movement is now ongoing and involves white-collar workers. White-collar unionization may be viewed as a continuation of earlier blue-collar unions insofar as the new workers desire collective bargaining and have a philosophy of strike to back up their demands and actions. Brooks asks some questions about this worker:

> Who are these workers of tomorrow? Are they blue-collar men, with the attitudes, work habits, and labor union loyalties of today's factory work forces? Or are they white collar workers with the wholly different attitudes, habits, and anxieties of that group? Is automation bleaching the blue collar? Or is it bluing the white collar? Or does it make any difference?[96]

One example where these questions are being asked is in the American Federation of Teachers, an affiliate of AFL-CIO. AFT, founded in 1916, had a no-strike policy until the early 1960's. Then, with the United Federation of Teachers strikes in 1960 to 1962, AFT moved to a strike policy. The quick growth of AFT from a membership in 1960 of 59,000 to 275,000 in 1971 shows a willingness of a significant number of teachers to join the labor movement.[97]

The shift in the numerical superiority of white-collar workers over blue-collar in the mid-fifties says something about the nature of industrialization. As a master trend it is revolutionizing itself and movements that have risen against it. Earlier organized white-collar workers were retail clerks, postal workers, railway clerks, teachers, and musicians organized both under the Knights of Labor as well as the AFL. In the

---

[92] Fred Thompson, *The IWW: Its First Fifty Years (1905-1955)* (Chicago: Industrial Workers of the World, 1955), p. 4.
[93] M. T. McDermott, *The Wobblies in the United States*, unpublished paper.
[94] Brooks, *op. cit.*, pp. 114-123.
[95] George S. McGovern and Leonard F. Guttridge, *The Great Coalfield War* (Boston: Houghton Mifflin Company, 1972).

[96] Brooks, *op. cit.*, p. 269.
[97] Stephen Cole, *The Unionization of Teachers: A Case Study of the UFT* (New York: Praeger Publishers, 1969). Ronald A. Manzer, *Teachers and Politics in England and Wales* (Toronto: Toronto Press, 1970). James M. Clark, *Teachers and Politics in France* (Syracuse: University of Syracuse Press, 1967). Norman Holsinger, *Unionism, "Class-Consciousness," and the Academic Intellectual: An Attitudinal Survey of Members and Non-members of the United Professors of California, AFL-CIO Local 1593*, unpublished masters thesis, California State University, Sacramento, 1973.

thirties, the Congress of Industrial Organizations (CIO) organized newspaper editorial employees, public employees in federal, state, county, and municipal areas, office workers, and retail and wholesale workers. The AFL-CIO merger in 1955 brought the white- and blue-collar workers together. Whether or not this will continue to reflect similarities rather than differences between the blue-collar and white-collar workers remains to be seen. It is quite possible that the growing number of white-collar workers will leave the good graces of the AFL-CIO or transform it to reflect the direction of the labor movement more to their liking as industrialism and bureaucracy advances in the U. S.[98]

Before leaving the labor movement and discussing socialist ideals, we must mention the attempts on the part of workers to have an international labor movement in reaction to the industrialization of the world. Economic and political conditions of the nineteenth century led the workers to increase their own political scale. Lorwin says:

> Workers in some countries found they often lost strikes because workers from other countries were imported as strike breakers. They became interested in preventing such occurrences not only by law but also by intercountry labor agreement. When industrial conflicts became prolonged and costly, the strikers in such cases sought financial and other aid from workers in other countries. As industries grew in size and developed national and international combinations and cartels, labor unions in different countries came to regard such "concentration of capital" as a threat which had to be counteracted by international organization of labor.[99]

This long history begins with William Lovett, who in 1838 called for an international labor organization. Then Flora Tristan in 1843 wrote the first concrete plan (in a booklet titled *L'Union Ouvriere*) calling for committees of correspondence in all the capitals of Europe.[100] Then came socialist input in the form of the Communist League (1847), the First International (1864 to 1876), the Second International (1889 to 1914), the Third or Communist International (1919 to 1943). Many other organizations have been formed since Lovett's first call until the present time: the International Secretariats of Crafts, around 1890, which became the International Federation of Labor (IFL) in 1913; and the International Federation of Trade Unions (IFTU) or Amsterdam International, which was dissolved in 1945 to be replaced by the World Federation of Trade Unions (WFTU). Then in 1949 came the International Confederation of Free Trade Unions (ICFTU), which is the outstanding labor international today.

The ICFTU Manifesto calls for bread, freedom, and peace and reads:

> Workers of all countries, races, and creeds: Join us in this mighty movement of free and democratic labor. Together we can conquer poverty and exploitation and create a world of abundance and security. Together we can destroy tyranny and oppression and create a world of freedom and human dignity. Together we can defeat the forces of war and aggression, and create a world of peace and justice.[101]

The ICFTU has a membership of about 54 million in 97 organizations in 73 countries and excludes communist-controlled, fascist, and government-sponsored labor organizations. Member unions must be voluntary, carry on collective bargaining, have the right to strike, be democratic in structure and management, and advocate peaceful methods for improving economic and social conditions.[102]

---

[98] For early comment on the white collar see C. Wright Mills, *White Collar* (New York: Oxford University Press, 1951). Adolf Sturmal, editor, *White Collar Trade Unions* (Urbana: University of Illinois Press, 1966). George Sayers Bain, *The Growth of White-Collar Unionism* (Oxford: Clarendon Press, 1970).

[99] Lewis L. Lorwin, *The International Labor Movement: History, Policies, Outlook* (New York: Harper & Brothers, Publishers, 1953).

[100] As quoted in Lorwin, *op. cit.,* p. 5.

[101] Laidler, *op. cit.,* p. 771.

[102] Lorwin, *op. cit.,* p. 286.

SOCIALISM AS A MOVEMENT FOR EQUALITY

As we have introduced each chapter with a quote, this section on socialism might be started with the following:

Socialism is a tendency, not a revealed dogma, and therefore it is modified in its forms of expression from generation to generation.[103]

For this reason, remarks in this introductory text on movements must necessarily turn out to be an oversimplification. The generations of the last two hundred years or so have modified socialist history so as to make it difficult to deal with meaningfully. Of course, those who think it to be revealed dogma will think we have been too elaborate in our brief introduction. As we did for the labor movement, we can limit ourselves to what we consider to be the dominant tendencies.

Previously, we related poverty and relative deprivation to the rise of the idea of equality and the middle ground called socialism in the nineteenth century (p. 116). It was within the context of the discussion on poverty that we said that there were two forms of socialism at present, A and B. Socialism A includes all schools of thought that set out to transform the social and economic system by abolishing capitalism either by violence or peaceful penetration. Socialism B is more collectivistic and amounts to progressive welfare legislation. Now we have to complicate this a bit by looking at what Harrington calls "the future of the socialist past."[104]

To simplify the ideas and movements that have claimed socialist ideals, we can say there are pre-*Manifesto* and post-*Manifesto* periods. We refer here to Karl Marx and Frederick Engels' *The Communist Manifesto* of 1848. It,

more than any other socialist document of recent times, made the past and the future ingredients in the present. In the words of Edmund Wilson:

The Communist Manifesto is dense with the packed power of high explosives. It compresses with terrific vigor into 40 or 50 pages a general theory of history, an analysis of European society and a program for revolutionary action.[105]

The general theory of history summarized in the *Manifesto* is so packed that it is referred to as a whole philosophy of history centered on a materialist metaphysic: historical materialism and dialectical materialism. It is, above all, a criticism of the prior idealistic view of history. The analysis of European society is essentially an anatomy of capitalism up to the middle of the nineteenth century. The program for revolutionary action is directed to the poor and underprivileged, of whom there have been many, both then and now. Finally, all of this was under the rubric of what Marx and Engels claimed to be "scientific socialism"; that is, not idealistic or religious socialism. What is lacking, in this and other Marx-Engels work, is that the picture of what the future was to be was very vague. This fact may account for not only the appeal of Marxism but its multifarious disputes, interpretations, and revisions by those in the socialist and communist movements.[106]

What about pre-*Manifesto* socialism? With the gradual collapse of feudalism, the estates, and old orders, we see the rise of capitalism, classes, and new orders. Said another way, the radical transformations we call the Commercial and Industrial Revolutions led to the many wars, movements, and revolutions in the countries affected by them (the British, American, French, Russian, and Chinese Revolutions are examples). These revolutions and the secular and urban trends of the last four hundred years have, in

---

[103] J. Ramsey MacDonald, in Jerome Davis, *Contemporary Social Movements* (New York: The Century Company, 1930), p. 97.
[104] Michael Harrington, *Socialism* (New York: Saturday Review Press, 1972), p. 3.

[105] Edmund Wilson, *To the Finland Station: A Study in the Writing and Acting of History* (Garden City, N. Y.: Doubleday & Company, Anchor Books, 1953), p. 157.
[106] Heberle, *Social Movements, op. cit.*, pp. 70-90.

turn, led to many blueprints for the ideal community. More's early sixteenth century book *Utopia* criticizes the British community rulers of his time for their opulence, oppressive policies, and sacred institution of private property, and he "calls for the recognition of equal social rights for all reasoning men through a return to primitive communism."[107] Bacon's *New Atlantis* (1622) saw science as savior; Andrere's *Christianopolis* (1620's) sought four hundred people who could be both Christian and communist; and Campanella's *City of the Sun* sought neither riches nor poverty with a four-hour work day.[108]

These utopian socialistic and communistic ideas were to be grounded in the New World. The Shakers set up the first communistic society at about the time of the American Revolution in the colonies. Mother Ann Lee inspired this millennial church group that sought to seclude themselves from the outer world and live the highest spiritual life. Equality of the sexes was paramount in this "religious communitarian" experiment.[109] Then came the secular communitarians called the Owenites. Robert Owen, British industrialist, socialist visionary, and reformer, reacting to the depression of 1816, came up with plans for "villages of cooperation" that were to have between five hundred and a thousand people. Failing in England, he went to America and set up a "community of equality" at New Harmony, Indiana, in which all property was to be held in common. He failed. Other Owenites went off to continue his example, like a woman named Frances Wright who set up the Neshoba community in Tennessee in 1826. She sought to solve the slavery problem by having freed slaves live in a cooperative community where there would be sexual, racial, and economic equality by abolishing family life and private property. It died in 1830 with the slaves packed off to Haiti.[110]

Another example of secular communitarianism or utopian socialism is the Associationists. Horace Greeley, editor of the *New York Tribune* and first president of the typographical union, was an associationist writer in the 1840's and sought an ideal community where the workers would unite together to secure good housing, education, labor, social relations, progress, and skill.[111] The most cited Association experiment was the Brook Farm phalanx where the communards wanted uniform pay rates, a ten-hour day, and free support of children under 10 years of age, old persons, and the sick.

Socialism to these generations before the 1840's and *The Communist Manifesto* rested on the possibility of escape from the realities of bureaucracy, industrialization, and cultural imperialism. The *Manifesto* pointed to these socialist escapes as well as to the realities of industrial capitalism. But this is an oversimplification in an important way because there were differences between socialists and communists before Marxism. Lichtheim comments:

> What distinguished "communism" from "socialism" at this stage was its proletarian character and its radical egalitarianism. . . . When the term "socialism" came into general use in France around 1830, it was evident that what was intended was an indictment of liberalism, specifically as an economic doctrine. In this sense the "communists" too were socialists. But the obverse was not true, for not all socialists accepted the principle of radical equality, which at this stage entailed a demand for the levelling of civilized institutions and a return to an egalitarian (and therefore natural) state. The early socialists, by and large, accepted civilization in general and the industrial revolution in particular.[112]

---

[107] Laidler, *History of Socialism, op. cit.,* p. 31.
[108] *Ibid.,* pp. 34-37.
[109] Albert Fried, editor, *Socialism in America: From the Shakers to the Third International* (Garden City, N. Y.: Doubleday & Company, Anchor Books, 1970), pp. 21-22. See also John H. Noyes, *History of American Socialisms* (New York: Dover, 1966). Charles Nordhoff, *The Communistic Societies of the United States* (New York: Dover, 1966).

[110] Fried, *op. cit.,* p. 73.
[111] Laidler, *op. cit.,* p. 101.
[112] George Lichtheim, *A Short History of Socialism* (New York: Praeger Publishers, 1970), p. 29.

An early Communist poster.

Historical conditions in Europe changed all this, and the axial year was 1848 with the abortive national democratic movement in Germany; serfdom disappeared in Europe except for Russia; there was a proletarian insurrection in France; Chartism failed in England; and *The Communist Manifesto* was published. Finally, says Lichtheim, 1848 was "the year when democracy and socialism separated—for in that year universal suffrage in France produced a bourgeois majority which relied upon the army and the peasantry against the working class."[113]

With the formation of the First International or the Working Men's International Association in 1864, the next generation had to define socialism as not being anarchist. The battle was

---

[113] *Ibid.*, p. 57. See also Rosenberg, *op. cit.*, pp. 59-170.

between Marx and the anarchist Bakunin and was a major contributing cause for the collapse of the International in 1876. As the labor movement and socialism movement spread around the world in the last part of the nineteenth century, Marxism had to deal with populism in Russia, anarchism or libertarian socialism in Europe, and positivism as well as Fabianism in England. The Second International from 1889 to 1914 centered upon the possibility for social democracy in Germany in the midst of war with France. This was the period of revisions of Marxist doctrine, and Eduard Bernstein was one of the leading revisionists. The following is from his book *Evolutionary Socialism:*

> . . . No one has questioned the necessity for the working classes to gain control of the government. The point at issue is between the theory of social cataclysm and the question whether the

127

Centennial - Paris Commune'

A potrayal of the 1871 Revolt in Paris.

TH. HEINE, in Simplicissimus

"I have no work to give you, but why don't you enlist?"

The unemployed follow this advice,

Copyright, International Copyright Bureau

And behave with such bravery in the first battle that

They soon find work—in Germany.

A German view of English capitalism in World War I. (From *Cartoons Magazine*, vol. 7, no. 2, February, 1915. H. H. Windsor, editor and publisher, Chicago.)

given development in Germany and the present advanced state of its working classes in the towns and in the country, a sudden catastrophe would be desirable in the interest of the social democracy.[114]

The Second International was ended by "shipped up" nationalism as Europe prepared for the "War to End all Wars"—World War I. In retrospect, the international workers' movement and the international socialist movement gained from the Second International, which set up an international socialist bureau, advanced the cause of

labor and social legislation around the world, coordinated and strengthened the democratic socialist ideas of the time, and did its best to combat militarism. This second attempt to give the working class an international rather than national political scale was virtually smashed by nationalism and the call to arms. Socialists and workers of Europe were forced to fight among themselves once again or get jailed.

The American Socialist Party, founded in 1901 by Eugene V. Debs, is a case in point. We said previously that Debs went from jail to socialism during the Debs Rebellion of 1894. During this period of growth for the Socialist Party, Debs eventually went back to jail for his socialism and the pacifist posture that flowed from it at that time. We have here a generation of socialists who define socialism in terms of the

---

[114] Albert Fried and Ronald Sanders, editors, *Socialist Thought: A Documentary History* (Garden City, N. Y.: Doubleday & Company, Anchor Books, 1964), pp. 424-425. For details see Peter Gay, *The Dilemma of Democratic Socialism: Eduard Bernstein's Challenge to Marx* (New York: Collier Books, 1962).

S. MAUD, in *The Big Kibetzer*

THE JEW'S FATHERLAND
"I have no Fatherland to live in, but I have many Fatherlands to die for."

Nationalism and the dilemmas of the Jewish people. (From *Cartoons Magazine,* vol. 7, no. 2, February, 1915. H. H. Windsor, editor and publisher, Chicago.)

possibility of international worker solidarity. This is forthrightly expressed in the *St. Louis Manifesto of the Socialist Party (1917):*

> The Socialist Party of the United States in the present grave crisis solemnly reaffirms its allegiance to the principle of internationalism and working class solidarity the world over, and proclaims its unalterable opposition to the war just declared by the Government of the United States.[115]

As the Socialist Party and other groups like the IWW were being persecuted under the Espionage Act of 1917, the Bolshevik Revolution was taking place in Russia. Socialists around the world were as unprepared for this as they were for a world war. World War I, internal doctrinal and tactical disputes, and the emergence of the Communist or Third International in 1919 left American socialists in disarray up to the present time. The thrust of labor and socialist internationalism was shunted until after World War II, when we had the formation of the International Confederation of Free Trade Unions and the reconstruction of the Socialist International in 1951. In the first congress of the International there was a change in the definition of socialism. Democratic socialism was the aim; collective security against totalitarianism was a principle as well as social and economic programming to eliminate poverty, oppression, exploitation, and mass unemployment.[116] In sum, cultural imperialism (in the form of the First, Second, and Cold, and recent wars), the rise of various forms of bureaucratic collectivism, and the ongoing internationalization of industrial capitalism continue to cause serious disagreements within and between socialist parties, labor parties, and communist parties throughout the world.[117]

Perhaps this is why American socialist Michael Harrington sees current socialism not only in visionary terms but also in terms of what to do tomorrow rather than in concern about the epoch.[118] To end this brief note on socialism as a movement for equality, we can turn to him and his socialist vision for this generation:

> It is the idea of an utterly new society in which some of the fundamental limitations of human existence have been transcended. Its most basic premise is that man's battle with nature has been completely won. As a result of this unprecedented change in the environment, a psychic mutation takes place: invidious competition is no longer programmed into life by the necessity of a struggle for scarce resources; cooperation, fraternity and equality become natural. In such a world man's social productivity will reach such heights that compulsory work will no longer be necessary. And as more and more things are provided free, money, that universal equivalent by means of which necessities are rationed, will disappear.[119]

IS INDUSTRIAL DEMOCRACY[120] POSSIBLE?

The labor movement as well as the socialist movement has a history of both vision and tactics

[115] Fried, *op. cit.*, p. 521.
[116] Laidler, *op. cit.*, pp. 759-761.
[117] Max Schactman, *The Bureaucratic Revolution: The Rise of the Stalinist State* (New York: The Donald Press, 1962). See also Daniel Bell, *Marxian Specialism in the United States* (Princeton, N. J.: Princeton University Press, 1967). Leo Huberman and Paul M.

Sweezy, *Introduction to Socialism* (New York: Modern Reader, 1968). Harry W. Laidler, *Socialism in Thought and Action* (New York: The Macmillan Company, 1970). Carl Landauer, *European Socialism: A History of Ideas and Movements,* Vols. 1 and 2 (Berkeley: University of California Press, 1959). John M. Laslett, *Labor and the Left: A Story of Socialist and Radical Influences in the American Labor Movement, 1881-1924* (New York: Basic Books, Inc., 1970).
[118] Michael Harrington, *Socialism* (New York: Saturday Review Press, 1972), p. 271. Socialist Party input into U. S. domestic policy through the Democratic Party in the area of social security has been considerable. See Robert M. Kloss, *Political Tendencies and Social Security from the New Deal to the Great Society,* unpublished doctoral dissertation, Louisiana State University, 1969.
[119] Harrington, *Socialism, op. cit.*, p. 344.
[120] The use of this term "industrial democracy" is one of compromise, albeit confusion. For the context of past uses of the term see Karl de Scheinitz, Jr., *Industrialization and Democracy: Economic Necessities*

THE DREAM THAT CAME TRUE

An early socialist view of capitalist America.

in its quest for equality under creeping bureaucracy, cultural imperialism, and industrialization. When we ask the question of the possibility of industrial democracy, we must, as students of both ideals and reals, note that democ-

and Political Possibilities (London: The Free Press of Glencoe, 1964). Eric Rhenman, *Industrial Democracy and Industrial Management: A Critical Essay on the Possible Meanings and Implications of Industrial Democracy* (London: Tavistock, 1968). Milton Derber, *The American Idea of Industrial Democracy 1865-1965* (Urbana: University of Illinois Press, 1970).

racy is still largely vision or at worst fraud, and industrialism is oftentimes all-too-real. After learning that they could not fight the industrial trend, early egalitarians had to change their vision and tactics. Production was revolutionized, and new classes and new definitions of democracy had to be posited. Birnbaum's observations on the relationship of the industrial trend to egalitarian movements is notable:

The history of industrial society is not the history of the extension of liberty. Gross and violent forms of domination have emerged in combination with technologically perfected means for the exercise of power; more subtle forms of domination have politicized the totality of culture. Where liberty has been extended, it has in fact been won in conflict which frequently entailed violence or the threat of it.[121]

It has been the labor movement (with democratic socialist tendencies) that has led the fight to win limited extensions of liberty and equality within the radical world trend of industrialization and its seeming necessity for new oligarchies. We need to ask the question about the possibility of industrial democracy because we

are undergoing the "industrialization of culture" itself![122] It will be possible if, and only if, the *humanistic* tendencies in bureaucracy, cultural imperialism, and industrialization are fought for and won by those movements with the vision and tactics to do so. New political groups composed of new as well as old working classes, new coalitions of the oppressed and fortunate, and new analysts and visionaries will have to "do their homework" in the hopes of understanding past successes and failures. This understanding is essential if further gains are to be made by the industrial egalitarians over the industrial oligarchies.[123]

---

[121] Norman Birnbaum, *The Crisis of Industrial Society* (London: Oxford University Press, 1969), pp. 55-56. See also Arthur Rosenberg, *Democracy and Socialism: A Contribution to the Political History of the Past 150 Years* (Boston: Beacon Press, 1965), pp. 287-363.

---

[122] Birnbaum, *op. cit.*, pp. 106-166.
[123] One possibility is that proposed by Michael Harrington in *Toward A Democratic Left: A Radical Program for a New Majority* (Baltimore: Penguin Books, Inc., 1969).

CHAPTER 8   ARCHAIC MODES OF CONTROL AND THEIR ANTITHESES

The more ancient the abuse, the more sacred it must seem.

Voltaire

We have discussed at some length the trends we believe will dominate the social world for the coming generations. The trends we have cited are also modes of control; bureaucracy, for example, as a system of rationality in social organization is likely to increase in the future as it has in the past. Bureaucracy is also a method of controlling (often manipulating) human beings. The question as to whether bureaucracy will be humanized is more important at this point than whether bureaucracy as a method of control will cease. We believe that it will not, in the near future, decline as a mode of control.

It may be asked if our trinity of trends is like the godhead, an Alpha and Omega without beginning or end. The truth of the matter is that these trends did have a beginning somewhere in human consciousness and that they may in the distant future be replaced by new trends and new means of control. We do know that modes of control have existed prior to the ones we have described, and we propose to examine these archaic modes of control as they relate to the human past. For it is certain that the present

generation cannot escape the consequences of the past.

FEUDALISM AND PEASANT REVOLTS

The agrarian way of life has been glorified by all manner of men, from certain Marxists who looked upon the estate system as a relatively humane form of precapitalism to conservatives who saw in feudalism a tranquility and wholeness in the ordered hierarchical society.

It is true that some look to the feudal system as a paragon of order. As for the individuals living under feudalism, "God made them high and lowly/And ordered their estate."

The view of feudalism as a benign social system is extremely questionable. Peasants were indeed close to the good earth, yet it would be no exaggeration to say that they were often driven into the earth by a system that allocated them no power. Feudalism is at base a system of land tenure in which men are allowed to occupy land by fiat and are expected by law to produce for themselves as well as for their "betters."

Feudalism in its variant forms is one of the oldest historical modes of control of individuals with the exception of slavery. While feudalism is an archaic mode of human relations, it is not dead in the twentieth century, as we shall see. Feudalistic societies are characterized by limited literacy among the masses, while the elites have enough literary abilities to monopolize intellectual life. This fact gives the nobility and rentiers the advantage of a unity and "consciousness of kind" denied the peasantry. Superstition and "the idiocy of the village" were divisive forces among the peasantry, most of whom were unable to converse with other nearby peasants in a meaningful way. When men are in a sense tied to the earth, they are in no position to show tolerance or understanding for the stranger, even if he, like them, shares the same problems.

And the world-wide peasantry does share problems. Most of these problems derive from the fantastic inequality so evident in the feudal system. Gerhard Lenski examines this feudal inequality in this way:

> In late fifteenth or early sixteenth-century Spain, the king was reputed to enjoy one-third of all the revenues of the land. . . . In eighteenth-century Prussia, the royal estates constituted "no less than one-third the total arable area," a figure which was matched by the royal estates in neighboring Sweden. Even these figures were surpassed in mid-nineteenth-century Russia, where the crown owned almost half the European territories; prior to the emancipation of the serfs, 27.4 million men and women were state peasants whom the Czars regarded as their property to dispose of as they wished. This explains how Catherine the Great and her son Paul were able to give away to various court favorites 1,400,000 serfs in the short period from 1762 to 1801 without seriously depleting the resources of the house of Romanov. In our own day the premier of Thailand, the late Marshal Sarit, accumulated an estate valued at $140,000,000 in only ten years in an Agrarian society with an annual per capita income of less than $100.[1]

Lenski's analysis of the tax structure for the peasants makes the causes of oppression obvious. In China peasants paid 40% to 50% of their produce to landowners. In India both Hindu and Muslin rulers were granted from one third to one half of peasant crops. In Turkey, the peasants were charged up to 50% of their produce. In medieval times the tradition of the *ispendyh* ruled Christian Europe. This rule said in effect that a noble or priest could claim any chattel or movable possession of a peasant (usually of course, the most valuable) upon the death of the peasant. It is possible also to perceive of the feudal system, not as a stable time in human history, but a period much like our own when greed motivated much fermentation. Consider, for example, the position of the French nobility in the eighteenth century. George Lefevere describes their position in *The Coming of the French Revolution:*

> [The great landowners] farmed out their rights to bourgeois agents who were relentless in collection of dues; they had minutely detailed manor-rolls drawn up, putting into effect dues which had become obsolete; they prevailed upon the king to issue edicts allowing them to appropriate a third of the common lands or to enclose their own fields and forbid the peasants to pasture their animals in them; they made use of the "planting right" to set out trees along the roads on land belonging to the peasants; they expelled the peasants from the forests.[2]

If we look to more modern times we can see that the position of the peasant within the old system does not change. Charles Robequin described the position of the Vietnamese peasant in 1944:

> [He] . . . often borrows both the seeds and the work buffaloes necessary to farm his land. When the harvest is bad he must also find funds with which to pay taxes and fulfill his religious and family duties. A money lender, whether merchant or big landholder, will readily advance a loan, but on very harsh terms. The debt will be repaid

---

[1] From *Power and Privilege: A Theory of Stratification* by Gerhard E. Lenski. Copyright 1966 by McGraw-Hill. Used with permission of McGraw-Hill Book Company.

[2] George Lefevere, *The Coming of the French Revolution,* R. R. Palmer, translator, (Princeton, N. J.: Princeton University Press, 1947), p. 14.

with difficulty, often at the cost of pawning the harvest, or even of the fields.[3]

Regardless of the misery and inequity we have described, the peasantry is not likely given to revolt. Yet, of course, the proper mixtures of hope and despair do come together at times to promote rebellion. When this happens among the peasantry, it is likely to take one of three forms—messianism, social banditry, or political revolution. The first two options are essentially nonpolitical or occasionally prepolitical in nature.

We will now examine a case of one of the earliest peasant revolts in European history, the Anabaptist uprising.

ANABAPTISTS—THE NEW JERUSALEM

One of the truly revolutionary medieval peasant movements was the Anabaptist schism of the sixteenth century in northern Europe. H. Richard Niebuhr writes in his *The Social Sources of Denominationalism* that

> The failure of the Reformation to meet the religious needs of peasants and other disfranchised groups is a chapter writ large in history. With all of its native religious fervor it remained the religion of the middle classes and the nobility. The Peasants War and the Anabaptist Movement were the result. . . . Thomas Muenzer, the arch-enemy of Luther, was Anabaptist as well as revolutionary leader.[4]

Further, Niebuhr quotes Luther as exhorting the peasants:

> Ye shall not resist evil, but whosoever shall compel thee to go one mile, go with him two . . . and whosoever smiteth thee thy right cheek turn to him the other also.[5]

A different kind of message was given by Luther to the peasants' masters in his pamphlet,

Against the Thieving and Murderous Hordes of Peasants.

> Here let whoever can give blows, strangle, stab—secretly or openly—and remember that nothing can be more poisonous, harmful, and devilish than a revolutionary; just as one must kill a mad dog, for if you do not slay him he will slay you and a whole land with you.[6]

Thus, official Lutheranism had become an established church with a predominantly aristocratic set of interests, according to Niebuhr. It was in this milieu that Muenzer and those who followed after him protested against the established order of things. Other apocalyptic movements, such as the German and Italian Flagellants, had convulsed Europe during the middle of the fourteenth century. They arose basically within the structure of the Catholic Church and were, in part, reactions to the plague that had destroyed almost one third of the European population some time before. The Anabaptist movement demonstrated strains of utopian thought hitherto unborn, however.

Thomas Muenzer was born in Thuringia in 1488 some five or six years later than Martin Luther. After his theological and scriptural study, Muenzer became a follower of Luther and broke away from Catholic orthodoxy. Muenzer became attracted to the chiliastic doctrines being preached at this time in Bohemia. The "last days" he felt were at hand. "First the Turks must conquer the world and AntiChrist must rule over it; but then—and it would be very soon—the Elect would rise up and annihilate all godless, so that the Second Coming could take place and the Millennium begin."[7] The Book of Revelation was increasingly quoted by Muenzer in an attempt to gain followers. He was finally expelled from Prague and began to wander about in central Germany preaching of the end of time and of the new order of things. Essentially, his was the notion of a community of the elect surrounded

---

[3] Charles Robequin, *The Economic Development of French Indo-China* (New York: Oxford University Press, 1944), p. 168.

[4] H. Richard Niebuhr, *The Social Sources of Denominationalism* (Cleveland: World Publishing Company, 1929), p. 34.

[5] *Ibid.,* p. 34.

[6] *Ibid.,* pp. 35-36.

[7] Norman Cohn, *The Pursuit of the Millennium* (New York: Harper and Row, 1961), p. 253.

by a wicked world. The elect were to be the poor, and in this sense, the "last were to be first." As Belfort Bax comments in his *The Rise and Fall of the Anabaptists*, "the original strain of ecclesiastical radicalism . . . received an accession of strength from the sentiment of an oppressed class in which political and economic considerations mixed themselves up with religious enthusiasm."[8]

Princes, according to Muenzer, had forfeited all claims to obedience on the part of the peasants. The nobility was in its essence ungodly and opposed to the will of Christ, and, thus, part and parcel of the AntiChrist of the Book of Revelation. The "cleansing" Muenzer spoke of frequently was not a nonviolent proposal.

> If the holy Church is to be renewed through the bitter truth, a servant of God must stand forth . . . and set things in motion. In truth, many of them will have to be roused, so that with the greatest possible zeal and with passionate earnestness they may sweep Christendom clean of ungodly rulers.[9]

By 1525 Muenzer felt his eschatological fantasies were approaching reality. He led a large[10] but unorganized army of peasants near Frankenhausen. His army was immediately sought out and soon destroyed by his princely opponents. The peasants scattered as they panicked, and Muenzer was later found in a cellar and beheaded on the twenty seventh day of May.

His ideas did not die with him, however. One reason for this was the extreme diversity of the Anabaptist sects. The theological issues that held the sects together were vague but revolved around rebaptism of believers, a rejection of infant baptism, and a rather meticulous observance of literal precepts found in the New Testament. For the most part,

> Their values were primarily ethical; for them

religion was above all a matter of active brotherly love. Their communities were modelled on what they supposed to have been the practice of the early Church and were intended to realize the ethical ideal propounded by Christ.[11]

Like later utopists, they sought to isolate their communities from nonbelievers, because of their self-concept as the "Elect." After the death of Muenzer, they suffered a great deal of persecution that, of course, reinforced their faith and their need for withdrawal.

By 1534 the power of the Anabaptists in the city of Muntzer increased greatly. Most of the Lutheran populace left at this point. According to Cohn,

> The majority of the remaining population was Anabaptist; and messengers and manifests were sent out urging the Anabaptists in nearby towns to come with their families to Muntzer. The rest of the earth, it was announced, was doomed to be destroyed before Easter; but Muntzer would be saved and would become the New Jerusalem.[12]

True communization of property was also affirmed at Muntzer.

> All I.O.U.'s, account books, and contracts were destroyed. All clothing, bedding, furniture, hardware, weapons, and stocks of food were removed and placed in central depots. It was announced that true Christians should possess no money of their own but should hold all money in common.[13]

This radical revision of the economic system was, in fact, a reversion to earlier modes of communal peasant life. It gave a kind of stability to the chaotic economic system of feudal Germany.

An even more revolutionary change in the social life of the faithful Anabaptist was to follow. Finding that the Old Testament sanctioned pologamy,[14] the Believers were asked to accept the principle of "plural wifery" as an article of faith. All unmarried women of marriageable age were required to marry a male member of the community. No marriage was valid if it had been

---

[8] Belfort Bax, *The Rise and Fall of the Anabaptists* (London: Swan Sonneschein, 1903), p. 16.
[9] Cohn, *op. cit.*, p. 261.
[10] Almost 8,000 peasants participated in this uprising; more than half were later killed.

[11] Cohn, *op. cit.*, pp. 273-274.
[12] *Ibid.*, p. 284.
[13] *Ibid.*, pp. 286-287.
[14] The more correct term is polygyny.

contracted with a nonbeliever. This broke several nuptial bonds and placed many women in the marriageable category. According to Cohn, "refusal to comply with the new law was made a capital offense and some women were, in fact, executed."[15]

Finally, Cohn states,

Divorce had to be permitted and this in turn changed polygamy into something not very different from free love . . . it seems certain that norms of sexual behavior in the Kingdom of the Saints traversed the whole arc from a rigorous puritanism to sheer promiscuity.[16]

At the height of its power, the Anabaptist leaders were able to control almost completely the lives of the membership. Bax describes the articles of the constitution of the Anabaptists in this way, "They were regulating the victually of the New Israel, the fabrication of clothes and other details affecting the industrial and economic life of the community."[17]

The year 1533 saw a blockade thrown around the New Jerusalem of the Anabaptists. A series of surprise attacks by the nobility and the capture of the Anabaptist "prophet," John of Leyden, brought an end to the sacred community. While the formal structure of the group was effectively rooted out by the authorities, the Anabaptist movement later gave birth to the Mennonite and Brethren utopist sects.[18]

In retrospect, Belfort Bax comments:

In such wise did the disinherited classes of that age envisage their social revidication. . . . The aspirations *au fond* legitimate as they were, of the medieval working classes of the 16th century, were historically retrograde in their form both as regards the end conceived, and the means by which it was believed that end would come to pass—and hence they were foredoomed to failure.[19]

---

[15] Cohn, *op. cit.*, p. 293.
[16] *Ibid.*, p. 294.
[17] Bax, *op. cit.*, p. 200.
[18] It also influenced the Baptists and Quakers to a degree.
[19] Bax, *op. cit.*, p. 389.

SOCIAL BANDITRY

As we have seen with the Anabaptist movement, the peasantry can infuse religious symbolism with political goals (that is, the seizure of power). The reason this is so is because the peasant is often faced with no secular alternative. He must revolt within the context of his own limited and parochial culture. If his analysis of the world were sociological and economic, he would strive for a secular solution to his problems. But he does not. Therefore his revolt will not follow the lines of a politically sophisticated industrial working class.

It would be wrong to imply, however, that the only mode of protest open to the peasant is a religious one. The British historian E. J. Hobsbawn in his seminal study *Primitive Rebels* has unearthed one of the most basic "prepolitical" social movements.

Bandits and highwaymen preoccupy the police, but they also ought to preoccupy the social historian. For in one sense banditry is a rather primitive form of organized social protest, perhaps the most primitive we know. At any rate in many societies it is regarded as such by the poor, who consequently protect the bandit, regard him as their champion, idealize him, and turn him into a myth: Robin Hood in England, Janosik in Poland and Slovakia, Diego Corrientes in Andalusia. . . . In return the bandit himself tries to live up to his role even when he is not himself a conscious social rebel.[20]

The social bandit then is in a real sense an individual representation for the wish fulfillment of many of the masses. If we were to look for social banditry, we would probably do well to look to underdeveloped countries, the nineteenth century south of Spain, Southern Italy, or Latin America. Yet the so-called developed nations are not without their social bandits. Consider the depression-haunted 1930's in the United States. The names of Pretty Boy Floyd, Bonnie and

---

[20] E. J. Hobsbawm, *Primitive Rebels: Studies in Archaic Forms of Social Movements in the Nineteenth and Twentieth Centuries* (New York: Frederick A. Praeger, 1959), p. 13.

Clyde, and John Westley Harding were implanted in the minds of the dirt-poor American "peasantry" who were at the time resentful of bankers, brokers, and realtors. The escapades of the bandits of the twenties and thirties made news because the public saw certain parallels between the farmboys "turned bad" and their own economic and social despair.

The idea that the social bandit robs the rich to give to the poor is a partial truth at best. It is a fact that the cooperation of the peasantry was necessary for the bandit to survive. Often the relationship between peasant and bandit was a symbiotic one. Peasant and bandit each worked either actively or passively for the protection of the other.

In the end, nonetheless, the social bandit represents a futile mode of protest. For while social banditry does provide a means of striking out at oppression, it "is a modest and unrevolutionary protest. It protests not against the fact that peasants are poor and oppressed, but against the fact that they are sometimes excessively poor and oppressed. Bandit heroes are not expected to make a world of equality. They can only right wrongs and prove that sometimes oppression can be turned upside down."[21]

Hobsbawm finds that the bandit typically acts in vengeance for private manners and is often nihilistic in his destruction of the property and lives of the very rich.

It is no accident that where the peasantry is armed with a political organization, social banditry cannot survive let alone flourish. In the end, as we have said, the role of the social bandit is futile. For he does not understand the structure of the society he has learned to rebel against. As Hobsbawm explains:

The future lay with political organization. Bandits who do not take to the new ways of fighting for peasant's cause, as many of them do as individuals, generally converted in jails or conscript armies, cease to be champions of the poor and become mere criminals or retainers of land-

lord's and merchants' parties. There is no future for them. Only the ideals for which they fought, and for which men and women made up songs about them, survive. . . .[22]

PEASANT REVOLUTIONARIES

If it is true that the peasantry is not easily awakened to social and economic realities, it is equally true that an aroused peasantry is not easily dissuaded from action. The case of the Italian peasant in 1891 is instructive. Throughout the 1880's Southern Italy, and especially the Sicilian island, had been in the grip of an economic depression. Also in Sicily, a transition was occurring from feudal domination to that of capitalism. The new bourgeoisie who controlled the land were quick to take advantage of the feudal benefits of agrarian land ownership but sidestepped many of the concomitant feudal responsibilities for their peasantry. The result was a miserable and severely oppressed people.

The peasantry did begin to band together for its own defense, not in a messianic movement, as did the Anabaptists, or with the aid of the social bandits. For it was at this time that peasant leagues, the so-called Fasci (not to be confused with the later Fascists), were organized. The Fasci were socialist in ideology and precipitated many riots and agricultural strikes on the island. Radically-minded intellectuals joined the peasant's conflicts, aiding in the formation of mutual defense societies.

A peasant woman, interviewed by a journalist in 1893 gave her views of the revolt.

We want everybody to work, as we work. There should no longer be either rich or poor. All should have bread for themselves and for their children. We should all be equal. I have five small children and only one little room, where we have to eat and sleep and do everything, while so many *signori* have ten or twelve rooms, entire palaces. . . .

Jesus was a true Socialist and he wanted precisely what the Fasci are asking for, but the priests do not represent him well, especially when they are usurers. When the Fascio was

---

[21] *Ibid.*, p. 24.

[22] *Ibid.*, p. 28.

founded our priests were against it and in the confessional they said that the Socialists are excommunicated. But we answered that they were mistaken, and in June we protested against the war they made upon the Fascio, none of us went to the procession of the Corpus Domini. That was the first time such a thing ever happened.[23]

The Fascio revolt, unlike the peasant uprisings before it, sought to use modern political methods. Yet it did have some characteristics of a religious faith for its followers. God was thought to be on the side of the Sicilian peasant as he was thought to be on the side of the Anabaptist poor. With God and the masses of peasantry on their side, the Fasci sought to take control of the local elections. In the town of Piana, the Fasci were successful in capturing the local elections. Since that time it has remained a bastion of Socialist and Communist party strength. The revolutionary spirit of the villagers was so strong that by 1943 when the Fascists were defeated, the Pianesi declared themselves an independent republic until cautioned by the Communists to avoid this.[24]

The situation just described reminds one of Barrington Moore's comment:

Where the peasants have revolted, there are indications that new and capitalist methods of pumping the economic surplus out of the peasantry had been added while the traditional ones lingered on or were even intensified. This was true in eighteenth-century France, where the peasant movement that helped to bring down the *Ancien regime* had strong anti-capitalist as well as strong anti-feudal features. . . . Again in China the peasant showed by his behavior that he resented the combination of the old tax-collecting official and commercial landlord embodied in the Kuomintang regime.[25]

Another prime example of Barrington Moore's fusion of capitalism and feudalism occurred in

Mexico at the turn of the twentieth century. In 1876 Porfiro Diaz, a former general in the Mexican army, took control of the country. Diaz was greatly interested in economic development, and he encouraged foreign capital to be invested in Mexico. Economic power soon became invested in the hands of a very few individuals, the *Cientificos*. The *Cientificos* were elitists who claimed to be "scientific positivists." Their aim was to modernize Mexico as rapidly and ruthlessly as possible. Indians and their way of life were seen as a barrier to the new Mexico. Indian communal lands

. . . were declared illegal and forced to divide into individual holdings. Land was turned into a marketable commodity, capable of being sold or mortgaged in payment of debts. Many Indians quickly forfeited their land to third parties, often to finance socially required ceremonial expenses. Practically all such land went into the hands of haciendas and land companies. It is estimated that more than two million acres of communal land were alienated in the Diaz period.[26]

The parcelling out of the Indians' land to the large haciendas was imminently destructive to their way of life. Many of the Indians and peasants were recruited to work on the national railways where they received a cash income for the first time. They also received ideas of a radical nature. Some of the railway workers came in contact with the anarcho-syndicalist I.W.W. In 1906 revolutionary strikes by the peasants were crushed by the *rurales*, a special police force recruited from among the most violent bandits in the rural areas.

By 1910, the revolution had broken out in both the south of Mexico around Morelos and in the northern border area of Chihuahua. The southerners were led by Emiliano Zapata and the northern revolutionaries by Pancho Villa.

In the next year, rebel forces had grown so strong that President Diaz left the country. This act in itself did not restore the peasants' land to

[23] Adolfo Rossi *L'Agitazione in Sicilia,* E. J. Hobsbawm, translator (Milano, 1894), p. 86.

[24] See Hobsbawm, *op. cit.,* p. 105.

[25] Barrington Moore, Jr., *Social Origins of Dictatorship and Democracy: Lord and Peasant in the Making of the Modern World* (Boston: Beacon Press, 1966), p. 473.

[26] Eric R. Wolf, *Peasant Wars of the Twentieth Century* (New York: Harper and Row, 1969), pp. 15-16.

them. The new president, Francisco Madero, promised land reform, but when the peasants with Zapata as their leader had disarmed, Madero failed to live up to his pledge. Zapata had been betrayed, and he began the struggle again:

> Let Senor Madero—and with him all the world— know we shall not lay down our arms until the ejidos of our villages are restored to us, until we are given back the lands which the hacendados stole from us during the dictatorship of Porfirio Diaz, when justice was subjected to his caprice.[27]

Zapata had developed an agrarian reform scheme called the *Plan de San Luis Potosi*. In it he outlined his nonpunitive attitude toward the elites along with his determination to give the peasants back their former land.

Both Zapata's and Villa's armies were limited in effectiveness, although they fought with real courage. They fought chiefly a defensive war and, of course, fought best on their own land.

Zapata was assassinated by an "ally" in 1919. Villa was less able than Zapata to think in political terms and was, in the end, ineffectual. Yet ironically, as Robert Quirk observed,

> The inarticulate, militarily ineffectual Zapata accomplished in death what he could not win in life. His spirit lived on, and in a strange, illogical, but totally Mexican twist of fate, he became the greatest hero of the Revolution. In the hagiography of the Revolution the *Caudillo* of Morelos continues to ride his white charger.[28]

The twenty years following the Mexican Revolution did see some of the reforms sought by Zapata. In 1934 President Cardenas began to distribute hacienda lands to the peasantry. More than 41 million acres were returned to the poor. Yet the results of the revolution were ambiguous, and the peasantry was never to gain the power envisioned by Zapata.

It would be possible to examine parallels to the Mexican peasant revolt in many parts of the world. The Russian Revolution of 1917 saw the *mujik* (peasant) rise up against czarist tyranny as they had done countless times in the past. In Vietnam the peasantry rebelled against the French who allowed "the communal lands to fall into the hands of speculators and dishonest village chiefs. . . ."[29]

Eric Wolf sums up the situation in this way.

> The peasant's role is thus essentially tragic: his efforts to undo a grievous present only usher in a vaster, more uncertain future. Yet if it is tragic, it is also full of hope. For the first time in millennia, human kind is moving toward a solution of the age-old problem of hunger and disease, and everywhere ancient monopolies of power and received wisdom are yielding to human effort to widen participation and knowledge. In such efforts . . . there lies the prospect for increased life, for increased humanity. If the peasant rebels partake of tragedy, they also partake of hope, and to that extent theirs is a party of humanity. Arrayed against them, however, are now not merely the defenders of ancient privileges, but the Holy Alliance of those who—with superior technology and superior organization—would bury that hope under an avalanche of power. . . . The peasantry confronts tragedy, but hope is on its side; doubly tragic are their adversaries who would deny that hope to but the peasantry and to themselves.[30]

Wolf here obviously has reference to the developed nations who see peasant revolts as dangers to "stability." Yet as we have pointed out, the misery of the peasant is not stable but increasingly caused by new modes of oppression.[31] The United States government has attempted to suppress peasant revolts and land reform in Guatemala, Cuba, the Dominican Republic, and Vietnam in the recent past. It remains to be seen whether American foreign policy will eventually

[27] Eyler N. Simpson, *The Ejido: Mexico's Way Out* (Chapel Hill: University of North Carolina Press, 1937), p. 51.
[28] Robert E. Quirk, *The Mexican Revolution 1914-1915* (Bloomington: Indiana University Press, 1960), pp. 292-293.
[29] Bernard Fall, *Le Viet-Minh. La Republique Democratique du Vietnam 1945-1960*, Cahiers de la Fondation Nationale des Sciences Politiques, No. 106 (Paris: Librarie Armand Colin, 1960), p. 265.
[30] Wolf, *op. cit.*, p. 302.
[31] For a documentation of this view see: Pierre Jalee, *Pillage of the Third World* (New York: Monthly Review Press, 1968).

consider the welfare of the poverty-striken masses as important as world stability.

PATRIARCHAL CONTROL—THE WOMEN'S MOVEMENT

It is improbable that we could ever chart with accuracy the beginnings of feudal control. It is even less probable that one could cite the beginnings of the domination of male over female. Certainly, with the exceptions of a few South Sea islanders, male domination has been the watchword of nearly every known culture.

An orthodox Hebrew prayer says, "I thank thee, O Lord, that thou hast not created me a woman." This thought has been echoed in nearly all the world's great religions, and not without reason; for if the role of men in an oppressive society is hard, the situation for women is often even more difficult. Why is this so, and why was one women's group forced to say in defense of themselves, "Before all else we are human

A new symbol for American women.

beings . . . we demand and respect the right of every individual to create his or her own life and to develop fully his or her own potential"?[32]

Surely no one could doubt that women were and are human beings; yet that is precisely the case. Male-dominated societies have indeed denied the humanity of women in much the same way that whites have refused to give human status to Orientals or blacks.

The ancient Romans, for example, had no compunctions about the double standard:

> Cato, in concise and prosaic language, describes the contrasting situations of an adulterous wife and an adulterous husband. "If you take your wife in adultery you may freely kill her without a trial. But if you commit adultery, or if another commits adultery with you, she has no right to raise a finger against you."[33]

Again we can cite the nineteenth century scholar, Sir Henry Maine. In Rome, ". . . the eldest male parent is absolutely supreme in his household. His dominion extends to life and death and is unqualified over his children and their houses as over his slaves.[34]

The women of the ancient Hebrews were regarded as little more than chattel. If a young man was to accuse his new wife of nonvirginity, a trial was held and if

> . . . the tokens of virginity be not found for the damsel, then they shall bring out the damsel to the door of her father's house, and the men of her city shall stone her with stone that she die because she hath wrought folly in Israel, to play the whore in her father's house; so shalt thou put evil away from among you.[35]

This crucial concern for virginity can be seen in two ways. First and most obviously it is a confirmation of the property rights of the male. As Simone de Beauvoir explains,

> Virginity is demanded for . . . immediate reasons

---

[32] "Women's Manifesto" (pamphlet).

[33] Otto Kiefer, *Sexual Life in Ancient Rome* (London: Routledge and Kegan Paul, 1934), p. 11.

[34] Sir Henry Maine, *The Early History of Institutions* (London: Murray, 1961), pp. 310-311.

[35] *Deuteronomy* 23:21-22.

when a man regards his wife as his personal property. In the first place, it is always impossible to realize positively the idea of possession; in truth, one never has any thing or any person; one tries to establish ownership in a negative fashion. The surest way of asserting that something is mine is to prevent others from using it. And nothing seems to a man to be more desirable than what has never belonged to any human being.[36]

Besides the idea of women as possessions, it seems to be deeply embedded in the psyche of many male-dominated societies that women have sexual power or magic. Usually, as in the case of Eve, this power is evil in intent or effect. For that reason, defloration is often an act of ritual importance. Indeed, it may symbolize man's concept of his domination over animal-magical nature in woman. The woman has often been perceived as a fearful creature because of her monthly production of menstrual blood and her seeming control of the life force in her capacity to give birth.

The primitive fear of women has, according to Beauvoir and others, created the desire to constrict, control, and restrict her activities as well as her body.

> Costumes and styles are often devoted to cutting off the feminine body from any possible transcendence; Chinese women with bound feet could scarcely walk, the polished fingernails of the Hollywood star deprive her of her hands; high heels, corsets, panniers, farthingales, crinolines were intended less to accentuate the curves of the feminine body than to augment its incapacity. Weighted down with fat, or on the contrary, so thin as to forbid all effort, paralyzed by inconvenient clothing and by the rules of propriety— then the woman's body seems to man to be his property, his thing.[37]

The female of the species is seen in western Judeo-Christian thought as potential evil, the source of sin and shame. It was Adam's defense

that "The woman whom thou givest to be with me, she gave me of the fruit and I did eat."[38]

We can, in fact, only speculate about the causes of woman's oppression. It is theoretically possible that woman's inability to hunt as well as men while she was biologically incapacitated by childbearing or child care, made her a less valued commodity. The fact remains that in most societies her lower status has given her the potentiality to be considered as an object, a thing, rather than a human of equal worth to the male.

One of the earliest to theorize on the origin of the oppression of women was Frederick Engels in his *The Origin of the Family, Private Property and the State*.[39] Engels, citing the work of the pioneer anthropologist Lewis Morgan, believed that the original state of mankind was matriarchal with tendencies toward group marriage. Men, Engels believed, were believers in the Great Earth Mother. They practiced a kind of pure communism in which women worked arduously but were given great respect.

Engels' theories concerning the original state of human society (that is, matriarchal group marriage) are disputed by most current anthropologists. Yet his other conclusions merit further examination. For according to Engels, a surplus in foods and luxuries by primitive tribes produced changes in their social structure. War provided prisoners and slavery; surplus created the ideal of private property. The idea of private property led to the subjugation of women:

> The savage warrior and hunter had been content to take second place in the house, after the woman; the "gentler" shepherd, in the arrogance of his wealth, pushed himself forward into the first place, and the woman down into second. And she could not complain. The division of labor within the family had regulated the division of property between the man and the woman. . . . We can already see from this that to emancipate woman and to make her equal of the man is and remains an impossibility so long as the woman is shut out

---

[36] Simone de Beauvoir, *The Second Sex* (New York: copyright Alfred Knopf, Inc., 1961), p. 143.
[37] *Ibid.*, p. 147.

[38] *Genesis* 3:12.
[39] Frederick Engels, *The Origin of the Family, Private Property and the State* (New York: International Publishers, 1942).

from social production on a large social scale, and domestic work no longer claims anything but an insignificant amount of her time.[40]

Engels is saying here what his colleague Marx had stated earlier in "The German Ideology":

> With the division of labour, in which all these contradictions are implicit, and which in its turn is based on the natural division of labour in the family and the separation of society into individual families opposed to one another, is given simultaneously the distribution, and indeed the unequal distribution, both quantitative and qualitative, of labour and its products, hence property: the nucleus, the first form of which lies in the family, where wife and children are the slaves of the husband. The latent slavery in the family though still very crude, is the first property.[41]

Marx and Engels both agree that the nuclear family with its emphasis on possession and a proper division of labor is responsible for the subjugation of women. Of course, they elaborate this to suggest that capitalism and the nuclear family turn personal relationships into impersonal commodities. Whether the nuclear family is a dehumanizing institution remains to be seen, but it is clear that early capitalism was not beneficial to working women. Most women in nineteenth century England worked as domestic servants, factory operatives, needlewomen, or agricultural workers. The needle trades produced what Charlotte Bronte called "genteel slavery." The Victorian ideal of refinement called for compulsory idleness among those ladies of "quality." Yet idleness was not the case for women of low status. Some English women, called drawers, dragged coal wagons through crevices in a mine too small for a horse to traverse. One woman, a Mrs. Harris, described her ordeal in the mines in this way:

> I have a belt around my waist and a chain passing between my legs, and I go on my hands and feet . . . my cousin looks after my children in the

daytime. I am very tired when I get home at night; I fall asleep sometimes before I get washed. I am not so strong as I was, and cannot stand my work so well as I used to do. I have drawn till I have had the skin off me; the belt and chain is worse when we are in the family way. . . .[42]

Kate Millet[43] cites the case of an American sweatshop, the Triangle Shirtwaist Company. On March 25, 1911, it burned, and one hundred and forty six of its young female workers either burned to death or died by falls from the flaming building. The two men who owned the sweatshop were tried for the tragedy. One was acquitted, while the other was fined $20!

In civil affairs women were little better off. Marriage meant a kind of "civil death" for women in England. Women had no legal right to their earnings. Millet quotes *Blackwell's Commentaries* to this effect:

> By marriage, the husband and wife are one person in law; that is, the very being or legal existence of the woman is suspended during marriage, or at least is incorporated and consolidated into that of the husband. . . . But though our law in general considers man and wife as one person, yet there are some instances in which she is separately considered as inferior to him, and acting by his compulsion.[44]

Lest we should have any residual myths about the current status of women, Helen Mayer Hacker[45] has written an article for *Social Forces* entitled "Women as a Minority Group." Both blacks and women are subject to the same oppression according to Hacker. Both are highly visible; both have been ascribed as having lower intellectual capacity (that is, smaller brains); both are said to be more emotional, primitive, or childlike; both are thought to be all right in "their place;" both use similar modes of accommodation (outwitting white folks or using femi-

---

[40] *Ibid.*, pp. 147-148.

[41] Karl Marx, "The German Ideology" in Robert C. Tucker, editor, *The Marx-Engels Reader* (New York: W. W. Norton and Co., 1972), p. 121.

[42] Quoted in Wanda Neff, *Victorian Working Women* (New York: Columbia University Press, 1929), p. 72.

[43] Kate Millet, *Sexual Politics* (Garden City, New York: Doubleday and Co., 1970), pp. 71-72.

[44] *Ibid.*, p. 68.

[45] Helen Mayer Hacker, "Women as a Minority Group," *Social Forces* 30 (1951), pp. 60-69.

A leftist view of the status of working women.

nine wiles); both have limitations on their educational opportunities; both are relegated to low paying occupations; both have been denied the right to vote; and both are feared competition for the jobs of white males.

We may add to Helen Hacker's analysis that it is no accident that women are seldom found in high status–high income professions such as medicine, law, engineering, or airline pilotry but are often found in low status positions such as secretarial sciences, nursing, social work, or elementary school teaching. Men are not willing to give up their societal privileges and do not expect to do so in the future. As myths about the constitutional inferiority of women are junked with similar unfounded truths about other minorities, women have begun to ask why it is that they share inferior opportunities in careers while men manage both fulfilling careers as well as the emotional security of family life. In America in the 1970's women have begun to ask other questions as well, questions such as why women have been forced to act as a kind of surplus labor supply (along with blacks) to provide a ready source of cheap and available workers. (Rosie the riveter, the World War II charmer, is no longer in

style as recession makes competition between male workers even more intense.)

At the end of World War II, approximately one third of the adult female population in the United States was in the work force. In 1972, almost one half of all women were in the work force. This would indeed seem to mark progress in the development of sexual equity. Yet this is not the case. Mary Keyserling, former director of the Labor Department's Women's Bureau, shows that "indeed during recent years there has been a significant decline in the percentage of women in more privileged occupations—professional, technical, and kindred jobs. Currently they represent 38 percent of all the workers in these jobs." [46]

Women's fortunes are greatly like that of black people, "the first to be fired, the last to be hired." The lower pay given women does derive from economic exploitation; however, this is not the only onerous fact associated with womanhood. Some derive from her status in the family itself.

In a society that bases its evaluation of the individual on his productivity, it is natural that women would enjoy little status since their work

145

in the home is considered nonproductive in an economic sense. The woman's role (for the more than half who stay in the home) is to drudge through dirty dishes, floors, and washings, to soothe and comfort her husband, and to take reflected glory from his would-be successes in his professional life.

Moreover, the woman is given moral responsibility for her husband and children. If the husband is not in attendance at church, the minister or priest often urges the wife to induce her husband to become more concerned with spiritual things. If the husband strays, the woman is seen as a failure in her role as moral exemplar. Again, she is the source of evil, and when a moral problem arises, "cherchez la femme."

As one author puts it:

> We see these housewives' energies drained by unproductive chores without even benefit of paycheck, and we see their leisure hours played out in . . . nibbling fashion. Shopping becomes a way of taking up time like a card game. . . . Such middle-class women have been left presiding over a ghost town in our technological era where automatic timers mind the stew pots and irons convert into ivy-holders as wrinkle-shed fabrics improve. . . . Women have two primary tasks when they are home. Mother and consumer. Both are essential to keep the system working. . . . Consumer spending accounts for nearly two-thirds of all purchases in the country. Over two million tubes of beauty products are sold every week. This is called "conspicuous consumption." Keep up with and surpass the Joneses! As our culture and economy progress, women are convinced that new luxuries are actually necessities that she absolutely cannot get along without.[47]

We have discussed the role of the women in the relatively affluent middle classes of the United States. As we have seen, her frustrations derive from a male-dominated, competition-oriented society. But what of women of other societies and classes? First, it is obvious that

women in oppressed classes or nationalities are twice cursed. Often they are attached to men who have tremendous anger because of their oppression. Often this anger is directed toward the closest target, their women and children. The woman is also in a position to be sexually exploited by wealthier males of the ruling class or nationality. It has been said that the women of Vietnam have suffered more than the highly mobile men in their war with American airpower.

There is no question that oppression of Russian women before the revolution was severe. The Leninists who took control of the post-czarist society were convinced that the way to free women was to reorganize the nuclear family. In the 1920's the Bolshevik leaders wrote that:

> The first condition for the liberation of the wife is to bring the whole female sex back into public industry . . . and this in fact demands the abolition of the monogamous family as the economic unit of society. . . . To further this aim, "we are establishing communal kitchens and public eating houses, laundries and repairing shops, infant asylums, kindergartens, children's homes, educational institutes of all kinds. In short, we are seriously carrying out the demand in our programs for the transference of the economic and educational functions of the separate household to society."[48]

These measures by the state did not have immediate effect on Soviet society. While some women did take advantage of their new freedoms, most preferred the traditional roles assigned them by the ancient regime. Yet it is true that many changes did take place in the Russian family, and many of them were unplanned. They stem from these facts: The chaos and disorder caused by the revolution itself divided many families. Increasing numbers of women joined the work force as a means of bringing home bread during the economic crisis following the revolution. Irregular work schedules made it

---

[46] Quoted in Lyn Well's *American Women: Their Use and Abuse,* Southern Students Organizing Committee, Nashville, Tennessee, 1968. (pamphlet)
[47] *Ibid.*

[48] Quoted in Rudolf Schlesinger, *The Family in the U.S.S.R.* (London: Routledge and Kegan Paul, 1949), p. 10.

difficult for the adults in families to relate to each other on a regular basis.

As Urie Bronfenbrenner explains, the period after 1935 brought in a new era of state policy toward the family and the role of women. It was in this year that a new law was created,

> ... making parents legally responsible for the misbehavior of their children. Shortly thereafter, the Soviet press embarked on a propaganda campaign inveighing against laxity and irregularity in sexual relations, condemning abortion, criticizing "light minded" attitudes toward the family and family obligations, and glorifying the virtues of motherhood and fatherhood. Then in 1936, the government promulgated a new decree declaring abortions illegal, giving special allowances to mothers of large families, extending the network of maternity homes, nurseries, and kindergartens, and introducing stricter regulations in marriage and divorce.[49]

What had happened was that the bureaucratic mentality had supplanted the revolutionary one, and the need for a strong "fortress of socialism" had replaced the desire for egalitarian experiments in Russia. To be sure, women have made some degree of progress in raising their status. Three of every four medical doctors are women. Universal education for women has given them opportunities heretofore reserved for men. Yet in the end, the revolution for women was stillborn. Some Russian women today have responsibility for both a job and the home as well. The benefits of this situation are not unmixed with problems.

Back in the United States the feminist movement of reaction to male domination has taken and continues to take many forms. Possibly the earliest mode of feminist struggle in the United States took place in the abolitionist agitation of the nineteenth century. Women leaders such as Elizabeth Cady Stanton and Susan B. Anthony were activists in both the antislavery and feminist movements.

As Eleanor Flexner explains:

> It was in the abolition movement that women first learned to organize, to hold public meetings, to conduct petition campaigns. As abolitionists they first won the right to speak in public and began to evolve a philosophy of their place in society and of their basic rights. For a quarter of a century the two movements, to free the slave and to liberate the woman, nourished and strengthened one another.[50]

We cannot describe here the tedious, often tortuous, years leading to the enfranchisement of women in America and England. Demonstrations, protests, parades, and the like were used by women who felt that the public conscience must be awakened to the needs of the "gentle sex." The women faced formidable opposition from entrenched males as well as from special interests such as the liquor corporations who saw the enfranchisement of women as a threat to their businesses. Generally speaking, the labor movement and the western populists were favorably disposed to voting rights for women.

It is true that few drastic changes occurred in American society with the advent of women's suffrage. Wives tended to vote in the same way as their husbands; male domination of the congress and the presidency ensured that few substantive changes in "sexual politics" would grow out of women's new rights.

After women did win the right to a certain degree of political freedom, their movement tended to fragment and stagnate. The conservative wing of the movement became the League of Women Voters, basically an "educational" group. Other more radical groups were almost literally laughed out of existence; thus the movement, for a long time, went into limbo.

The next big upsurge in the women's movement began to take place, not coincidently, with

---

[49] Reprinted by permission of the publisher from Urie Bronfenbrenner, "The Changing Soviet Family," in Donald R. Brown, editor, *Women in the Soviet Union.* (New York: Teachers College Press, copyright 1968 by Teachers College, Columbia University), p. 101.

[50] Eleanor Flexner, *Century of Struggle: The Women's Rights Movement in the United States* (Cambridge: Belnap Press, 1966), p. 41.

the beginnings of civil rights activities in the American South. Like their antecedents in the Suffragette movement, a number of well-educated white women began to take an interest in the oppression of black men and women. Again young women marched, picketed, and demonstrated for the rights denied black Americans. Yet with their increased activism came the realization that, like blacks, women were always set at menial tasks; decision-making was always in the hands of men. Some of the idealistic young women began to understand that subtle forms of oppression were in effect in their own lives as well as those of the poor or racially oppressed.

It was with this understanding that,

> In 1967 a women's caucus at the S.D.S. convention presented a "manifesto" to the convention. Liberal in tone, this document was enough to cause chaos and ridicule on the convention floor. It asked that "radical" men deal with their own problems of male chauvinism, and that they take advantage of the abilities and potential contribution of women within the organization. Mild as this may now seem, it was relegated to be "studied" for later action. A year later, a similar resolution was also laughed off the floor.[51]

Some radical women began to believe that "people don't get radicalized by fighting other people's battles;" in other words, women who had been in the vanguard of the movements for racial equality, peace, or an end to poverty began to reassess their own interests.

In the late 1960's then, women's groups began to proliferate, especially among those with higher education. Most women's organizations began with consciousness-raising sessions to assess the role of sexual oppression in their own lives. The answers derived from these consciousness-raising sessions came from basic questions: What are my abilities and potentials? Why am I, as a woman, unhappy with my life (or a large portion of it)? Who and what are denying me full expression of my abilities? And further, who or what force is responsible for my oppression?

Some women responded to these questions in a basically reformist and traditionally political way. Women who held responsibility in the Democratic or Republican parties pushed for legislation for equal pay and equal work for women, abortion reform, and free child-care centers to free women from the constant need to stay in the home. Movement organizations such as Betty Freidan's N.O.W. (National Organization for Women) represent this line of thinking. To them, as to Aristotle, an evil man is only an ignorant one; people who understand oppression will fight against it. The basic problem is to inform men of their oppression of women and to change their images of women as sex objects or inferior beings. One of the chief means of doing this lies in education itself.

One feminist who is also a student of sociology has uncovered a number of conservative biases toward women in the discipline. She writes:

> I have been particularly sensitive to the sociologists' analysis and treatment of the roles of women in our society. The family as an institution and as a primary group has been a favorite subject of sociologists and is the area in which widest attention has been given to the "functions" of women. Therefore, the marriage and family textbook is one of the best mediums for testing the sociologists' objectivity (or lack of it) in regard to the rights, needs, and potentials of women in our society.
>
> Unfortunately, many of these textbooks seem to be authored by social scientists of the school of thought known as structural-functionalism. Put simply it's a defense of the *status quo* (i.e. certain time honored institutions, cultural values and norms persist because they contribute to the social order). . . .
>
> The authors of such books believe that a woman's place is primarily and properly in the home, and while they cannot deny that most women are no longer satisfied with just "occupation housewife" they do lament it. Ruth Cavan describes homemaking as the "chief and most absorbing role of the women" and says in terms of its importance, it is unfortunate that it has lost prestige through the years. . . . Wallace Denton argues, also, that the present American attitude that housework is drudgery should be re-

[51] Marilyn Salzman Webb, "Building the Women's Movement" *Guardian* (November 22, 1969), p. 7.

placed by "a sense of pride in domestic skills and achievement."[52]

One of the prime strategems of reform-oriented women is an exposition of the miseducation of men and women about women's psychology and abilities. This, of course, calls for educational reforms that many of the women's liberationists regard as an essential step toward human liberation.

Not all women in the movement see political, economic, and educational reform as the answer, however. For some, male dominance is so pervasive and universal that the only solution is withdrawal from male company. It would be a silly ad hominem argument to understand the women's movement as a simple reaction to lesbian tendencies. Given this fact, it is still true that a minority of women in the movement see lesbianism as the only consistent means of opposition to male domination in America.

One feminist and lesbian offers this analysis of the lesbian alternative:

> A woman who is totally independent of men—who obtains love, sex, and self-esteem from other women, is a terrible threat to male supremacy. She doesn't need them, and therefore they have very little power over her. . . .
> Lesbians, because they are not afraid of being abandoned by men, are less reluctant to express hostility toward the male class [sic] who are oppressors of women. Hostility towards your oppressor is healthy.[53]

Among the more radical feminists, a conflict continues between those who hold that a male-dominated society is inevitable in capitalism, and those, such as radical lesbians and others, who argue that males will dominate females in any social system in which both maintain close relations.

Rita Laporte, a radical lesbian, attacks the Marxist view of women's liberation:

My conclusion is that unconsciously marxists apply male supremacy no less than all other men. In reasoning that the means of production should be placed in the hands of the people, they conclude that women, as one means of production—the production of babies—must likely be in the hands of the people.[54]

Laporte does not trust the economic equality sought by the Marxists either:

> Some of us, she argues, are better able to manage the means of production, the finances, the legal intricacies necessary to run our complex society than are others. Some of us will continue to garner a greater share of the gross national product than others. A society that tries to give equal material reward for unequal contribution will not last long.[55]

A socialist critic of Laporte, Mary Alice Waters, disputes Laporte's biological determinism.

> Throughout her article Laporte makes comments that equate "male" with violence, conquest, destruction, and glory seeking, while female is synonymous with peace, privacy, and homemaking. . . . But all the characteristics she accepts as being "male" attributes are in reality characteristics not of men *per se* but of class society, or a competitive system based on each one for herself or himself, a system where the strongest do take advantage of the weaker. To place women in power instead of men, without fundamentally changing that system, would alter nothing.[56]

And thus the argument goes on. Are men or the capitalistic system itself the culprit in the oppression of women? Both men and capitalists will watch with some interest the outcome of this ideological struggle in the current women's movement.

Of course, radical feminists with a Marxian orientation would argue that capitalism and its

[52] Pat Roberts, "Bread and Roles ala Sociology," *New Prairie Primer* (Feb. 9, 1970), p. 11.
[53] Martha Shelly, "Women of Lesbos," *Kaleidoscope* (June, 1970), p. 2.

[54] Rita Laporte, "Political Theology or Practical Government," *The Ladder* (October, 1971), p. 7.
[55] *Ibid.*
[56] Mary Alice Waters, "Are Feminism and Socialism Related?" in Linda Jenness, editor, *Feminism and Socialism* (New York: Pathfinder Press, 1972), p. 19. Reprinted by permission of Pathfinder Press.

stepchild, the nuclear family, must be radically transformed if women are to be truly liberated. The abolition of the competition-oriented society would provide an end to male-female competition for the scarce job, but what of the family unit itself? Has it not survived even in the socialist countries? Of course it has. Two young intellectuals from the "other side of the iron curtain" argue that changes must be made in the family structure of both socialist and capitalist nations if women are to be freed. They ask:

> What criteria must be met by the new family structure? (1) It must be a democratically structured community which allows the early learning of democratic propensities. (2) It must guarantee many sided human relations including those between children and adults. (3) It must guarantee the development and realization of individuality. The basic precondition of this is the free choosing and rechoosing of human ties even in childhood. (4) It must eliminate both the conflicts originating in monogamy and those originating in its dissolution. This is the type of solution to be sought in the new type of family, which we will call the commune.[57]

The commune, as perceived by the writers, would have three basic rules. First everyone in the commune must work both inside and outside the commune. Second, all adults must share in the care of the children, and third, any individual would be free to leave the commune at any time. Then, according to the writers, the commune

---

[57] Mihaly Vajda and Agnes Heller, "Family Structure and Communism," *Telos* (Spring, 1971), p. 101.

would be voluntaristic but supportive, and egalitarian but not stifling.

THE FUTURE OF ARCHAIC MODES OF CONTROL

We have discussed at some length two of the oldest means of suppression known to mankind, feudalism and the patriarchal social system. While both are old means of oppression, the solutions to their problems are often vastly different. It is likely, nonetheless, that the domination of feudal and patriarchal control is on the wane. Technology has drastically changed the lives of both peasants and women and not always for the better. But it has, in many regions of the world, provided the communications needed for the self-consciousness of oppression. Peasants around the world are beginning to realize, painfully it is true, that they are not tied to the soil. Women come to the knowledge that they are not tied to their biology, and many of the myths used to justify these oppressed classes of humanity have been taken aback by modern science.

It is not clear at this time whether peasants in revolt will choose to stay on the land. It is also unclear at present if women will choose to stay in the nuclear family. There is a good deal of evidence to suggest, however, that great transformations in the social life of peasants and women will occur in the coming decades. If the reformist and revolutionary leaders in both movements have their say, it is certain that those changes will be egalitarian.

PART THREE

MOVEMENT OUTCOMES: REALITY AND POSSIBILITY FOR OUR TIME

The radical emergence of bureaucracy, cultural imperialism, and industrialism as well as the many movements of reaction to them point up the social dynamics of history. We are left with a few final questions: how have these movements been consciously and systematically nullified, contained, or stopped? What strategies, symbols, and tactics are available to the keepers of social control and order? And last, is our time to be different from times past in what happens to movements in history? Are we at least at the beginning of the end of ideology, if not at the end? Are we, in like manner, somewhere towards the end of utopia?

Answers to such questions flounder between reality and possibility. The reality is that our master trends and movements are made up of people who define them according to the situation they find themselves in. Smug, sometimes greedy elites who are profiteering from bureaucracy, cultural imperialism, and industrialization tend to see movements threatening their position and made up of people to be either controlled or smashed. Oppressed peoples who want a "piece of the action"—be it in the form of bread, nonalienating labor, peace, or the right to make their own history—tend to see movements as hope. Confusion reigns, however, as bread becomes cake, labor becomes drudgery, peace becomes the necessity to fight, and only people in the right office or place can make history.

Chapter 9, "Negating the Negation: Elite Controls of Social Movements," deals with the fact that people in power do not confront movements with passivity. They look to the options ranging from the manipulation of symbols and official force to official sanction of counter-revolutionary, reactionary, or conservative movements. Studied ignorance, ridicule, co-optation with minimal reform, and official and unofficial violence make up the list of tactics open to them. Four examples of elite controls of social movements are then discussed: (1) clerical conservatism, as a movement of reaction that sees the necessity for war, poverty, and harsh government because man is basically evil; (2) bourgeois conservatives and pseudo-conservatives who are in a paradoxical position because on the one hand they must resist change to preserve the privileges they have gained, while on the other hand, their need for profit and economic growth makes profound and unplanned changes; (3) the reactionary right that blames outside agitators, conspirators, and so forth for all of the social ills and attempts to "undo" egalitarian reforms of a past age; and finally (4) European fascism that revolves around action, blood, and violence for shoring up large corporations and instilling identity.

Chapter 10, "Syntheses, Possibilities, and Dilemmas of Future Movements," reviews the possibilities for the success of movements. First is the necessity of movements to solve the problem of scale; second, leadership must learn the control and use of technology as well as understanding the necessity of planning. Small victories and "ego integration" are considered necessary for successful movements. Finally, there is a discussion on the flux and divergence of movements and the possibility of movements against the "colonialization of the future."

CHAPTER 9   NEGATING THE NEGATION: ELITE CONTROLS OF SOCIAL MOVEMENTS

We hope no one would imagine that elites confront social movements with passivity, for in any society, social movements are given the amount of attention called for by any threat to the ruling class. Nor should we imagine that the options of the threatened elites are few in number, for they generally have control of the shared symbols of a society as well as its physical resources.

We will examine the options of the elites as they deal with movements of an increasing degree of threat to the status quo. Generally speaking, two broad options avail themselves to the rulers of society. The first involves the manipulation of symbols and official force to destroy or render harmless the radical movement. The other option may involve official sanctions of counterrevolutionary, reactionary, or conservative movements. This latter option "negates the negation" of social movements by the effect of countervailing forces. First let us appraise the first options open to elites threatened by insurgent social movements.

STUDIED IGNORANCE

Social movements need communications, especially mass communications to recruit and socialize their membership. If the movements are in the process of beginning recruitment, lack of access to communications can abort the movement. In preliterate societies, this is of course less true since informal communication is of greater importance. By way of contrast, black American rioting and insurgency from 1965 to 1968 was highly publicized; after that period of time mass action by blacks was downplayed by the media in the United States. This was done with the hope that the potentially prepolitical actions by blacks would not spread via media attention.

To selectively ignore insurgent movements can succeed only to the extent that the movements have not developed potentials for their own mass communications. With a few successes, a social movement can demand atten-

153

tion, and at this point its treatment by the establishment press is not favorable. Yet the old cliché that "a bad press beats none at all" is probably true. Critics of the so-called youth movement in the United States attribute its growth to the great media attention given the youth. This is not altogether a false accusation, and so long as the youth movement (a nonmovement in our terms) represents no threat to the existing social order, it can be tolerated, especially in its more zany or entertaining aspects.

RIDICULE

It has been said that the three topics of most western humor revolve around sex, religion, and death. All of the aforementioned are sources of tension within the human community, and one of the psychological functions of humor is tension release. Ridicule is a form of humor that probably has another purpose. Usually it is used to demean the status of another individual or group. Ridicule has been used with some success in keeping people "in their place."

One of the more vicious white supremacy jokes circulated in the American South was to term the moderate N.A.A.C.P. the "National Association of Apes, Coons, and Possums." Dehumanization has always been one of the by-products of colonialism, and when decolonial movements take root, they are subject to the symbolic dehumanization of racist ridicule.

The women's movement in America has not escaped ridicule by males on the street as well as by the male-dominated media. The Women's Liberation movement quickly became "women's lib," or even "ladies lib." Both of the latter titles diminish the importance of the word "liberation," which lends dignity and purposiveness to the image of the movement.

More importantly, many elements of the media have chosen to deal with the nonpolitical events (or more correctly nonevents) that have come to characterize the movement. A case in point is the constant reference to the "bra-burners" in the contemporary feminist movement. It is true that a handful of women calling themselves "women's liberationists" did burn their bras on a midwestern college campus. While their act may have been exciting (in a libidinal sense at least) to male reporters, it is quite peripheral to the central goals of the movement, which are economic and political.

All of the above examples show the trivialization of movements through manipulation of symbols. This is effective only to a point: when the Black Panthers walked into the California State Legislature armed with semiautomatic weapons, they were not, needless to say, greeted with ridicule. For when violent confrontation becomes imminent, ridicule gives way to more serious forms of social control.

CO-OPTATION AND MINIMAL REFORM

When a social movement does become a serious threat to the well-being of economic or political elites, other brakes can be applied to those who would rearrange power. One strategy would be to separate the leadership of a movement from its followers. Bribes such as the ones offered Emiliano Zapata (discussed earlier) are the most overt examples of such a ploy. Yet more subtle pressures and appeals can be made as well.

Consider the case of Roy Wilkins and Martin Luther King. Both black leaders had considerable following among the black middle classes. Roy Wilkins, as the leader of the N.A.A.C.P., also had good relations with President Lyndon Johnson. When the war in Vietnam began to escalate, Dr. King began increasingly to perceive the conflict as racist in nature, as well as counterproductive to the goal of the civil rights movement at that time. Roy Wilkins pleaded in the black community for support of President Johnson and his war, arguing that the civil rights movement had been aided by the President in the past and that any break with his policy could lead to an end to his support for black demands. King's argument was that the war claimed proportionately far more black bodies than white and that it was not in the interest of the black masses. Martin Luther King lost whatever influence he possessed with the White House at that time, whereas Wilkins retained his favor with the President. What had happened was that the leadership of the black middle classes had split over an issue generated by the policy-making elites in the U.S. society.

Playing off one faction of a movement against another is not necessarily a conscious ploy by the elites of a given society. Nevertheless, it is a tempting possibility for elites who wish to generate chaos in enemy ranks. Such a split was generated within the ranks of the Irish Republican Army when the British offered Ireland her freedom from colonial status, but without the six northern and predominantly protestant colonies.

If, indeed, elites are forced to compromise with the threat of a social movement, they are likely to do so in the way least likely to compromise their dominant position. During the great economic depression in the United States in the 1930's, many potentially radical social movements stood to gain from the widespread despair of the unemployed. The elites in American society stood ready to isolate these radical movements (mostly socialist, communist, or anarchist in nature) by accusing the leadership of unpatriotic attitudes, mindless violence, and unchristian ideals. Moreover, the appeal of the radical movements was undercut by the promise of more moderate reform.

Frances F. Piven and Richard Cloward describe the situation well in their book, *Regulating the Poor: The Functions of Public Welfare.*

> In a feudal or oligarchical polity, the poor could demonstrate their discontent only by begging, stealing, marching, burning, or rioting. These mass disturbances were a form of political action, a means by which the poor occasionally forced some degree of accommodation from their rulers. But civil disorder is far more costly and threatening in a highly organized and complex society, especially as urbanization and industrialization increase.[1]

[1] Frances F. Piven and Richard A. Cloward, *Regulating the Poor: The Functions of Public Welfare* (New York: Vintage Books, 1972), p. 39.

It is to avoid this civil disorder that the poor have been enfranchised with the vote:

> During periods of electoral upset political leaders proffer concessions to win the allegiance of disaffected voting blocs. It is this objective—the political "reintegration" of disaffected groups—that impels electoral leaders to expand relief programs at times of political crisis engendered by economic distress. Indeed it was this objective that accounted for the initiation of a national public welfare system during the great depression.[2]

VIOLENCE—OFFICIAL AND UNOFFICIAL

Violence, the ultimate measure of authority in a state, is seldom used capriciously. The only exception to this is the totalitarian state, as described by Hanna Arendt. One reason for its measured use by authorities derives from the fact that violence often has unpredictable results. It can, if massive enough and thoroughgoing enough, root out and destroy a movement dangerous to the elites in a particular society. Yet violence may draw sympathy to a cause; it may in fact deepen the commitment of the rebels. One can never be sure of the far-reaching effects.

With this in mind we can often see the use of violence in an official or unofficial capacity as an option open to those who would thwart the social change advocated by social movements.

In Mississippi in 1876, the movement for black rights began to meet the unofficially sanctioned violence of the lynch mob.

> . . . in Washington county, four Negroes complained that they had been driven from their homes and had "lain in the weeds for weeks." They had committed no crime, but had been persecuted "because of our political opinions." Another Negro had received notice from the "Klu Klux" to leave home within twenty-four hours. After a Negro riot at an election at Artesia, the Democratic *Jackson Clarion*, probably the most influential paper in the state, sent out a call to all (white) Mississippians to "quench in blood"

[2] *Ibid.*, p. 40.

the Negro's lust for blood. The "unconquerable Anglo-Saxons" it said, "must have in every riot, an eye for an eye and a tooth for a tooth."[3]

This call for unofficial violence by the semiofficial newspaper has been matched by the fact that officials in many counties have winked at violence generated toward members of an egalitarian social movement.

In Italy in 1922, the Republican government often confronted the socialist movement as an enemy. The Fascists, unofficial "allies" of the Republicans, attacked the socialists viciously. Often the socialists were disarmed by the police before the conflicts. According to Ernst Nolte,

> The targets of the [Fascist] squads were all socialist institutions, no matter whether they were affiliated with revolutionary or reformist factions. . . . They were looted, burned down, forced to liquidate. . . . These expeditions could always rely on the financial backing of powerful circles and the tacit, not to say practical, consent of the authorities. The fact that the agrarians supplied the trucks and paid for the gasoline, that the industrialists regarded the Fascists as the legitimate defenders of their interests, is one of the main theses of the socialist argument and it is confirmed by the Fascist *Chiurco*.[4]

Many other examples besides the preceding could be cited; they all point to the idea that the political "center" and Right often "gang up" on the Left to maintain the status quo. As often as not, this involves extralegal tactics.

The so-called third world is now a battleground for a social revolution and controversy over the "containment" policies of those countries that have a vested interest in preservation of the current social systems. These countries, too, are the scenes of much official and unofficial violence. Moreover, the middle classes in the United States have seen their sons and daughters involved in violence when students of

Southern University, Jackson State, and Kent State were shot and killed by national guardsmen and police.

The use of violence is one recourse open to elites in an attempt to preserve their privileges. Another set of options may revolve around the ability of elites to generate countermovements. It is this possibility we will now discuss.

CLERICAL CONSERVATISM

The same Industrial Revolution that produced liberal democracy and movements such as parliamentary and revolutionary socialism, produced movements of reaction as well. Since the French Revolution, the notion of progress and human perfectability had been proclaimed by the political Left in Europe. The free market of capitalism would allow the best to come forth from each man, according to liberals such as Adam Smith or Herbert Spencer. On the other hand, the free market as such must be destroyed, according to later socialist thought; yet the tools of the marketplace technology can be used to alleviate human misery and to create the new "socialist man."

Yet the idea of progress had its skeptics, and not unreasonably so, for those who disdained progress were those most threatened by it—the feudal aristocracy. According to the European conservatives, the French Revolution with its anarchy and violence was the only alternative to total loyalty to the institutions of the patriarchal family, the church, and the state. According to the philosophical conservatives such as de Bonald,[5] de Maistre, or Chateaubriand, man is

---

[3] Albert D. Kirivan, *Revolt of the Rednecks: Mississippi Politics 1876-1925* (New York: Harper and Row, 1951), p. 6.

[4] Ernst Nolte, *The Three Faces of Fascism* (New York: Mentor Books, 1969), p. 257.

[5] de Bonald attacked liberal thinking such as Montesquieu's *Spirit of the Laws* in his *Theorie du Pouvoir*, published in 1840. Joseph de Maistre (1754-1821) also attacked what he felt were the destructive tendencies of capitalism, protestantism, and liberalism. Chateaubriand was the editor of the early French journal *La Conservateur*. Other conservatives of note of the early period were intellectual giants such as Edmund Burke and Fredrick Hegel.

by nature sinful and antisocial. Authoritarian institutions, even harsh ones like the hangman's noose, are seen as necessary to control "natural man" with his propensities toward evil. War, poverty, and unjust government are just punishments given by God to unjust men.

In one way, the European conservatives anticipated a Marxian argument against capitalism; that is, that capitalism tended to "deracinate" or uproot the peasant classes by promising them gains in material wealth while destroying their identity and security. To the aristocrats and their clerical brethren, capitalism with its emphasis on rationality and change was a threat to the established order as well as to aristocratic and churchly privilege. Capitalism must be replaced with the corporate state in which class conflicts are nonexistent and social climbing is minimal. This concept of the corporate state the clerical and aristocratic conservatives shared with the later, more dynamic fascist movements.

In point of fact, European conservatives wished a return to the status quo ante and the feudal estate system. The Catholic Church, fearing liberal reforms that would change its special relationship to the state, coalesced with the aristocracy to fight radical change. For example, Pope Leo XIII's encyclical *Rerum Novarum* of 1891 was a manifesto defending old ways and aristocratic loyalties. Often the clerical conservatives organized themselves into political parties such as the German Catholic Center Party. The clerical conservatives were also given to making theologically strange coalitions, such as the one Pope Pius X made with Charles Maurras, an atheist[6] but staunch defender of "the old way."

In the end, of course, the European aristocracy could not withstand the onslaught of the new men of power, the entrepreneurial and business classes. Some of the aristocracy were able to convert their self-proclaimed natural superiority to mere financial dominance. Others became

declassé. The political power of the church began to dwindle greatly after World War I, and conservative Catholic parties were replaced to an extent by centrist or moderately socialist groups such as the Christian Socialists.

BOURGEOIS CONSERVATIVES AND PSEUDOCONSERVATIVES

The parvenues so despised by the European aristocracy were men of trade and commerce. As we have observed earlier, the dynamics of capitalism produced great concentrations of political and economic power in the hands of a new elite. Businessmen, as representatives of that elite, were not given to much reflection on the past; the future and continuous growth captivated the imaginations of the captains of industry. Yet every group holding to power derives a rationale for that possession of power. When in conflict with the forces of aristocracy and church, the bourgeoisie put forth doctrines of reform insisting on an end to special privilege. Yet when the owners of the means of production confronted the demands of the working class, the bourgeoisie, by and large, came out against social reforms such as socialized medicine or the social security program. Thus, we can understand the change from liberal reform to conservative resistance on the part of the bourgeoisie as a function of their change from an out-of-power group to a dominant socioeconomic class.

The business community has indeed become the locus of power in Western Europe, the United States, and Japan.

Like other elites holding great power over men's lives, the entrepreneurial classes have a penchant for the status quo. However, the modern capitalist conservative has a different set of problems than his predecessor in conservatism, the European feudal elite. The old aristocracy had opposed all forms of social change as threatening the social order. *Yet the paradoxical position of the bourgeois conservative is that he, on the one hand, must resist change to preserve his*

---

[6] See Edward R. Tannebaum, *The Action Francaise* (New York: John Wiley and Sons, 1962).

privileges in society, while on the other hand his need for financial profit and economic growth makes profound and often unplanned changes in the larger society. An example: most American businessmen consider automation of factories an excellent way of increasing productivity and profit. Yet the implementation of this technological advancement creates numerous dislocations in the society because of problems of overproduction, job displacement, and unemployment. For the entrepreneur, the situation then becomes one of initiating great technological changes while trying to avoid responsibility for the potentially costly solutions. The new conservative is the great technological and (perhaps unintentionally) social innovator. Nevertheless, like the old conservative of Europe he must constantly argue for social stability. His situation is not unlike that of the cowboy who mounted two horses and rode off in opposite directions.

William Newman underscores this point in his book, *The Futilitarian Society:*

The businessman, once he is faced with the results of his deeds, therefore, refuses to acknowledge that they entail a different kind of society, and as a result he fights every proposal that the "radicals" bring in to redress the things he has done. "Radicals" are in fact so busy bringing about the social and political changes made necessary by the businessman's activity that they seldom have time for anything else, for any kind of long-range revolution. But the businessman does not see what the radicals are driving at because he does not want the social and political change he has made necessary. One may take as an example of his inability to see the consequences of his acts the recently introduced compact cars. Having created a situation in which urban life has come to a condition of near crisis through the overproduction of automobiles, what is the businessman's solution to the problem he has created? It is not to contemplate the creation of a new kind of urban existence, of new social and political measures to deal with the failures of city life. No, his solution is—to produce more but slightly smaller cars. Did every family have one big car? Now they should have one big and one small car. As a solution to urban

congestion it leaves something to be desired, but one can see the point, the point being (a) that there was profit to be made from compact cars, and (b) a real solution would mean social innovation.[7]

It has been argued that America has never had a true aristocracy (although the plantation owner in the South attempted to play this role). This means that bourgeoisie in America cannot appeal to sacred tradition or haute culture to preserve their dominance. They are more likely to defend their position by references to high productivity, higher living standards, and the like. In one respect, however, modern conservatives have retained the ideological beliefs of European conservatives; that is, that they have resisted cultural changes and foreign influence. Critics of conservative economic policies are often labeled with the charge of insidious or unpatriotic ideas: "Free enterprise is the American way." Thus, the idea springs forth that a true American national will hold to capitalism with the same fervor that a true Frenchman will hold to the myth of Joan of Arc. On the whole, however, bourgeois conservatives have been quite open to change in their geopolitical attitudes when opportunities for trade and new markets come forth. Both rightists and leftists in the United States were amazed at Richard Nixon's activities in 1972 as he fought against "international communism" in South Vietnam while opening new trade relations with the communist giants, the U.S.S.R. and China. Critics of the President accused him of economic motives for both activities. Nonetheless, Nixon had the support of most of the business community for both activities.

We can understand the political stance of the bourgeois conservative as an attempt to maintain the stratification system of his society. Therefore, we should not be surprised when the business community, a traditional foe of govern-

---

[7] From *The Futilitarian Society* by William J. Newman; reprinted with the permission of the publisher. Copyright © 1961 by William J. Newman.

mental interference in business affairs, applauds government subsidies and loans such as those to the giant Lockheed Aircraft Company and the Penn Central Railways in 1970 and 1971. Most conservatives, including the American Medical Association, also come to appreciate the value of governmental subsidies to the medically needy when those subsidies are administrated by private organizations, such as the physicians' own Blue Cross Insurance organization. Also, in the 1970's many conservatives came to believe in the idea of the guaranteed annual income as an improvement over the "welfare mess." While this action may have seemed to be radical for some, it represented no change in the relative status of the haves and have-nots in American society. It was praised by some conservatives and, of course, condemned by those more bound to the traditions of rugged individualism.

If we then understand bourgeois conservatism as an attempt to maintain class differences in the larger society, it should become clear that programs such as the social security plan and others popular with the masses are not against the interests of the elites if these programs tend to mediate against more radical reforms and, of course, if they are not seen as overly expensive.

Bourgeois conservatism is, at root, a reaction of the ruling corporate elite to the labor movement in its varied forms. Like the labor movement, the conservative countermovement has at times been fragmented by nationalism. It is obvious from past and present trade wars that competition in trade has become a real source of international tension. Conservatives are often forced to contend with foreign competition as well as labor problems, and for this reason restrictive trade legislation has been passed to protect industries such as textiles and electronics in the United States. The chance for cooperation between bourgeois conservatives of many nations does, however, exist with the establishment of huge multinational corporations such as those in petroleum, the automotive industry, and bank-

ing. Many of these financial giants dominate the economic landscape in the third world companies. W. Walt Rostow has articulated the hopes of the bourgeois conservatives for the third world with his *The Stages of Economic Growth.*[8] Rostow maintains (counter to socialist thinkers) that the third world countries try to encourage foreign investment to further development. This is, of course, the conservative argument for international economic activities. Members of the labor movement have on occasion accused the multinational corporations of simply looking to the third world for a cheap, unorganized labor pool. Conservatives return with the argument that labor in the developed countries has "priced itself out of the market" with its demands.

Our discussion of bourgeois conservatism should not blind us to the fact that members of the bourgeois class are not unified in their attitudes toward the political world. Some individuals from the dominant economic class have put forth radical political views, as we shall see later; others under certain historical circumstances have opted for dynamic fascism. Moreover, capitalism itself has taken many forms, from the benign welfare states of Scandinavia, to the phenomenal growth of Japanese corporate activities, to the near indentured service system of racist South Africa. These social and historical differences in capitalism help to explain the relative rigidity of elites in a given system. This, in turn, can provide clues as to the degree of flexibility inherent in a given bourgeois philosophy. Where economic and social contradictions are rampant, we can expect the bourgeois to use repression as a mode of stifling dissent from the underclass. Such is the case currently in the Republic of South Africa. When racial or class divisions are less evident, as in Sweden, we can expect a more tolerant and progressive elite.

---

[8] W. Walt Rostow, *The Stages of Economic Growth* (Cambridge: Cambridge University Press, 1960).

THE REACTIONARY RIGHT

If social movements, such as those generated by labor agitation, generate their own antithesis, we can expect to find such antithetical movements in a dynamic economy such as the United States. A case in point is the growth of the so-called "radical Right" in American politics after World War II. The attacks on liberals and moderates by Senator Joseph McCarthy in the 1950's produced a good deal of anticommunist hysteria in American politics. McCarthy, of course, lost respectability when he began to attack the military for its softness on communism.

In the early 1960's, the John Birch Society and its leader Robert Welch made headlines by

A right-wing portrayal of internationalism. (From *Common Sense*, April, 1961.)

160

attacking President Eisenhower as a "conscious dedicated member of the communist conspiracy."[8a] The Birch Society, as well as other reactionary groups of that genre, advocated elimination of welfare and social security programs, preventive war with the communists, and an end to "social experiments" such as sex education or school integration. Unlike bourgeois conservatives, the American rightists sought basic social changes to increase social distance and economic inequity. Clearly the reactionary Right differed from bourgeois conservatives in its extreme interest in conspiratorial plots and subversion. Communists and fellow travelers were perceived in all levels of government. The reactionary Right sought an answer for nearly all social problems (that is, disorders) by blaming external sources of dissent (outside agitators).

It was no accident that the reactionary Right showed its greatest strength in the deep South, the Southwest, and the Western United States. Most sociologists attributed the rise of what they called the extreme Right to status inconsistencies among the declassé or nouveau riche, that is, groups that had great wealth and little social prestige, or groups that were losing prestige. For the most part, the anger of these groups was directed at those groups thought to be ascending to power in the United States such as blacks, government bureaucrats, intellectuals, the poor, and nonconformists of all stripes.

While on one hand the reactionary Right was encouraged by those with threatened social status, it was also encouraged by elements of the very government it often attacked. As Daniel Bell reports:

> To a surprising extent, much of the radical right agitation . . . was unleashed by the Eisenhower administration itself. In 1958, the National Security Council issued a directive, as yet still unpublished, which stated that it would be the policy of the United States government . . . "to make use of military personnel and facilities

[8a] Robert Welch, *The Politician,* copyright by Robert Welch, 1963, p. 6.

to arouse the public to the menace of communism."... In August, 1960, ... the United States Naval Air Station at Glenview, Illinois sent out invitations to community leaders and businessmen, inviting them to a seminar on "Education for American Security."... The conference was addressed by a number of high ranking naval officers. But it also included Dr. Fred C. Schwarz, the organizer of the Christian Anti-Communism Crusade [and] E. Merrill Root, ... endorser of the John Birch Society.... The speeches during the sessions ... not only attacked communism but condemned as well "liberals," *The New York Times*, the American Friends Service Committee, pacifists, "naive ministers," and so on.[9]

The military "seminars" were carried on in the United States from the mid 1950's until 1961 when a memorandum from Senator Fulbright and Secretary McNamara pressured the Pentagon to place restraints on right-wing political activities by officers currently in service.

Another source of strength for the reactionary Right in America was the large corporation. Again Bell explains, "... a significant number of corporations have been contributing financially to the seminars of the radical-right evangelists."[10] Bell goes on to list the corporations sponsoring the rightist propaganda sessions. Not surprisingly, many of the corporations cited by Bell are among the largest recipients of defense contracts.

These tendencies show the support of the radical right by elites in the business community and military establishment. It is in fact an old tactic for the centrists in power to cooperate with the reactionary Right to prevent egalitarian changes. A case in point occurred during the decades following the American Civil War when black and white farmers threatened to form a "popular front" against conservatives in the plantation system. As the white North turned its

back on the South, conservative plantation owners split the coalition of poor black and white farmers with the use of stridently racist rhetoric and the encouragement of violence by white racists. " 'I told them to go to it, boys, count them out,' admitted the conservative Governor William C. Oates of Alabama. 'We had to do it. Unfortunately, I say it was a necessity, we could not help ourselves.' "[11]

The combination of violence, white supremacy ideology, and legal manipulation was successful in destroying the integrated Southern populist movement. Many Southern planters did not approve of the excesses of groups such as the Ku Klux Klan; yet they found in such groups means to preserve the privilege and power of the plantation system. History would show later that neither poor whites nor poor blacks would profit from the archaic system.

We have not used the word extreme in reference to the reactionary Right because the word is on a sliding scale and subject to a great deal of individual interpretation. The reactionary Right is characterized by the attempt to undo egalitarian reforms of a past age. In this sense it differs from conservatives who accept most reforms of the past, while resisting current or future egalitarian changes.

The reactionary Right looks with great misgivings on democratic processes, since self-government for the masses could lead to changes taking power from elites (that is, the masses could, if they had power, choose socialism or whatever).

One other factor in the development of the reactionary Right is its support by at least some of the elites in the more "respectable" center of politics. It must not be forgotten that a European conservative attempted to use Fascists for his own purposes. As he later found to his chagrin, the Fascists' successes did not guarantee a conservative state.

---

[9] Daniel Bell, "The Dispossessed" in Daniel Bell, editor, *The Radical Right: The New American Right Expanded and Updated* (Garden City, N. Y.: Doubleday & Company, 1964), pp. 6-7.
[10] *Ibid.*, p. 24.

---

[11] Quoted in C. Van Woodward, *The Strange Career of Jim Crow* (New York: Oxford University Press, 1955), p. 61.

EUROPEAN FASCISM

On the surface, the ideas of Fascism seem to approximate those of European conservatism; namely, the ideals of nationalism, hierarchy, antilabor sentiment, and extreme ethnocentrism. It is also true, as we have said, that conservatives have at times actually supported Fascist movements. Nonetheless, Fascism is not merely a variant of conservatism, and this can be shown by its dynamic and action-oriented program.

Every moment has a "carrying class," and Fascism is no different in this respect. Most scholars agree that one of the constituent classes of Fascism is the upper-middle class, which became apprehensive about the economic implications of liberal democracy.

Consider, for example, Adolf Hitler's speech to the Rhineland industrialists in January of 1932.

> Private property, [Hitler argued], can be justified on the ground that men's achievements in the economic field are unequal, but it is absurd to construct economic life on achievement of personality, while in political life this authority is denied, and thrust in its place is the law of the greatest number—democracy.
>
> Communism is more than just a mob storming about in our German streets. It is taking over

A Nazi propaganda poster. (From George L. Mosse: *Nazi Culture,* New York: Grosset & Dunlap, 1968.)

162

the entire Asiatic world. Unemployment is driving millions of Germans to look on Communism as the logical theoretical counterpart of their actual economic situation. This is the heart of the German problem. We cannot cure this state of affairs by emergency decrees.

There can only be one basic solution—the realization that a flourishing economic life must be protected by a flourishing, powerful state. Behind this economic life must stand the determined political will of the nation ready to strike, and strike hard.[12]

Hitler was clearly arguing for Fascism as a

defense against economic radicalism. He presented the Nazi movement as a bulwark against those preaching egalitarianism or an end to social privilege. As we know, Hitler came to power and was given the opportunity to carry out his program. Did he make good on his pledge to preserve the dominance of the German corporation with its massive economic power? Franz Neumann, writing in 1944, believed that Hitler did more than fulfill his promises to the economic giants. At that time Neumann analyzed the German economy and found the following:

The process of monopolization has received an enormous stimulus from a large number of factors. The study of structural changes seems to

---

[12] Quoted in Louis L. Snyder, *The Weimar Republic* (New York: Van Nostrand Co., 1966), pp. 209-210.

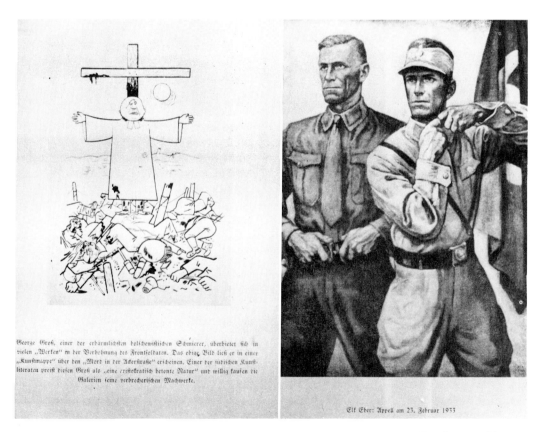

Geerge Groß, einer der erbärmlichsten bolschewistischen Schmierer, überbietet sich in vielen „Werken" in der Verhöhnung des Frontsoldaten. Das obige Bild ließ er in einer „Kunstmappe" über den „Mord in der Ackerstraße" erscheinen. Einer der jüdischen Kunstliteraten preist diesen Groß als „eine aristokratisch betonte Natur" und willig kaufen die Galerien seine verbrecherischen Machwerke.

Elf Eber: Appell am 23. Februar 1933

Nazi art. (From George L. Mosse: *Nazi Culture,* New York: Grosset & Dunlap, 1968.)

indicate that there is scarcely any economic measure, of whatever nature, which does not ultimately conduce to concentration and centratization.

In particular, the following factors are vital in that gigantic process: organization (the process of confiscating Jewish businesses); Germanization (the confiscation of foreign owned businesses), technological changes; the weeding out of small and medium scale businessmen; and the corporate structure. Apart from these factors . . . there is inherent in the bureaucratic structure of state and of business and in the scarcity of numerous materials a trend toward the encouragement of the big and destruction of the small. The state bureaucracies prefer dealing with one big business or with a few big businesses instead of with hundreds of small and medium business[es].[13]

Neumann proceeds to explain more of the interchange between the large corporation and the corporate Nazi state. Labor unions were destroyed; socialists were imprisoned or killed, while Jewish property was given to huge German cartels. Thus was Hitler's Düssledorf promise fulfilled.

The large corporation was, nonetheless, only one of the constituencies for the Fascist movement. In Rumania, Italy, and Germany, ex-army officers and enlisted men provided another source of strength for the mass rallies and violence that characterized the movement as it sought power.

One of the pioneering studies in the "political ecology of Nazism" was done by Rudolf Heberle, who analyzed social areas of Germany with their percentage of the Nazi vote. Heberle's findings in Schleswig-Holstein led him to the conclusion that "the main support of the Nazis came from the small independent family farmers rather than from the owners of estates and large farmers."[14] Fascism was not without its appeal

to other classes such as the small business owner in urban areas who felt threatened by the economic dislocations of capitalism and the fear of socialism. S. J. Woolf extends this idea to Italian Fascism: "The two most fundamental and consistent characteristics of Italian Fascism were its nature as a mass party, and the employment of economic conservatism, in the interests of bourgeois capitalism."[15]

Fascism's dynamics revolved around action, blood, and violence. The "philosophy of the deed" was to replace the speculation of the bourgeois philosopher. Anti-Semitism, for the German and Rumanian Fascists, was an issue built on the ethnocentrism of bygone years. But it was more than this. It became a principle of self-definition as potential party members were forced to prove that they had no Jewish ancestry. Anti-Jewish violence became a force that could unite the entire *volk* regardless of social class or political opinion. By drawing rigid lines to exclude Jews, gypsies, and "other inferiors," the Fascists were able to set themselves apart from the world and give an identity to dislocated masses. On the one hand, this psychological security or identity was promised the dislocated, and on the other, the bourgeois were promised economic security. In propaganda at least, the Fascists were able to exploit the personal problems of many of the European masses.

We have discussed some of the sociological and economic roots of Fascism, yet a few words on the psychological aspects of the movement may be in order. Fascism has been described by some observers as a rage for order. In another sense it is an ordered variety of rage. Death and destruction are seemingly a part of the Fascist idealogues' mentality. The Rumanian Fascist Legionari sang songs such as the following:

> Legionari do not fear that you will die young
> For you die to be reborn and are born to die
> For we are the death team that must win or die.

---

[13] Reprinted with the permission of Farrar, Straus & Giroux, Inc. From *Behemoth: The Structure and Practise of National Socialism 1933-1944* by Franz Neumann. Published in 1963 by Octagon Books. Copyright 1942, 1944 by Octagon Books.

[14] Rudolf Heberle, *Social Movements: An Introduction to Political Sociology* (New York: Appleton-Century-Crofts, 1951), p. 228.

[15] S. J. Woolf, "Italy" in S. J. Woolf, editor, *European Fascism* (New York: Random House, 1969), p. 45.

Death, only the legionari death is a gladsome wedding for us.[16]

Nazis such as Horst Wessel (who had died in street brawling) were glorified by street demonstrations and anthems. The mysticism of the Fascist preoccupation with death often assumed a kind of pseudoreligious fervor. The nonrational and the emotional were glorified in a way that many intellectuals saw as a return to gemeinschaft, the insular and secure folk community. Many prominent writers and philosophers saw in the initial stages of Fascism an anchor of security for the uprooted masses of Europe. Unfortunately, Fascism did not bring security. Instead it achieved a level of terroristic assaults on the politically "nondesirable" that has never been equalled in modern times. Hannah Arendt describes it thus:

> Terror as the counterpart of propaganda played a greater role in Nazism than in Communism. The Nazis did not strike at prominent figures as had been done in the earlier wave of political crimes in Germany . . . instead, by killing small socialist functionaries or influential members of opposing parties, they attempted to prove to the population the dangers involved in mere member-

ship. This kind of mass terror, which still operated on a comparatively small scale, increased because neither the police nor the courts seriously prosecuted political offenders on the so-called Right.[17]

We have described Fascism as what Barrington Moore, Jr., calls "revolution from above." This means that bourgeois democratic institutions such as the parliament are seen by some elites as a possible threat to their privileged status. Social democratic movements and the political forms representing those movements must be crushed according to the line of these aristocratic or bourgeois elites. When the tactics used by the elites and the uprooted masses involve terrorism to crush the uprisings by the laboring classes, Fascism is the result.

Some Marxist intellectuals have described Fascism as the logical extension and inevitable result of capitalism. It is our view that no movement is inevitable. Fascism did arise as a defense of capitalism in Germany and Italy, yet in Great Britain and Sweden, capitalism adapted itself to the far more benign welfare state. In short, while human history structures and limits choice, it does not obviate it.

---

[16] Quoted in Z. Barby, "Rumania" in Woolf, *Ibid.,* p. 158.

[17] Hannah Arendt, *Totalitarianism* (New York: Harcourt, Brace, and World, 1968), p. 42.

CHAPTER 10 SYNTHESES, POSSIBILITIES, AND DILEMMAS OF FUTURE MOVEMENTS

It is only for the sake of those without hope that hope is given to us.

Walter Benjamin

A REVIEW OF POSSIBILITIES FOR SUCCESS AND FAILURE

Social movements, as we have said, are born out of the potentialities for humans to turn personal problems into social issues. Those personal problems are generated, in part at least, by the master trends cited earlier in this book. The social trends mentioned, imperialism, industrialization, and bureaucratization, shape our lives for better or often—as we have noted—for worse. Yet, if movements are to succeed in transforming these trends or forms of control into more humane forms of social relations, adherents of the movements must somehow learn from the successful aspects of the dominant trends.

From cultural imperialism with its racism and other antihumanistic tendencies, social movement leadership must learn to think in national not regional terms and eventually in international not national scale. Have any movements achieved this scale of vision? Per-

haps liberalism and socialism have come the closest, although it may be argued that both have yet to internationalize their dreams. Liberalism, with its emphasis on international free markets, has made some degree of progress in breaking down nationalistic barriers, for example, in the creation of the common market. Yet it has as frequently failed, as we can witness with the development of trade wars, barriers, and the like. Socialism, too, has attempted to break down the nationalistic barriers separating the interests of the world's working class. It too has met with only minimal success; nationalistic loyalties have often blotted out the worldwide working class solidarity dreamed of by Marx and other radicals of his time. Yet it may be that the growth of multinational corporations by the business elites will force international consciousness.

Other social movements have attempted to raise the scale of their concerns to a multinational level. In Africa, the Pan African Congress has attempted to create an anticolonialist struggle on a continental scale. Bertrand Russell and

Linus Pauling were instrumental in the creation of international peace-seeking organizations for scientists. Their success has been moderate at best. Nevertheless, the worldwide perspective is needed if a movement is to avoid the parochial concerns that make it irrelevant to its potential constituency around the world. For it is true that the trends discussed in this book affect nearly all the world's population. For that reason we can add to the Marx's famous dictum, "Ecologists of the world, unite," or "Anticolonialists of the world, unite." This is to say that most of the problems that inflict themselves upon us have their roots in worldwide structures and conditions.

We would add to the first proposition the idea that movement leadership must also learn the control and use of technology if it is to effect its purposes. We have discussed at some length how technology has been used as a kind of adjunct to human slavery in the early industrial period. It is both banal and true to assert that technology is without morality and can be used for good or evil. It is important to go beyond this statement to ask when technology has been used for antihumanistic ends. Basically, we would argue, this has been true when technology has been advanced without the knowledge or consent of the great "unwashed masses."

Egalitarian social movements based on labor, anticolonialist, sex, or youth constituencies must come to terms with the implications of technology for their movement. Technology can destroy jobs, perfect sedative drugs, or create networks of communication. How do these discoveries change the task of social movements in our day? More concretely, how did the discovery of the transistor, for example, change the lives of those in the third world? It is true that the only change in many traditional villages is that the rural folk walk around with a radio to their ear all day. Is this the beginning of the "global village"? Is this type of radio a new means of social control, or has it a revolutionary potential? No movement can safely ignore either the revo-

lutionary potential of mass communications or the counterrevolutionary possibilities.

A third and most crucial facet of concern to movement leadership revolves around the issue of planning. The idea of planning is by no means the prerogative of stultified bureaucratic structures, and if antibureaucratic movements are to succeed in even a partial way, they must not fall into the trap of mysticism or romanticism. It is more likely that planning for tactics and strategy will be productive in social action than dependence on revelation, divine intervention, or messianic leadership.

If we were to add together all our ingredients for a successful social movement, the enlargement of scale, the use of technology, and the application of planning to human affairs, it would appear that we were advocating the institutionalization of social movements—the very thing many movements are trying to avoid. Let us state the case simply: we are not arguing that institutions in themselves are frustrating to human potentialities. What we do believe is that institutions are in constant need of formulation, reform, and, on occasion, of destruction. Stated another way, authority is needed in human affairs; yet the legitimacy of current institutions must constantly be challenged and, in doing so, questions must be asked which are never considered by the institutional elites. However, most movements are more prone to take action that directly challenges the claims of institutional legitimacy than to ask questions about that legitimacy.

A case in point is the National Welfare Rights Organization, which constantly probes into the inequities and injustices of the welfare system. Those whose lives are touched by the oppressive welfare system are in the best position to understand its destructive nature. Welfare Rights activists do not challenge the legitimacy of the political system. What they do attempt is political action to "humanize" the welfare system, if not supplant it with a more humane institution. Their efforts are, of course, hampered by their lack of power and social "respectability."

167

In a different situation, revolutionary movements criticize existing institutions at the same time that they create "dual sovereignty" by the establishment of alternative institutions—police, educational, judicial, and economic. While we cannot out of hand reject the possibility, it is difficult at present to see the ascendence of revolutionary movements in Western Europe or America. Yet a few organizations such as the Black Panthers in the United States have attempted to create alternative institutions (or dual sovereignty) within the black community.

MORE ON SUCCESSFUL MOVEMENTS

We have defined a social movement as an organized and collective attempt to alter the labor and property relations of a society, in short, its economic system. Movements may take a reformist or revolutionary tack. Whichever road they take is a long one, and group solidarity is possible only when the membership of the organization receives psychological reinforcement from time to time. This means those involved in the movement organization must have small victories, especially if the changes sought by the group are vast. Organizations of southern blacks, who had as their final goal the abolition of a racist society, could point to smaller victories, the successful boycott of a racist store, or a successful suit to desegregate courtrooms (and restrooms!). These victories are perhaps more symbolic than substantive; however, they do give supporters the drive to continue the fight for equality.

Another important factor in the success of more radical movements has to do with the idea of ego integration. By ego integration, we refer to the process whereby the individual personality or character structure becomes aligned with the movement's goals. Ego integration can only be achieved as individuals undergo constant self and group evaluation. This is not, of course, needed in moderate groups. Nonetheless, in groups that have radical change as their goal,

ego integration becomes a necessity. Ego integration has been used by religious groups for some time. The meditation techniques of the Friends, the confessional in Catholicism, and mutual criticism among the Anabaptist sects are examples.

Mayer Zald and Roberta Ash cite figures that indicate "that the Socialist party had a more rapid decline in membership than the Socialist Workers Party during the McCarthy era. . . . This despite the fact that the Socialist Workers Party's ideology was more left-wing and more subject to charges of un-Americanism."[1] The inference here is that the ego integration of the Socialist Workers was greater than that of the less exclusive Socialist party. Ego integration occurs as party indoctrination and the rigors of group activities shape the individual's commitment to the movement.

Several of the movements described in this book attempt with varying success to integrate the egos of their membership into the collective goals of the movement. The Ujamaa experiments in Tanzania, the French student movement, Socialist and worker's councils, and the Cultural Revolution of China represent some of the attempts to change the individual's life-style along with institutional change. What this amounts to is a kind of mobilization of the human psyche, which may be repugnant to the liberal mind, yet necessary to successful revolutionary struggle.

This commitment to a cause associated with ego integration is often won at hard cost to the individual. Indeed, many individuals have gained commitment to their cause after long hours of distributing literature, violence or near-violence with antagonists, or other unpleasant experiences. What we are saying here is that a successful movement must have the capacity to absorb human sacrifices. In other words, a movement that requires no sacrifice or commitment

---

[1] Mayer N. Zald and Roberta Ash, "Social Movement Organizations," *Social Forces* 44 (1966), p. 332.

will always have a tenous membership. On the contrary, those movements that can successfully demand the time, the emotional commitment, and the personal or financial sacrifice will (all other things being equal) always have a dedicated core of disciplined workers.

THE CONFLUX AND DIVERGENCE OF MOVEMENTS

The world being the generally imperfect sphere that it is, leaders of social movements often must compromise their purist convictions for success. It is certain that the many egalitarian movements current in the United States have great potential for social transformation. Yet it is equally certain that they will be unable to effect significant change without cooperation or perhaps even merger.

Many movements, it is certain, are unwilling or unable to cooperate even when common survival is at stake. A prime example of this occurred in post-World War I Germany when the Social Democratic movement (right-wing socialists) were unable or unwilling to cooperate with the revolutionary socialists to form a popular front against Fascism. In the end, both movements were destroyed by the fascistic revolution from above. Ideological differences, such as those expressed by the Social Democrats and the Socialist revolutionaries, are not the only source of cleavage.

Let us examine the case of two more recent egalitarian movements in the United States. The first, the women's movement, seeks sexual equality in a male-dominated society. The second, the black liberation movement, seeks an end to racial oppression in a society that has denied blacks equal rights. Although the movements are built on separate status groups, it seems obvious that a generally more egalitarian society would benefit both blacks and women.

Yet consider the argument against the (white) women's movement as given by black activist Linda Larue:

If white women have heretofore remained silent while white men maintained the better position and monopolized the opportunities by excluding blacks, can we really expect that white women, when put in direct competition for employment, will be any more open-minded than their male counterparts when it comes to the hiring of black males and females in the same positions for which they are competing? From the standpoint of previous American social interaction, it does not seem logical that white females will not be tempted to take advantage of the fact that they are white, in an economy that favors whites. It is entirely possible that womens liberation has developed a sudden attachment to the black liberation movement as a ploy to share the attention that it has taken blacks 400 years to generate. In short, it can be argued that womens liberation not only attached itself to the black movement, but did so with only marginal concern for black women and black liberation. . . .[2]

This rejection of the women's movement is not confined to black women, of course. Still, it is more than interesting that two groups who are deprived in life and career chances can fail to perceive their common dilemma. Or is their dilemma really common? In America, are women basically *white* or *black* women or white or black *women*? In other words, which status, race or sex, has most oppression associated with it? The answer to this question is somewhat problematic, although black people in America certainly incur more physical oppression than white women. Yet to return to Linda Larue's basic proposition, will the white women's movement simply take possible jobs away from black males in the already scarce job market? Larue believes this will be the case.

It may be argued, nonetheless, that this is the wrong question to ask. A more crucial query may be, Why are jobs scarce in this society? or Why are deprived groups involved in a struggle for fixed positions in a competitive society? The last two questions propose a class-based rather than status-based analysis. For it is obvious that

---

[2] Linda Larue "The Black Movement and Women's Liberation," *The Black Scholar* 1, no. 7 (1950), p. 37.

two status groups struggling against each other are not threats to the social order. As Gunnar Myrdal once said, when the troughs are empty, the horses bite each other. The idea that the ascendency of one group (women) would be destructive to another (blacks) may derive from a view that is not large enough in scale. Nevertheless, as long as this view is prevalent in the movements, the possibilities of coalition are slim.

MOVEMENTS AGAINST THE "COLONIZATION OF THE FUTURE"

It may be argued that the task of social movements in underdeveloped (or rather misdeveloped) nations is fundamentally different than in those in the advanced capitalist phase of development. The problems of the third world are simple, if grim; they revolve around bread and land and the inadequacy of both for the peasantry. These problems also exist in the developed countries, yet in a more subtle and complex form. It may well be that our definition of social movements as an attempt to transform labor and property relations may be inadequate for the future. For as fewer individuals are needed in production in American society and as welfare reforms are grudgingly instated, it is possible that physical needs at a minimal level may indeed be met for the masses of people in the United States. If indeed this does become the case, other concerns may prompt social movements.

Listen to Zbigniew Brzezinski's analysis of future life in the developed world.

Human conduct will become less spontaneous and less mysterious—more predetermined and subject to deliberate "programming." Man will increasingly possess the capacity to determine the sex of his children, to affect through drugs the extent of their intelligence and to modify and control their personalities.

... The information revolution, including extensive information storage, instant retrieval, and eventually push-button visual and sound availability of needed data in almost any private home, will transform the character of institutionalized

collective education. The same techniques could serve to impose well-nigh total political surveillance on every citizen, putting into much sharper relief than is the case today the question of privacy. Cybernetics and automation will revolutionize working habits, with leisure becoming the practice and active work the exception—and a privilege reserved for the most talented.[3]

The future, as described by Brzezinski, is hardly utopian. According to his view, technology will "transvalue" antiquated concerns about work, leisure, and self-fulfillment.

Herbert Marcuse sees the same future with different eyes:

Pacified existence. The phrase conveys poorly enough intent to sum up, in one guiding idea, the tabooed and ridiculed end of technology, the repressed final cause behind the scientific enterprise.[4]

Like Brzezinski, Marcuse argues that man must continue to seek control over nature through further applications of technology. Technology has liberative as well as repressive possibilities. As for its repressive side,

In the contemporary era, the conquest of scarcity is still confined to small areas of advanced industrial society. Their prosperity covers up the inferno inside and outside their borders; it also spreads a repressive productivity and "false needs." It is repressive precisely to the degree to which it promotes the satisfaction of needs which require continuing the rat race of catching up with ones peers and with planned obsolescence, enjoying freedom from using the brain, working with and for the means of destruction.[5]

Marcuse concludes by saying that, "Comfort, business and job security in a society which prepares itself for and against nuclear destruction may serve as a universal example of enslaving contentment."[6]

---

[3] Zbigniew Brzezinski, "America in the Technetronic Age," *Encounter* 30, no.1 (1968), pp. 17-18.
[4] Herbert Marcuse, *One Dimensional Man: Studies in the Ideology of Advanced Industrial Society* (Boston: Beacon Press, 1964), p. 235.
[5] *Ibid.*, p. 241.
[6] *Ibid.*, p. 243.

WILL DYSON, in London Daily Mail

WONDERS OF SCIENCE

This remarkable drawing by Will Dyson, "the cartoonist of revolt," is one of a collection by that artist recently placed on exhibition at the Leicester galleries, London. It is said to be the largest cartoon ever published in Great Britain, having been given an entire page in the Daily Mail.

A pacifist view of war. (From *Cartoons Magazine,* vol. 7, no. 2, February, 1915. H. H. Windsor, editor and publisher, Chicago.)

A view of man's past and current possibilities. (©*Punch*, London.)

Marcuse's view is that future trends portend the use of massive force to "contain" the aspirations and revolutions of the third world, while at home, "engineers of the soul" pacify dissent through manipulation, surveillance, and co-optation. Marcuse has been accused of over-pessimism, and perhaps this is true. Yet, if his

picture of the future (and present) is correct, do potentials exist for an end of repressive technology and social irrationality? Perhaps. Marcuse does see certain groups as critical in mentality and desirous of real change. They are: " . . . the substration of outcasts and outsiders, the exploited and persecuted of other races and other colors, the unemployed and the unemployable. . . . The fact that they start refusing to play the game may be the fact which marks the beginning of the end of a period."[7]

In other words, movements of the "underclass" may challenge the legitimacy of the future brave new world.

In summation, we would like to argue that future social movements are inevitable, as inevitable as the inequality that breeds them. " . . . The lasting determinant of social conflict," Ralf Dahrendorf argues, "is the inequality of power and authority which inevitably accompanies social organization."[8] Dahrendorf is probably correct that complete social equality will never come to pass. It is equally unlikely that oppressed classes will ever give up their desire for equality. This is the dilemma and the dialectic of social movements.

---

[7] *Ibid.*, p. 246.
[8] Ralf Dahrendorf, *Class and Class Conflict in Industrial Society* (Stanford: Stanford University Press, 1959), p. 64.

172

APPENDIX

INTELLECTUALS, POWER, AND SOCIAL MOVEMENTS

No discussion of social movements would be complete without a discussion of the men and women of ideas—the intelligentsia and their relationship to the elites who dominate the economic and political power. Intellectuals for the most part are political animals, and leaders of social movements would be unwise to ignore their potential support or threat.

We will analyze here the relationship between the intellectual and social movements and trends. Our first task will be to define the ephemeral person we call the intellectual. This task is not, as we shall see, an easy one. Melvin Seeman, for example, writes that, "I have defined the intellectuals as a group for whom the analysis of ideas in their own right (i.e. for no pragmatic end) is a central occupation." [1]

Seymore Lipset's definition is at once more comprehensive and precise; he considers intellectuals as

> . . . all those who create, distribute and apply culture, that is, the symbolic world of man, including art, science and religion. Within this group there are two main levels: the hard core of creators of culture—scholars, artists, philosophers, authors, some editors and some journalists; and the distributors—performers in the various arts, most teachers, most reporters. [2]

Merton relates a variant of this statement in *Social Theory and Social Structure:* "We shall consider persons as intellectuals in so far as they devote themselves to cultivating and formulating knowledge. They have access to and advance a cultural fund of knowledge which does not derive solely from their direct personal experience." [3] Merton goes on to further divide intel-

[1] Melvin Seeman, "The Intellectual and the Language of Minorities," *American Journal of Sociology* 64 (July, 1958), p. 26.

[2] Seymore Lipset, *Political Man: The Social Basis of Politics* (New York: Doubleday & Company, 1958), p. 311.
[3] Robert K. Merton, *Social Theory and Social Structure* (New York: Free Press, 1957), p. 209.

lectuals into two categories, the "bureaucratic" and the "unattached" intellectual.

Another interesting group of definitions of the intellectual represents a set of normative expectations. Indeed, Toynbee,[4] Mills,[5] Mannheim,[6] and Benda,[7] at an earlier point in history, conceived of the intellectual as a possible moral exemplar as well as a dominant force in history. The intellectual is sometimes represented here as being a potentially "moral elite" as well as a man of intellectual creation.[8] It is beyond the scope of this work to comment on this idea, yet there is some irony in the fact that in many segments of American society the term intellectual connotes "moral decay" (especially to the good burghers residing in university towns).

In essence, the concept of intellectual must include three ideas: (1) a self-consciousness of one's position in the society, that is, the taking of the role of the intellectual type; (2) a set of normative standards manifest in a reference group or ideology; and (3) a system of rewards[9] provided by some segment of the society for successfully carrying out the role expectations demanded by that society.

The requirements for playing the role are simply a modicum of intellectual ability, requisite training, and socialization. For the purposes of this study, the intellectual role may be defined as one in which normative expectations include the production of ideas that justify, confront, or extend power. Thus, the intellectual holds a particularly important relationship to those elites who participate in the crucial decision-making processes of a society.

Following this delimited concept of the intellectual role, one can proceed to explore possible relationships between "power" and the "intellectual" as a social type. One such relationship, or rather nonrelationship, is the possibility that the creative man of learning may refuse to admit the existence of power, or indeed, may deny the existence of society. While this may be a viable epistemological position, it is one that has little relevance to the political milieu, and for this reason, it cannot be treated in this book.

Three basic relationships between power and the intellectual will be explored in the following section. The intellectual types will be analytically separated into: (1) legitimatizers of power, (2) substantive rationalists, and (3) functional rationalists. (See the chart opposite.)

LEGITIMATIZERS OF POWER

Two types of intellectuals can be seen historically as having justified power by the creation and support of ideologies, the "conservative" and the "ideologue."

THE CONSERVATIVE

All ruling elites are threatened from time to time, and none can use only sheer force or coercion to stay in power. Hobbes, de Bonald, de Maistre, Burke, and Hegel have in many ways functioned as advocates of the conservative ideology. Conservative intellectuals conceptualize

[4] Arnold J. Toynbee, *A Study of History* (London: Oxford University, 1946).

[5] C. Wright Mills, *The Sociological Imagination* (New York: Oxford University Press, 1959).

[6] Karl Mannheim in his *Man and Society in an Age of Reconstruction* (New York: Harcourt Brace and Company, 1950), p. 83, sees intellectuals as sublimating "those psychic energies which society . . . does not fully exhaust. In this way they stimulate objective knowledge as well as tendencies to introversion, introspection, contemplation and reflection. . . ."

[7] Julian Benda, *The Betrayal of the Intellectuals,* Richard Aldington, translator (Boston: Beacon Press, 1955).

[8] Both Benda and Raymond Aron see the intellectual as fallen from grace and forsaking the special moral responsibility concomitant to his role. See Aron's *The Opium of the Intellectuals* (Garden City, New York: Doubleday & Company, 1955).

[9] According to Don Martindale in *Social Life and Cultural Change* (Princeton: Van Nostrand and Company, 1962) "Intellectual roles are not basically dissimilar from any others. They represent the stable patterning of individual behavior with respect to conceptual activities and skills. They provide certain rewards to their occupants. . . . Intellectual roles are unique only with respect to their peculiar content with intellectual activities and skills."

INTELLECTUALS, POWER, AND MOVEMENTS: POSSIBLE RELATIONSHIPS

ROLE-FUNCTION:	LEGITIMATIZERS OF POWER		SUBSTANTIVE RATIONALISTS (ADVOCATES OF CHANGE)		FUNCTIONAL RATIONALISTS (BUREAUCRATIC INTELLECT)
SUBCLASS:	CONSERVATIVE ADVOCATES	IDEOLOGUES	REVOLUTIONARY	REFORMIST	
EMPIRICAL EXAMPLES:	Monarchists	Bonapartists	French philosophes	Abolition- ists, civil libertarians	Systems analysis in business, govern. and military action
SOURCE OF POWER:	Ruling elite (traditional)	Ruling elite (new)	Deprived masses disenfranchised with organizing potential	Deprived mas- ses with enfran- chisement or potential for it	Technological, bureaucratic systems (control of resources)
FORM OF SOCIAL INTEGRATION DESIRED:	Cultural integration (archaic)	Normative integration	Cultural inte- gration (new steady state)	Normative integration	Functional and com- municative integration on institutional level
SOCIAL ACTION DESIRED:	Compliance	Compliance	Mobilization in revitalization or revolutionary movements	Participation in reformist norm-oriented groups	Planned action to further specific aims of particular institutions
DESIRED GOALS:	Organic equilibrium	Maintenance of current elites	New utopian equilibrium	Delimited constitutional changes	Increased functional integration leading to "progress" or "development"

society as a totality. Further, conservative advocates seek total "cultural integration" in the society. A lack of cultural integration is conceptualized by Landecker as:

> . . . inconsistency among cultural standards . . . first in the form of contradictory demands made by universals (universal standards) or if several specialties with societal reference are at variance with one another, cultural inconsistencies exist, i.e. labor and management.[10]

According to Russell Kirk, a "modern" conservative, conservatism revolves around six ideas: (1) a belief that divine intent rules society; (2) affection for the variety and mystery of traditional life; (3) the conviction that civilized society requires orders and classes; (4) a belief that property and freedom are inseparable; (5) faith in prescription, distrust of calculators, and a belief that man is governed by emotion and not by reason and that, therefore, he must be controlled; (6) a conviction that innovation is a devouring conflagration more often that it is a torch of progress.[11]

The church, the monarchy, and the aristocracy of the ancient regime have been staunchly supported as the legitimate sources of power in the Western world by the conservative intellectuals yet they have been stripped of most of their power in the political arena (with the exception of certain areas of Latin America). Thus, the fate of the traditionalist conservative today is not bright. Technology and "democratic" ideals have

---

[10] Warren S. Landecker, "Types of Integration and Their Measurement," *American Journal of Sociology* 56 (1951), p. 332.

[11] Russell Kirk, *The Conservative Mind* (Chicago: Henry Regenry, 1964), p. 18.

emasculated his ruling elite and left him as a rather quixotic and irrelevant social type.

Any social system, however, develops aspects of the "sacred" if it endures over a given period of time. Capitalism has continued to provide a base for the conservative intellectual in America. Wilbert Moore and Melvin Tumin[12] have argued that "ignorance" is one key mode for the maintenance of social cohesion in a given society. In American society (and indeed in all others), ignorance is a useful state of being for the conservative advocate since, according to Moore and Tumin, it functions as a preservative of privileged position, a reinforcement of traditional values, a preservative of fair competition, a preservative of stereotypes, and the basis for the maintenance of incentive appropriate to the system.[13]

Therefore, it would seem that any relatively stable social system producing a relatively stable class of elites would provide fertile ground for the development of conservative intellectual types. Eric Fromm[14] argues very persuasively that the Soviet Union, as well as the United States, is an essentially conservative and static social system.

THE IDEOLOGUE

Societies are not always static, of course, and shifts of power through mass revolutions, reform coups, or palace revolts occur frequently in nonconstitutionalist forms of government. Legitimatizers are required to justify power after the fact of its change to produce compliance on the part of all nonelitists in the state. Coser points out that, "Intellectuals may fashion new legitimations in historical situations in which the old ones no longer seem sufficient to shore up the legitimation or they may create entirely novel systems of legitimation in order to justify new systems of power."[15]

Coser sees the Bonapartists and Polish Marxist Revisionists of a later date as ideologues dedicated to the justification of "new Power."

It is important to note here that the ideologue seeks a different variety of integration than does his conservative counterpart. Landecker states that "Integration in relation to standard and persons is called normative integration and is in accord with such norms."[16]

The task of the ideologue, then, is to see that the norms of the ruling elites are complied with in the fullest sense. They seldom need to justify entire systems of values but rather specific norms created by the new men of power.

ADVOCATES OF PLANNED CHANGE (SUBSTANTIVE RATIONALISTS)

REVOLUTIONARIES

All purveyors of knowledge are potentially revolutionary with regard to their society. As societies reach "critical epochs," intellectuals are often at the forefront of those groups demanding changes. This is especially true when intellectuals are out of favor with those holding political and social power. For example:

The French historian Roustan asserts that the philosophes had a direct and strong influence upon the revolutionary development that exploded in 1789. Poverty, despair and mistreatment inflamed the masses but without the intellectuals there would be no revolution. . . .[17]

The French philosophes offer an excellent empirical example of the ideal type—the "substantive rationalist," because as Remmling points out, "The philosophes worked with the conception that three prejudices operate to cause errors

[12] Wilbert E. Moore and Melvin M. Tumin, "Some Social Functions of Ignorance," *American Sociological Review* 14 (December, 1949), p. 787.
[13] *Ibid.*
[14] Eric Fromm, *May Man Prevail?* (New York: Anchor Books, 1961).

[15] Lewis A. Coser, *Men of Ideas* (New York: Free Press, 1965).
[16] Landecker, *op. cit.*, p. 332.
[17] Gunter W. Remmling, *Road to Suspicion* (New York: Appleton-Century-Crofts, 1967), p. 113.

and deceptions which distort men's relationship to the objects constituting their world: idols, interests, priestly fraud."[18]

Joseph Hamburger's work *Intellectuals in Politics: John Stuart Mill and the Philosophic Radicals*, points to a similar situation in 1829 in England.

> The philosophic radicals approached being pure intellectuals in politics. Because they felt no close identification with any of the established parties, classes, or other groupings of society, their conduct as politicians could be guided by their sympathies, hostilities, and attachments to which most politicians are subjected.[19]

Two possible factors in the intellectual's commitment to change are as follows. First, the intellectual may perceive inconsistencies in value systems to a greater extent than those whose vocation does not include critical reflection. Second, these inconsistencies may in turn be translated into personal dissonance for the intellectual. Weber describes this most vividly in his analysis of the Hebrew prophet as intellectual:

> The intellectual seeks in various ways . . . to endow his life with a pervasive meaning, and thus to unify with himself, with his fellow men and with the cosmos. It is the intellectual who transforms the concept of the world into the problem of meaning.[20]

Thomas O'Dea sees this variety of intellectual as the man

> . . . who in terms of his advancement of knowledge and his conserving functions with respect to the accumulated knowledge of the past, builds and preserves the bridge over the void. At the same time in terms of the critical aspects of his role, he is the man who exposes the weakness of that very bridge. . . .[21]

Pointing out weaknesses in societal bridges is not likely to endear the substantive rationalist to ruling elites, especially if they are rigid in techniques of social control. Yet the revolutionary intellectual in many cases, driven as he is by the need to invest history with meaning, is not likely to be deterred. Perhaps the mood of this social type can be best expressed by Proudhon, who represents in many ways the tenor of the revolutionary intellectual:

> Today's civilization is indeed in a critical stage . . . all traditions are used up, all beliefs abolished. . . . Everything contributes to sadden people of good will. We shall struggle in the night, and we must do our best to endure this life without too much sadness. Let us stand by each other, call out to each other in the dark, and do justice as often as opportunity is given.[22]

Of course, the crisis in values is only one reason for the motivation of the substantive rationalist's desire for change. In many societies, intellectuals are faced with a kind of status incongruence that is likely to produce the desire for the reorganization of society. For example, T. B. Bottomore states that

> There is much evidence that the political attitudes of intellectuals are influenced very strongly by their social class origins; for example, there was a striking difference in France between the students of the Ecole Libré des Sciences Politiques recruited . . . from the upper class and strongly right wing and the students of the Ecole Normal recruited . . . from working class and peasantry and predominately left wing in their attitude.[23]

The intellectual elite desiring radical social change must depend on the "deprived" masses for support. By aligning his interests with that of the masses, strong impetus for change is affected. Eric Hoffer sees the intellectual in a constant tension with the "masses," needing their support yet loathing his dependence.

[18] *Ibid.*, p. 137.
[19] Joseph Hamburger, *Intellectuals in Politics: John Stuart Mills and the Philosophic Radicals* (New Haven: Yale University Press, 1965), p. 173.
[20] Max Weber, *The Sociology of Religion* (Boston: Beacon Press, 1963), p. 125.
[21] Thomas F. O'Dea, *American Catholic Dilemma* (New York: New American Library, 1958), p. 34.

[22] Pierre Joseph Proudhon, quoted by Karl Lowith in *Meaning in History* (Chicago: University of Chicago Press, 1949), p. 73.
[23] T. B. Bottomore, *Elites and Society* (Middlesex, England: Penguin Books, 1966), pp. 75, 76.

The intellectual's concern for the masses is as a rule a symptom of his uncertain status and his lack of an unquestionable sense of social usefulness. It is the activities of the chronically thwarted intellectual which makes it possible for the masses to get their share of the good things of life. When the intellectual comes into his own, he becomes a pillar of stability and finds all kinds of lofty reasons for siding with the strong against the weak.[24]

Hoffer is probably correct that the alliance between intellectuals and "mobilized" masses in a social movement is always a tenuous one. Lenin, for example, had no place for intellectualizing within his revolutionary cadres.

The revolutionary intellectual, then, perceives himself as having no stake in the existing social order. Since the existing order does not provide adequate gratification for him (either in access to power or in status) or an adequate frame of reference for a system of coherent values, he attempts to change the "cognitive mazeway"[25] of his society by revolutionary means to seek a new "steady state" or equilibrium. Revolutionary movements are in the end utopian in nature. Revolutionaries, just as conservatives, seek cultural integration. Revolutionary cultural integration must be on new and "more just" levels of solidarity, however. Both revolutionary intellectuals and conservatives are likely to conceive of society as a totality, and both in different ways seek to give it unity.

REFORMISTS

Alienation from existing norms and values in a society is a matter of degree, and although many intellectuals show dissatisfaction with given elements of the society, they except certain crucial values in that society from their questioning. Many would accept the opinion of Edgar

Zilsel: "If the critical spirit expanded to the whole field of thinking and acting it would lead to anarchism and social disintegration."[26]

The reformist intellectual is in a very real way a substantive rationalist as well as is the revolutionary. The reformist, however, stays inside the value structure of his society and speaks with the same "vocabulary of motives," as do his more conservative compatriots, but the reformist challenges specific norms or the gap between the norm and the actual behaviors of members of his social system. To do this he must have, to some degree, a modus vivendi with those in political or economic power. He must not seem to be a threat to their existence, at any rate, or he may be forced out of the common value system. The reformist, too, may use the deprived masses as a source of power; yet these masses must be enfranchised or have the potential for enfranchisement. This is one great difference between the revolutionary and the reformist and one reason that in totalitarian societies, such as the Republic of South Africa, reformist intellectuals are silenced or pushed into becoming fullblown revolutionaries. Societies that cannot tolerate the democratic left are always threatened by revolutionary and nonconstitutionalist leftists.

The reformist is different from the revolutionary, also, in that his conception of society is not holistic in nature. His approach is essentially a pragmatic and fragmentary one. Typically, he is relativistic in terms of his value system as well. It is important to note that it is not the content of his message that makes one a reformer, however. The civil rights worker in the northern part of the United States may be tolerated or even given some degree of aid by the power structure of some communities, whereas many communities in the deep South regard the young idealists as revolutionaries.

Both the revolutionary and the reformist face

---

[24] Eric Hoffer, *The Ordeal of Change* (New York: Harper and Row, 1967), p. 46.
[25] This term was gleaned from Anthony F. C. Wallace in his article, "Revitalization Movements," *American Anthropologist* 58 (April, 1956).

---

[26] Edgar Zilsel, "The Sociological Roots of Science," *American Journal of Sociology* 47 (January, 1942), p. 544.

a difficult time in an affluent society such as that of the United States or western Europe. Kenneth Keniston remarks that

> Given a widespread conviction that deliberate attempts at reform lead to excesses worse than those they seek to correct, the easiest solution for the individual or the culture is never to voice the principle by which reform might be guided. Disillusion of overly high hopes has produced cynicism—not the cynicism of the naive opportunist, but the more corrosive cynicism of the man or the culture which has seen its hopes dashed.[27]

FUNCTIONAL RATIONALISTS

C. P. Snow's classic statement on the gulf between scientific and humanistic cultures in western society leads one to an understanding of the "third" camp in the world of intellectuals, that of the scientist-engineer.

> Literary intellectuals at one pole—at the other scientists, and as the most representative, the physical scientists. Between the two a gulf of mutual incomprehension—sometimes (particularly among the young) hostility and dislike, but most of all lack of understanding.[28]

More important to this study than the communications gap between intellectuals is the relationship between the intellectual and his source of power. The intellectual termed here a functional rationalist is defined as anyone who consciously attempts to further the division of labor in a society. Thus, the intellectual in this case would differ from the bureaucrat in that the bureaucrat simply fulfills the role demands of his position. The functional rationalist intellectual attempts to extend the functional integration of his organization by furthering or increas-ing specialization (that is, by means of research), or he hopes to further the communicative integration of his organization by increasing the precision of information flow and by rechanneling the networks.

It is obvious that the source of power of this intellectual is the bureaucratic, large-scale organization. It is undoubtedly true as well that any individual in a large-scale organization has a vested stake in a degree of stability in the larger society that has produced the bureaucratic organization.

Bottomore comments on the nature of this intellectual variety in this way,

> Two features of the recent history of intellectuals in industrial societies need to be considered. The size and the internal differentiation of the intellectual elite have both increased, especially at the lower levels, with the expansion of university education and the growth of scientific, technical and professional occupations.
>
> It may be as a consequence of these developments that intellectuals have tended to become less radical critics of society as a whole and to be more concerned with solving the kind of short term specific problem which arises out of the complex activities of the industrial societies in which they live.[29]

Robert Michels has commented on the trend toward functional rationality within the intellectual community in Germany:

> In German industry, for example, 39 per cent of the salaried directors and other employees came from intellectual environments. Penetration or deviation? Both, but perhaps more the first than the second. Given the uncertainty of the future and in addition the desire for money and speculation, it is not marvelous if our times particularly are characterized by the intellectual classes suffering grave losses to the professions that the Germans call "practical."[30]

The grafting of intellectuals to the pragmatic business of building organizations may or may not produce a sense of alienation within the

---

[27] Kenneth Keniston, "Alienation and the Decline of Utopia," *The American Scholar* 29 (Spring, 1960), pp. 107-108.
[28] C. P. Snow, *The Two Cultures and the Scientific Revolution* (New York: Cambridge University Press, 1959), p. 4.

[29] Bottomore, *op. cit.*, pp. 76-77.
[30] Robert Michels, *First Lectures in Political Sociology* (New York: Harper and Row, 1949), p. 109.

individual, depending upon the organization that utilizes the services of the intellectual.[31]

Robert Boguslaw's excellent book, *The New Utopians*,[32] sees the designers of systems (programming analysts and the like) as new men of power. The source of power of these intellectuals lies within the bureaucratic framework of government, industry, or business—more particularly in the cybernetic system.

> The programmer himself, through the specific sets of data he uses in his solution to a programming problem and the specific techniques he uses for his solution, places a final set of restrictions on action alternatives available, within a computer-based system.
>
> It is in this sense that computer programmers, the designers of computer equipment, and the developers of computer languages possess power. To the extent that decisions made by each of these participants in the design process serve to reduce, limit or totally eliminate action alternatives, they are applying force and wielding power in the precise sociological meaning of these terms.[33]

These cybernetic "new utopians" are unlike the classic (substantive rationalist) utopians in several important ways. For although both believed "planning" to be essential to the facilitation of social change, the classic utopian was likely to take a holistic point of departure in dealing with the society, whereas the data systems specialists plan within the value system of their particular organization. In addition, the new utopians have not only

> . . . lost the humanistic orientation that motivated so many of the classical utopian efforts, but also

they proceed from a philosophical base in which traditional values of western societies seem to be self consciously excluded. . . . The workaday new utopians seem to have implicitly turned Max Weber's Ethic on its head to read, "Hard work is simply a temporary unautomated task. It is a necessary evil until we get a piece of gear, or a computer large enough, or a program checked out . . . until then you working stiffs can hang around—but for the long run we really don't need or want you."[34]

The functional rationalist intellectual seems to be guided by two values: first, the goal orientation upon which his organization is based, and second, efficiency. Because he fulfills or attempts to fulfill the standards and tasks set for him by his organization, he increases greatly the potential for power of those who set the values for his bureaucratic organization. Whether he deals in "hardware" (that is, the development of sophisticated weaponry) or in "software" (human engineering, such as motivational research or the creation of political images), he has become a kind of unwilling, or in some cases unknowing, revolutionary.

CONCLUSION

Social and political power does not stem from simple control of limited resources; it also involves the struggle for men's minds. The intellectual has always been a general in these wars of influence. Western society has seen the rise of ideological and utopian systems of thought, one stemming from the need of elites to maintain the stability of their society, the other from the need for change generic to the condition of the deprived. Both conservative and revolutionary intellectuals have understood society to be a unity. Therefore, both have prescribed action or inaction in terms of their holistic Weltanschauung.

Ideologues and reformists, while differing in intent, see society pragmatically. In this way

---

[31] See Robert Presthus, *The Organization Society* (New York: Alfred A. Knopf, 1962). Presthus develops an "index of alienation" to portray the perceptual disparity between the common image the research scientists and military organization men have of themselves and of each other. See also Jan Hajda "Alienation and Integration of Student Intellectuals," *American Review* 26, no. 5 (1961).

[32] Robert Boguslaw, *The New Utopians: A Study of System Design and Social Change* © 1965. Reprinted by permission of Prentice-Hall, Inc., Englewood Cliffs, New Jersey.

[33] *Ibid.*

[34] *Ibid.*, p. 25.

they differ from their conservative and revolutionary brethren.

No intellectual has ever been truly unattached or objective in purveying one or another social philosophy. The power of the conservative and ideologue has always resided with the interests of an elite. Likewise, the leftist intellectual is politically impotent without communication with the deprived masses.

Sources of power shift because of technological and organizational advances, however, and the intellectuals in ascendency in the modern technologically advanced western societies are the functional rationalists, the specialists furthering the division of labor in society. In many ways the impact of the functional-rationalist's thought radically restructures the cultural

mazeways as much as does any revolutionary's. Yet the functional rationalist does not take cognizance of the totality of society in his planning. His point of view is rational and pragmatic.

Future currents of power in human society are likely to revolve around the issues of (1) whether intellectuals perceive their social order as a totality or a fragmented network of problems, (2) whether intellectuals will seek "rationality" or tradition as a guide for the confrontation and control of social change, and most importantly (3) whether the substantive rationality of the utopian will continue to conflict with the functional rationality of the engineer.

Saint-Simon and others dreamed of a fusion of science and humanism. At this point in history, however, it remains a dream.

ANNOTATED BIBLIOGRAPHY

Alinsky, Saul D. "The War on Poverty—Political pornography" *Journal of Social Issues,* 1 (January, 1965). A polemic by one of America's late radical activists. Alinsky shows great frustration with the "cooptation" manifest in the "war on poverty."

Allen, Robert L. *Black Awakening in Capitalist America* (New York: Anchor Books, 1970). This is one of the best sources on the black power movement in the U.S. Allen criticizes "cultural nationalism" and black capitalism which he finds fraudulent. Allen proposes a cooperative economic system for blacks.

Anderson, Walt, editor. *The Age of Protest* (Pacific Palisades, California: Goodyear Publishing Company, Inc., 1969). A popularized account of the political activism of the 1960's.

Arendt, Hannah. *Totalitarianism* (New York: Harcourt Brace and World, 1968). Arendt's book is a philosophical tome comparing the tactics of terrorism in Stalinist Russia and Nazi Germany. Occasionally obscurantic, Arendt does have great value for the advanced student of social movements.

Aron, Raymond. *The Opium of the Intellectuals* (Garden City, New York: Doubleday & Company, 1955). Aron's work here is an attack on European intellectuals and their affinity for Marxism.

Aron, Raymond. *Progress and Disillusion: The Dialectics of Modern Society* (New York: The New American Library Mentor Book, 1968). This book uses the dialectical metaphor skillfully in discussing industrialization and other trends. Aron, an acute observer, is a Gaullist and is essentially conservative in his approach to the idea of progress.

Ash, Roberta. *Social Movements in America* (Chicago: Markham Publishing Company, 1972). This excellent book uses an essentially conflict approach to the study of social movements in the U. S. It is perhaps the most valuable of its kind—using history and sociology in a very readable fashion.

Bain, George Sayors. *The Growth of White-Collar Unionism* (Oxford: Clarendon Press, 1970). An important contribution to the literature on the potentially radical impact of middle-class professional unionism.

Bakula, B. B. "The Effect of Traditionalism on Rural Development: The Omurunazi Ujamaa Village, Bukoba" *University of Dar Es Sallaam: Studies in Political Science* (No. 2).

Balandier, George. *Ambiguous Africa: Cultures in Collision* (New York: Pantheon Books, 1966). Balandier, a humanistic anthropologist deals with social change, especially urbanization in Africa. A compassionate and balanced view of the changing scene.

Balandier, George. *The Sociology of Black Africa,* Douglas Garman, translator (New York: Praeger Publishers, 1970). Perhaps the best introduction to the social and political forces sweeping through Africa today.

Baldwin, James Mark, editor. *The Dictionary of Philosophy and Psychology,* Vol. 2 (New York: Peter Smith, 1940).

Barby, Z. "Rumania," in S. J. Woolf, editor, *European Fascism* (New York: Random House, Inc., 1969). Barby presents a brief but incisive account of Rumanian Fascism using an interesting blend of sociological and psychological perspectives.

Bax, Belfort. *The Rise and Fall of the Anabaptists* (London: Swan Sonneschein, 1903). This classic work, sympathetic to the left-wing Christians of medieval times, is still of great import in the understanding of utopian movements.

Bay, Christian. *The Structure of Freedom* (New York: Atheneum Publishers, 1965). Bay's book is a highly creative attempt to fuse the knowledge of modern sociology and psychology with the classical philosophical problems of human freedom—an important book.

Becker, Howard and Barnes, Harry Elmer. "The Quest for Secular Salvation: Social Reform in Relation to the Sociological Impulse" in *Social Thought from Lore to Science,* Vol. 2 (New York: Dover Publications Inc., 1961). Becker and Barnes, long familiar to students of sociology, has excellent sections on the development of the idea of social "form" and reform.

Bell, Daniel. *Marxian Socialism in the United States* (Princeton, New Jersey: Princeton University Press, 1967). Bell, a disillusioned socialist, looks at Marxism with a jaundiced eye. This book expresses Bell's desire for an "end of ideology." Bell's work has been severely criticized by leftists.

Bell, Daniel, editor. *The Radical Right: The New American Right Expanded and Updated* (Garden City, New York: Doubleday & Company, 1964). This is an important though uneven series of essays on the origins and positions of the radical right in the U. S. The weakness of this book lies in its cursory treatment of the economic factors in the genesis of the so-called radical right.

Bell, Daniel. *Work and its Discontents* (New York: League for Industrial Democracy, 1970). This is one of Bell's best works—a discourse on the alienation of the blue collar worker. "Must" reading for middle-class college students who wish to "build bridges" to the working class.

Bendix, Reinhard. *Nation Building and Citizenship* (New York: John Wiley & Sons, Inc., 1964). Nation-building, a preoccupation of the Cold War, is taken up by this political sociologist as another attempt to get at the copresence of equality and inequality.

Bennis, Warron. "Beyond Bureaucracy" in Irving Louis Horowitz and Mary Symons Strong, editors, *Sociological Realities* (New York: Harper & Row, Publishers, 1971).

Berger, Peter and Luckmann, Thomas. *The Social Construction of Reality: A Treatise in the Sociology of Knowledge* (Garden City, New York: Doubleday & Company, 1966). This is an important introduction to the sociology of knowledge. Extremely readable and comprehensible.

Bernard, Jessie. *Social Problems at Mid-Century: Roles, Status and Stress in a Context of Abundance* (New York: Holt, Rinehart and Winston, Inc., 1957).

Birnbaum, Norman. *The Crisis of Industrial Society* (London: Oxford University Press, 1969). Birnbaum represents the best in the scholarship in the revival of the neo-Marxist tradition in sociology. These essays are important contributions to one's understanding of industrialization.

Blauner, Robert. "Internal Colonialism and Ghetto Revolt," *Social Problems,* 16 (Spring, 1969). This article has been reprinted in innumerable books of readings and with good reason; it is crucial to the understanding of race relations in the U. S.

Blumberg, Paul. *Industrial Democracy* (New York: Schocken Books, Inc., 1969). Quoting C. Wright Mills, "I have tried to be objective. I do not claim to be detached," Blumberg on the relevance and future of workers' management. The dynamics of socialist ideology point in the direction of increased workshop democracy.

Blumer, Herbert. "Collective Behavior" in Alfred M. Lee, editor, *New Outlines of the Principles of Sociology,* second ed. (1946), rev., (New York: Barnes and Noble Books, 1951). A classic summation of theories and principles of collective behavior with a symbolic interactionist approach.

Blumer, Herbert. "Social Movements" in A. M. Lee, editor, *New Outline of the Principles of Sociology* (New York: Barnes and Noble Books, 1951).

Bookchin, Murray. *Post Scarcity Anarchism* (Berkeley: The Ramparts Press, 1971). A new leftist enters into the not-so-new debate between Marxists and anarchists with the latter perspective. Especially significant in terms of Bookchin's political assumptions concerning technology and abundance.

Boskoff, Alvin. "Social Change: Major Problems in the Emergence of Theoretical and Research Foci" in Howard Becker and Alvin Boskoff, editors, *Modern Sociological Theory in Continuity and Changes* (New York: The Dryden Press, 1957).

Boulding, Kenneth E. *A Primer on Social Dynamics: History as Dialectics and Development* (New York: The Free Press, 1970). Boulding criticizes the dialectical conflict-oriented theory, which should be supplanted by developmental and non-conflictual ideals. Basically Boulding argues here for reform rather than radical change.

Bourges, Herve. *The French Student Revolt: The Leaders Speak,* B. R. Brewster, translator (New York: Hill & Wang, 1968). A good primary source on the ideology and world-view of the French radical youth.

Bowditch, John and Ramsland, Clement. *Voices of the Industrial Revolution* (Ann Arbor: University

183

of Michigan Press, 1968). Excellently edited little book with excerpts and biographical sketches of some of those concerned with the economic and social issues unleashed by the Industrial Revolution. Nice overview for the mercantilist period to the nineteenth century.

Brady, Robert A. *Business as a System of Power* (New York: Columbia University Press, 1943). This thirty-year-old book charts corporate irresponsibility in the United States and is not in the least dated.

Breitman, George. *The Last Year of Malcom X* (New York: Schocken Books, Inc., 1968). The last year of Malcolm's life produced a radical reorientation of his thought. An excellent analysis of Malcolm's increasing commitment to socialism.

Brinton, Crane. *Anatomy of Revolution* (New York: Vintage Books, 1952). This is *the* classic work on revolution by a non-Marxist scholar. While much research has been done since Brinton's time, it remains a crucial beginning in the theoretical work on revolution.

Bronfenbrenner, Urie. "The Changing Soviet Family" in Michael Gordon, editor, *The Nuclear Family in Crisis* (New York: Harper & Row, Publishers, 1972).

Brooks, Thomas R. *Toil and Trouble: A History of American Labor* (New York: Delacorte Press, 1964). A realistic history of the toil and trouble encountered by the American worker in the last 300 years or so. Calls for increased *political* activity by organized labor—who must take drastic action to grow or else atrophy.

Brzezinski, Zbigniew. "America in the Technetronic Age" *Encounter,* 30 (January, 1968). This article outlines the possible futures technology holds for us and, from a humanistic point of view, the possibilities are not encouraging.

Campbell, Ernest and Pettigrew, Thomas. *Christians in Racial Crisis* (Washington D. C.: Public Affairs Press, 1959).

Cantril, H. *The Psychology of Social Movements* (New York: John Wiley & Sons, 1941). Cantril's work was a pioneering effort, yet it seems in many ways dated today.

Chinnery, E. W. F. and Hadden, A. C. "Five New Religious Cults in British New Guinea," *Hibbert Journal,* 4, 1917.

Chinoy, Eli. *Automobile Workers and the American Dream* (New York: Random House, Inc. 1955). This is a fascinating bit of research by Chinoy on the matter of blue-collar alienation.

Christie, Richard. "Eysenck's Treatment of the Personality of Communists" *Psychological Bulletin,* 53 (November, 1956).

Citizens Board of Inquiry. *Hunger U. S. A.* (Boston: Beacon Press, 1968). This important book that documents the extent of hunger and starvation in America is unfortunately not out of date. It points to the vast contradictions in federal policy which allow rich rentiers to reap federal benefits while the poor are expected to fend (or not fend) for themselves.

Clark, James M. *Teachers and Politics in France* (Syracuse: Syracuse University Press, 1967). Teachers as a pressure group in the political process receive well-documented treatment for the French case. The Fédération de l'Education Nationale (FEN), as the largest and most powerful union of educators in France, gives insight into militant unionism—like the strike against de Gaulle's assumption of power in 1958 and support of negotiation with Algerian rebels.

Cohn, Norman. *The Pursuit of the Millennium* (New York: Harper & Row, 1961). An important and well-written book about the Anabaptist movement. Cohn is a conservative and sees great evil in all utopian or messianic movements.

Cole, Stephen. *The Unionization of Teachers: A Case Study of the UFT* (New York: Praeger Publishers, Inc., 1969). A critical incident in the struggle of American teachers is explored by Cole. From the United Federation of Teachers in New York City comes the repeal of its no-strike strategy. A new political tendency for white-collar unionism in motion.

Cook, Fred J. *The Warfare State* (New York: Collier Books, 1964). This is a popularized introduction to the study of the military-industrial complex, yet it is packed with good information on the military behemoth in the U. S.

Dahrendorf, Ralf. *Class and Class Conflict in Industrial Society* (Stanford: Stanford University Press, 1959). Dahrendorf uses a neo-Marxist analysis (his politics are centerist) to understand the stratification system in the Western world. He basically argues with Marx's ghost—and sometimes wins.

Das, Nabagopal. *Experiments in Industrial Democracy* (New York: Asia Publishing House, 1964).

Davis, Jerome. *Contemporary Social Movements* (New York: The Century Company, 1930). A classic introduction to social movements. Davis, a progressive, was sympathetic to the plight of the "have-nots" and shows this in his work.

Davies, James C. "Toward a Theory of Revolution" *American Sociological Review,* 27 (February, 1962). Davies' article is well-known in sociological circles and represents a real attempt to understand the genesis and stages of revolution.

Dawson, C. A. and Gettys, W. E. *Introduction to Sociology,* revised ed. (New York: The Ronald Press Company, 1935).

de Beauvoir, Simone. *The Second Sex* (New York: Alfred Knopf, Inc., 1961). One of the precursors of the Women's Liberation Movement. She and her friend Sartre represent a humanistic and existential varient of Marxist thought and praxis.

Derber, Milton. *The American Idea of Industrial Democracy, 1865-1965* (Urbana: University of Illinois Press, 1970). Deals with the evolution of the collective bargaining model in the U. S. Claims it is flexible enough to cope with the general historical condition of the American experience. Good questions on industrial participation.

de Tocqueville, Alexis. *The Old Regime and the French Revolution* (New York: Harper Brothers, 1956). The classic on revolutionary France. Should be read by all in conjunction with his *Democracy in America.*

Deutscher, Issac. *On the Chinese Cultural Revolution* (London: Bertrand Russell Peace Foundation, 1967). An independent scholar and usually dispassionate scholar does a hatchet (dare we say "pickaxe") job on the Maoist revolution from above.

Diop, David. *Coups de Pilon*, Wilfred Cartey, translator (Paris: Presence Africaine, 1956). Poetry in the new tradition of "negritude" by a West African intellectual.

Domhoff, G. William. *Who Rules America* (Englewood Cliffs, New Jersey: Prentice-Hall, Inc., 1967). This analysis builds on the prior work done by C. Wright Mills and adds empirical method to Mills' theories.

Draper, Hal. *Berkeley: The New Student Revolt* (New York: Grove Press, 1965). A good descriptive work portraying sequentially the trials of university turbulence in the 1960's.

Durant, Will and Ariel. *Rouseau and Revolution The Story of Civilization*, Vol. 19 (New York: Simon and Schuster, 1967).

Durkheim, Emile. *The Division of Labor in Society*, George Simpson, translator (Glencoe, Illinois: The Free Press, 1947). Durkheim's work is in a real sense an answer to the Marxian vision of class conflict. This early work is still de rigueur for all serious students of sociology.

Durkheim, Emile. *The Elementary Forms of Religious Life: A Study in Religious Sociology* (New York: The Macmillan Company, 1915). Durkheim's analysis of religion is essentially functionalist in nature. Religion is seen as a source of social solidarity; God is "society symbolically transformed."

Ehrenreich, Barbara and John. *Long March, Short Spring: The Student Uprising At Home and Abroad* (New York: Modern Reader, 1969). This approach to student movements has a Marxist bent to it and touches on the "shortcomings" of the movements from a rather orthodox Marxian perspective.

Eisele, Volker. "Theory and Praxis: The View From Frankfort," *Berkeley Journal of Sociology* 16, (1972). The Frankfort school of sociology—a radical neo-Marxist-Freudian approach is detected here. For those interested in the notion of a "critical" sociology, this is an excellent source.

Eisenstadt, S. N. *Modernization: Protest and Change* (Englewood Cliffs, New Jersey: Prentice-Hall, Inc., 1966). This book is somewhat disappointing since it gives only fragmentary ideas about the concept of modernization. It is, in fact, a poor substitute for the work done by Horowitz and others.

Elkin, Frederick. "God, Radio and the Movies" in Bernard Rosenberg and David White, editors, *Mass Culture* (New York: The Free Press, 1957).

Ellis, William T. *Billy Sunday: The Man and His Message* (Philadelphia: The John C. Winston Co., 1914).

Elms, Alan C. "Pathology and Politics" in *Change: Reading in Society and Human Behavior* (Del Mar, California: C. R. M. Books, 1971).

Engels, Frederick. *The Origin of the Family Private Property and the State* (New York: International Publishers, 1942). This book has recently come to be considered a serious work by many radical women. Engels' analysis of the prehistoric family depends on the work of Lewis Morgan which has been challenged by more recent anthropologists. Nevertheless, the idea of women as property is still important to the understanding of sexual oppression.

Fall, Bernard. *Le Viet-Minh. La Republique Democratique du Vietnam 1945-1960, Cahiers de La Fondation Nationale des Sciences Politiques*, No. 106 (Paris: Librarie Armand Colin, 1960).

Fanon, Franz. *Black Skin White Masks* (New York: Grove Press, 1967). Fanon on the psychology of colonized identity and a little politics.

Fanon, Franz. *The Wretched of the Earth* (New York: Grove Press, 1968). What can we say? This is a requirement for anyone who attempts to understand the dynamics of anticolonial struggle. An important statement on revolutionary violence.

Feuer, Lewis S. *The Conflict of Generations* (New York: Basic Books, 1969). Feuer's book is both a ponderous tome (1,200 pages) and a tirade. The use of unadulterated Freudian psychology to understand (and therefore reject) the youth movement is at best questionable.

Flexner, Eleanor. *Century of Struggle: The Woman's Rights Movement in the United States* (Cambridge: Belnap Press, 1966). This is a really excellent historical analysis of the women's movement.

Frazier, E. Franklin. *Race and Culture Contracts in the Modern World* (Boston: Beacon Press, 1957). Frazier's world-wide analysis of "the cycle of race relations" gives one a rather cool, that is to say, unemotional view of imperialism. Nevertheless Frazier's work is extremely valuable for a comparative view of race relations.

Freund, Julian. *Max Weber* (New York: Vintage Books, 1969). A fine analysis of Weber's work.

Fried, Albert, editor. *Socialism in America: From the Shakers to the Third International* (Garden City, New York: Anchor Books, 1970). This is a rather limited sourcebook of original materials from socialist party platforms and the like.

Fried, Albert and Sanders, Ronald, editors. *Socialist Thought: A Documentary History* (Garden City, New York: Anchor Books, 1964). Another small paperback of some value to the beginning student of socialism.

Fromm, Erich. *Escape From Freedom* (New York: Farrar and Rinehart, 1941). Fromm applies his sweeping social psychology and his ingrained Christian-Judaic ethic to the question of social freedom.

Fromm, Erich. *The Sane Society* (New York: Fawcett Books, 1965). The same man with just a little more politics.

Galbraith, John Kenneth. *The New Industrial State* (Boston: Houghton Mifflin Company, 1967). Galbraith is a rare creature—an economist with a sense of aesthetics. His work here is especially interesting as he points to the autonomous nature of the bureaucratic economic organizations both in the U. S. and Russia. How does one exercise control over the giant corporation, or rather how can the public avoid being controlled by such corporations? An excellent contribution.

Gans, Herbert J. "Social and Physical Planning for the Elimination of Urban Poverty" in Bernard Rosenberg, I. Gerver, and F. W. Howton, editors, *Mass Society in Crisis: Social Problems and Pathology* (New York: The Macmillan Company, 1964).

Gay, Peter. *The Dilemma of Democratic Socialism: Edward Berstein's Challenge to Marx* (New York: Collier Books, 1962). Nearly anything written by Peter Gay is excellent, and this analysis of the struggle between parliamentary socialism and revolutionary socialism is no exception.

Gerassi, John. *The Great Fear in Latin America* (London: Collier-Macmillan Ltd., 1963). A scathing attack not only on the corupt regimes of Latin America, but also the imperialist policy of the United States. Gerassi presents a nation by nation view of the potential for and struggle toward social justice in Latin America.

Gerth, Hans H. "The Nazi Party: Leadership and Composition" *American Journal of Sociology,* 14 (1940). Hans Gerth is one of the finest of the emigré sociologists to come to America. His analysis of the polity of the Nazi machinery is indeed classic in its insights.

Gerth, Hans and Mills, C. Wright. *Character and Social Structure: The Psychology of Social Institutions* (New York: Harcourt, Brace and World, Inc., 1953). Gerth and Mills have written a definitive work in social psychology. Especially important is the concept of the "vocabulary of motives" as a tool to understand the relationship between personality and social structure.

Gerth, Hans and C. Wright Mills. "Politics as a Vocation" and "Science as a Vocation" in *From Max Weber: Essays in Sociology* (New York: Oxford University Press, 1946).

Geschwender, James A. "Explorations in the Theory of Social Movements and Revolutions" *Social Forces,* 46 (June, 1968). Geschwender attempts here to create axioms in the theory of revolution. His theories are logical and sound.

Graham, Billy. *Peace With God* (Garden City, New York: Doubleday & Company). Billy Graham is not a social theorist, nevertheless he represents a point of view that is individualistic, conservative and antistructural change.

Graham, Hugh Davis and Gurr, Ted Robert. *The History of Violence in America* (New York: Bantam Books, 1969). This volume was prepared for the President's official committee on the causes and prevention of violence. It was (naturally) ignored by the President. Yet it is of great value to the serious student of social movements. Violence is part and parcel, it seems, of the American past and present.

Grieve, A. F. "Vows (Christian)" in James Hastings, editor, *Encyclopedia of Religion and Ethics* (New York: Charles Scribner, 1925).

Gusfield, Joseph R. *Protest, Reform, and Revolt: A Reader in Social Movements* (New York: John Wiley & Sons, Inc., 1970). As a rule, sociological readers are poor substitutes for carefully conceived books; Gusfield's reader is an exception, and it contains several crucial articles, both theoretical; and historical.

Hacker, Helen Mayer. "Women as a Minority Group," *Social Forces,* 30 (1951). The first effort to compare the status of white women and black men. The article, though over 20 years old is still relevant today.

Handler, M. S. "Malcolm X Splits with Muhammed" *New York Times* (March 9, 1964).

Harrington, Michael. *The Accidental Century* (Baltimore: Penguin Books, Inc., 1965). This is an excellent attempt by Harrington to relate aesthetics, politics, and economics. Harrington's reformist socialist bias leads him to the conclusion that individual greed rather than collective (substantive) rationality have guided the past century.

Harrington, Michael. *The Other America* (Baltimore: Penguin Books, Inc., 1962). This book was credited with making Americans aware that poverty is pervasive in the affluent society.

Harrington, Michael. *Socialism* (New York: Saturday Review Press, 1972). Not the first book on socialism, not the last, it forthrightly concentrates on the future of the socialist past. By concentrating on democratic Marxism, the book welds vision with reality for the leftist coalitions to come.

Harrington, Michael. *Toward a Democratic Left: A Radical Program for a New Majority* (Baltimore: Penguin Books, Inc., 1969). This is a polemical and programatic attempt to acquaint radicals with the possibilities of a middle-class–blue-collar coalition for change.

Hayek, F. A. *The Counter-Revolution of Science: Studies on the Abuses of Reason,* Parts I and II. (Glencoe, Illinois: The Free Press, 1952). Hayek, a rightist Austrian economist delivers a stinging attack on the logical positivists who founded sociology. More than this, he attacks the idea of social planning or any "rationalized" social system.

Heberle, Rudolf. *Social Movements: An Introduction to Political Sociology* (New York: Appleton-Century-Crofts, 1951). This work, the magnum opus in the literature on social movements has an international reputation and deservedly so.

Hiches, John D. *The Populist Revolt: A History of the Farmers' Alliance and the People's Party* (Lincoln: University of Nebraska Press, 1961). The populist movement in America is one of the least understood and most important movements in this country's agrarian past. This scholarly treatment of the movement is a real contribution to the literature.

Hobsbawm, E. J. *Primitive Rebels: Studies in Archaic Forms of Social Movements in the Nineteenth and Twentieth Centuries* (New York: Frederick Praeger, 1959). Hobsbawm, an historian, has written the definitive work on "prepolitical" movements in southern Europe. The transition from the sacred to the secular in political thought is charted in this work.

Hoffman, Abbie. *Revolution For the Hell of It,* (New York: Pocket Books, 1970). A multi-media manifesto of the late and semi-great Yippie movement. It was a time when it was thought by some that what America needed was a good dose of cultural shock therapy, and Hoffman tells it like it was.

Holsinger, Norman. *Unionism and Class-consciousness Among Academic Intellectuals: The Case of the United Professors of California, California State University, Sacramento,* unpublished masters thesis, California State University at Sacramento, 1973, "Introduction." An example of the kind of theses to come on the growing white-collar unionism. The place of academic intellectuals is central to the future of this process.

Huberman, Leo and Sweezy, Paul M. *Introduction to Socialism* (New York: Modern Reader, 1968). An "orthodox" account of Marxian socialism for the novice. Lucidly written.

Hunt, R. N. Carew. "Socialism" in J. Gould and W. Kolb, editors, *A Dictionary of the Social Sciences* (New York: Free Press, 1964). A good, short but definitive statement on socialism.

Huxley, Aldous. "The Politics of Ecology," *The Center Magazine,* 2 (March, 1969).

Jalee, Pierre. *Pillage of the Third World* (New York: Monthly Review Press, 1968). This is an angry book, Marxist in orientation. It documents the techniques of the economic exploitation of the third world by the "have" nations.

Johnston, Sir H. H. *The Colonization of Africa* (Cambridge Historical Series—no date given).

Keniston, Kenneth. *Young Radicals: Notes on Committed Youth* (New York: Harcourt, Brace, and World, 1968). A psychological statement on the make up of "young radicals." Though thoroughly useful, it falls short. This is due primarily to its limited (psychological) perspective.

Keys, Ancel. *The Biology of Human Starvation* (Minneapolis: University of Minnesota Press, 1950). An interesting technical account of the famous Minnesota experiments in physiological change due to starvation. Keep in mind while reading this book that three fifths of the world's population goes to bed hungry each night.

Kiefer, Otto. *Sexual Life in Ancient Rome* (London: Routledge and Kegan Paul, 1934). This book is more scholarly than erotic (is more for historians than pornographers). It does give an interesting account of patriarchal control.

King, C. Wendell. *Social Movements in the United States* (New York: Random House, 1956). A distinctly underwhelming effort.

Kirivan, Albert B. *Revolt of the Rednecks: Mississippi Politics 1876-1925* (New York: Harper & Row, 1951). This is a rather detailed technical account of the strange mixture of populism, elitism, and racism governing Mississippi politics for the last century. Strangely enough, it does not cover racial conflicts to any great extent.

Kloss, Robert M. *Political Tendencies and Social Security from the New Deal to the Great Society,* unpublished dissertation, Louisiana State University, August, 1969. A three-year study hastily completed in one year on the "linch-pin" of the New Deal, the Social Security Act of 1935 and its several amendments. Arrogance prevents me from saying it is bad.

Kolaja, Jiri. *Workers Councils: The Yugoslav Experience* (New York: Frederick A. Praeger, 1966). A good, sympathetic but critical analysis of the Yugoslav's attempts to democratize industry.

Korpi, Walter. "Working Class Communism in Western Europe: Rational or Nonrational," *American Sociological Review,* 36 (December, 1971). This article is a good antidote to the idea that radical commitment is somehow based on nonrational or psychogenic factors.

Kunen, James Simon. *The Strawberry Statement: Notes of a College Revolutionary* (New York: Random House, 1968). It's the humor side of campus radicalism, and Kunen adds a nice perspective to "campus unrest."

La Barre, W., McAllester, D. P., Slotkin, J. S., Steward, O. C., and Tax, S. "Statement on Peyote," *Science,* 104 (1959). Shows that the use of peyote within the structural context of a religious framework is not deleterious to the individual.

Lachs, John. *Marxist Philosophy: A Bibliographical Guide* (Chapel Hill: The University of North Carolina Press, 1967). Sources galore for the beginning student of Marxist-Leninism. Comments are both helpful and hindering. A must for the shelf of anyone uttering Marx's name.

Laider, Harry W. *History of Socialism* (New York: Thomas Y. Crowell Company, 1968). This classic is in paperback and as such is a real bargain for those unfamiliar with the growth of the various sectarian and philosophical branches of socialism. It is a generally sobering volume written in a sympathic way by a social democratic.

Laidler, Harry W. *History of Social Movements* (New York: Thomas Y. Crowell Company, 1942).

Laidler, Harry W. *Social-Economic Movements* (New York: Thomas Y. Crowell Company, 1944). Updated and expanded as *History of Socialism*. An earlier version of *The History of Socialism*.

Laidler, Harry W. *Socialism in Thought and Action* (New York: The Macmillan Company, 1970). A lucid account of socialism by a nondogmatic advocate of reformist socialism.

Laing, R. D. *The Divided Self* (London: Penguin Books, 1970). An attempt to view mental illness in a totally existential framework. He contends that sickness is more like existential isolation than pathology.

Landauer, Carl. *European Socialism: A History of Ideas and Movements* (Berkeley: University of California Press, 1959). Vols. I and II. This book is de rigueur for all serious students of socialism.

Lang, Kurt and Gladys. *Collective Dynamics* (New York: Thomas Y. Crowell Company, 1961). See also "Collective Dynamics: Process and Form", in Arnold M. Rose, editor, *Human Behavior and Social Processes* (Boston: Houghton Mifflin, 1962).

Lanternari, Vittorio. *The Religions of the Oppressed: A Study of Modern Messianic Cults* (New York: Mentor Books, 1965). This is a fascinating yet scholarly view of revitalization movements around the world. It is a veritable encyclopedia and is reasonably priced in paperback. Buy it!

Laporte, Rita. "Political Theology or Practical Government," *The Ladder* (October, 1971). A lesbian manifesto with an anti-Marxist appraisal of the women's movement.

Larue, Linda. "The Black Movement and Women's Liberation" *The Black Scholar*, 1 (May, 1970). A view of the (white) womens' movement by a black woman who does not see kinship in the common oppression of blacks and women.

Laslett, John M. *Labor and the Left: A Story of Socialist and Radical Influences in the American Labor Movement 1881-1924* (New York: Basic Books, Inc., 1970). Six U. S. unions and the place of various types of socialism are related in detail. Well-researched attempt on the socialist–trade-union alliances of the past point to industrialization as the major cause for the failure of American socialism.

Lazarsfeld, Paul F., Sewell, William H., and Wilensky, Harold, editors. *The Uses of Sociology* (New York: Basic Books, 1967).

Lefevere, Georges. *The Coming of the French Revolution,* R. R. Palmer translator (Princeton, N. J.: Princeton University Press, 1947). A handy primer on the French revolution. Lucid, well written, with a good class analysis.

Lenski, Gerhard E. *Power and Privilege: A Theory of Stratification* (New York: McGraw-Hill Book Company, 1966). This is an extremely creative and scholarly attempt to understand social distance and stratification through an evolutionary framework. Somewhat questionable is Lenski's contention that industrialism lessens social inequality.

Lewallen, John. "Ecocide: Clawmarks on the Yellow Face," *Earth* (April, 1972).

Lewallen, John. "Grand Mix Meets American Pie," *Clear Creek* (April, 1972).

Lewis, John Wilson. *Party Leadership and Revolution in China* (London: Cambridge University Press, 1970). An excellent non-Marxist account of the leadership struggles in the Peoples Republic of China during the Cultural Revolution.

Lewis, Oscar. "The Culture of Poverty," *Scientific American*, 245 (October, 1966). The idea of the "culture of poverty" is a very controversial one in the social sciences. Radicals see it as "blaming the victims" for their own exploitation. Lewis' argument is presented here in full on the "pro" side of the argument. His opponents see structural not cultural bases of poverty.

Lichtheim, George. *A Short History of Socialism* (New York: Praeger Publishers, Inc., 1970). As a *short* history of socialism from the standpoint of the history of ideas, for the modern reader it is unsurpassed. The relationship of socialism to liberalism is clarified.

Lichtheim, George. *Imperialism* (New York: Praeger Publishers, Inc., 1971). Lichtheim's work on *Imperialism* is given from the social democratic viewpoint. Capitalism, he points out, is not the only source of imperialism. Much of the book is an argument against Maoist and Leninist perspectives on imperialism.

Lincoln, C. Eric. *The Black Muslims In America* (Boston: Beacon Press, 1961). Lincoln's doctoral dissertation is a classic description of the Muslim movement among the most deprived of the urban black population.

Lipset, Seymour. *Agrarian Socialism* (Berkeley: University of California Press, 1950). This is one of Lipset's best efforts—an attempt to understand the radical populism in the prairie provinces of Canada.

Lipset, Seymour. *Political Man: The Social Bases of Politics* (New York: Doubleday & Company, Anchor Books, 1963). This book is required reading for nearly every political sociology course. One questions whether this should be. Much of the material in the book is dated; much of it exhibits the smugness which C. Wright Mills characterized as a "celebration of American life." The book has a pluralist antiradical, anticonservative bias.

Lipset, Seymour Martin and Bendix, Reinhard. *Social Mobility in Industrial Society* (Berkeley: University of California Press, 1964). One of the first comparative studies to judge the relative "openness" of American and European society. Lipsit and Bendix conclude there isn't much difference in rates of social mobility between the two continents.

Lorwin, Lewis L. *The International Labor Movement: History, Policies, Outlook* (New York: Harper and Brothers, Publishers, 1953). Views international labor organizations as having pragmatic-reformist tendencies. Limited by the Cold War climate of opinion.

Mackenzie, Norman. *Secret Societies* (New York: Collier Books, 1967). This is a fun book—learn the secret rituals of the Masons, Ku Kluxers, and the Thuggees!

Maine, Sir Henry. *The Early History of Institutions* (London: Murray, 1961). A dated classic in anthropology. Maine has interesting ideas on the genesis of marriage.

Malcolm X. *The Autobiography of Malcolm X* (New York: Grove Press, 1965). This is it. Who can deny the significance of any book that has altered the direction and tone of an entire movement for human liberation?

Malcolm X. *Malcolm X Speaks* (New York: Merit Publishers, 1965). More of Malcolm, primarily from speeches after his religious split with the American Black Muslim leadership. This also must be read.

Mannheim, Karl. *Essays in the Sociology of Knowledge* (London: Routledge and Kegan Paul, Ltd. 1952). Mannheim has gone Marx one better in his work on the sociology of knowledge. Mannheim's "relationalism" seems much like an extreme epistemological relativism; social position determines one's mentality.

Mannheim, Karl. *Ideology and Utopia: An Introduction to the Sociology of Knowledge* (New York: Harcourt, Brace and Company, 1936). This is *the* modern work in the sociology of knowledge.

Mannheim, Karl. *Man and Society in an Age of Reconstruction* (New York: Harcourt, Brace and Company, 1940). This is Mannheim's best effort in his argument for a democratic, planned society. Planning and democracy are crucial to avoid the "negative selection" of fascism.

Manzer, Ronald A. *Teachers and Politics in England and Wales* (Toronto: Toronto Press, 1970). Deals with the role of the National Union of Teachers in the making of National Educational policy since 1944 in England and Wales. As a pressure group, the N. U. T. has achieved limited success.

Marcuse, Herbert. *Eros and Civilization* (Boston: Beacon Press, 1955). Marcuse's work here is with the destruction of libidinal drive in capitalism. This book was a great stimulant to the American and European "new left."

Marcuse, Herbert. *One Dimensional Man: Studies in the Ideology of Advanced Industrial Society* (Boston: Beacon Press, 1964). Capitalism has developed forms of control unknown to Marx. Critical thought in philosophy, art, and the social sciences has been stunted. A nearly total indictment of American society.

Marcuse, Herbert. *Reason and Revolution: Hegel and the Rise of Social Theory* (Boston: Beacon Press, 1960). An argument for the revolutionary potential of Hegelian thought. Hegel, the old conservative, might have disliked Marcuse's "toying" with his ideas.

Marshall, T. H. *Class Citizenship and Social Development* (New York: Anchor Books, 1965) An important collection of essays in the battle between "inequality" and "equality." British sociology at its best.

Marx, Karl. *Economic and Philosophical Manuscripts of 1844,* Martin Milligan, translator (London: Laurence and Wishard Ltd., 1959). The early Marx here, concerned with humanism, the fetishism of commodities, and alienation.

Marx, Karl. "The German Ideology" in Robert C. Tucker, editor, *The Marx-Engels Reader* (New York: W. W. Norton and Company, Inc., 1972). The transition between the early Marx and the "mature" Marx of late years.

Marx, Karl and Engels, Frederick. "Wage, Labour and Capital" in *Selected Work in Two Volumns,* Vol. 1. (Moscow: Foreign Languages Publishing House, 1955). A technical analysis of the economic exploitation of early capitalism.

May, S. and Plaza, George. *The United Fruit Company in Latin America* (Washington D. C.: National Planning Association, 1958). An exposé of the power of American neocolonialism in the third world.

McClosky, Herbert. "Conservatism and Personality," *Political Science Review,* 42 (April, 1958). An interesting argument (related in an empirical study) for the idea that conservatives are "alienated," "anomic," and so forth. Later studies have lessened the worth of this study by putting severe limits on its validity.

McCord, William. *The Springtime of Freedom: The Evolution of Developing Societies* (New York: Oxford University Press, 1965). This is an essential conservative (anti-Marxist) approach to the problem of economic development. McCord contends that democracy is nearly impossible in a developing nation.

McDermott, M. T. *The Wobblies in the United States,* unpublished paper.

McGovern, George S. and Guttridge, Leonard F. *The Great Coalfield War* (Boston: Houghton Mifflin Company, 1972). You should have voted for George just for this book. He did his doctoral dissertation on the Ludlow massacre.

Mead, Margaret. *New Lives for Old* (New York: William Morrow, 1956). An excellent description of social change in a pacific culture. The impact of modernization is described thoroughly.

Merton, Robert K. *Social Theory and Social Structure* (Glencoe, Illinois: The Free Press, 1949). All graduate students in sociology know this one, and it is well worth famHarizing oneself with the ideas in this fertile volumne.

"Mexican American Set Free" *Student Action* (no date given).

Michels, Robert. *Political Parties* (Glencoe, Illinois The Free Press, 1949).

Michels, Robert. *Political Parties: A Sociological Study of the Oligarchical Tendencies in Modern Democracy* (New York: Hearst's International Library Company, 1915). Michels is a pessimist. Even egalitarian organizations such as labor unions or socialist parties have elitist tendencies. Relax Robert, all the evidence isn't in yet!

Miller, S. M. "Poverty, Race and Politics" in Irving L. Horowitz, editor, *The New Sociology* (New York: Oxford University Press, 1965).

Millet, Kate. *Sexual Politics* (Garden City, New York: Doubleday & Company, 1970). Why are the most lionized literati of our time borish sexists? The shadow knows. So does Kate Millet.

Mills, C. Wright. *The Marxists* (New York: Dell Publishing Company, 1962). A good primer for those who know absolutely nothing about Marxism but have an open mind.

Mills, C. Wright. *The Power Elite* (New York: Oxford University Press, 1957). Marx, mixed with Mosca and Mannheim gives Mills an analysis of the military-industrial complex and its dominance in a massified society of impotent individuals.

Mills, C. Wright. *The Sociological Imagination* (New York: Oxford University Press, 1959). Should be required for every sociologist who doesn't want to sell out to grantsmanship, one-upmanship, or respectability. Right on Charles Wright!

Mills, C. Wright. *White Collar* (New York: Oxford University Press, 1956). The first study of the middle classes in America, their loss of political and economic independence, and their false consciousness.

Mondlane, Eduardo C. *Mozambique: A Country at War* (London: Harold Darton and Associates, 1968). The struggle in Mozambique from the guerillas' point of view.

Mooney, James. *The Ghost-Dance Religion and the Sioux Outbreak of 1890* (Chicago: University of Chicago Press, 1965). This volume is over 70 years old and has been reprinted for it is full of useful information on the Ghost dance.

Moore, Barrington. *Social Origins of Dictatorship and Democracy: Lord and Peasant in the Making of the Modern World* (Boston: Beacon Press, 1966). Barrington is an academic radical. His standards of scholarship are the highest, and his concern for the have-nots is always evident. An excellent book.

Muhammed, Honorable Elijah. "Be Yourself", *Muhammad Speaks*, 10 (November 6, 1970).

Musoke, I. K. S. "Building Socialism in Bukoba: The Establishment of Rugazi Ujamaa Village," *University of Dar Es Salaam: Studies in Political Science*, (No. 2).

Nee, Victor. *The Cultural Revolution At Peking University* (New York: Monthly Review Press, 1969). A sympathic little volume on the beginnings of the cultural revolution.

Neff, Wanda. *Victorian Working Women* (New York: Columbia University Press, 1929). This book gives one some slight idea of the horror of women in the vicious grip of early capitalism.

Nehru, Jawaharlal. *The Discovery of India* (New York: The John Day Co., 1946).

Neumann, Franz. *Behemoth: The Structure and Practice of National Socialism 1933-1944* (New York: Harper & Row, 1944). This may well be the most important analysis of Nazism ever written. Using a Marxian and economic analysis, Neumann shows the merger of monopoly capitalism and totalitarianism.

Newman, William J. *The Futilitarian Society* (New York: George Brazmiller, 1961). This book is an interesting treatise on the conservative mentality. Newman uses parody, philosophy, and history to attack fogies young and old.

Niebuhr, Richard H. *The Social Sources of Denominationalism* (Cleveland: World Publishing Company, 1969). A profound contribution to the sociology of religion. Not too flattering to the Christian denominations he speaks of.

Nisbet, Robert A. *Social Change and History: Aspects of the Western Theory of Development* (New York: Oxford University Press, 1969). Perhaps the most cogent and well thought out conservative views of social change.

Nisbet, Robert A. *Tradition and Revolt: Historical and Sociological Essays* (New York: Random House, 1968). An extremely erudite vision by Nisbet of the necessity for tradition and organic growth.

Nkrumah, Kwame. "The Basic Needs of African Socialism," *Pan Africa* (April 19, 1963).

Nolte, Ernest. *The Three Faces of Fascism* (New York: Mentor Books, 1969). Nolte's huge tome on Fascism is the result of years of research. It is basically philosophical rather than sociological and sees Fascism as a resistance to transendence.

Nordhoff, Charles. *The Communistic Societies of the United States* (New York: Dover Publications, Inc., 1966). A good survey of the early utopian experiments. Read it before you take to the woods to form your own commune.

Noyes, John H. *History of American Socialisms* (New York: Dover Publications, Inc., 1966). Noyes likewise is a good commentator on the communal scene—all the better because he created his own utopian community in upstate New York.

Nyerere, Julius K. *Education for Self-Reliance* (pamphlet), Government Printer, Dar Es Salaam, Tanzania, 1968.

Nyerere, Julius K. *Socialism and Rural Development* (pamphlet) Government printer, Dar Es Salaam, Tanzania, 1967.

Nyerere, Julius K. *Ujamaa: Essays on Socialism* (Nairobi: Oxford University Press, 1968). Nyerere's philosophy of socialism is not philosophically elaborate, but it is unique. Europeans as well as Africans are looking to Tanzania as a source of hope for a more human society.

O'Neal, James. *The Workers in American History* (New York: The Rand School of Social Science, 1921). From the dedication: "To the workers of America, who are now besieged by the Powers that Prey, in the hope that this small volume will reveal to them how present tyrannies came to be and how they may be abolished." How cooperative labor in the factories came to be is outlined by O'Neal. Competitive labor in the factories must be supplemented with cooperative ownership and control, says O'Neal, who has the optimism of the American socialist of 50 years ago.

Ossowski, Stanislaw. *Class Structure in the Social Consciousness* (New York: The Free Press of Glencoe, 1963). Perhaps the most underread book of this generation. A must for those interested in "class formation."

Pettigrew, Thomas. "Personality and Sociocultural Factors in Intergroup Attitudes, a Cross National Comparison," *Journal of Conflict Resolutions*, 2 (January, 1958). Pettigrew's research has shown the limitations of a purely psychological approach to the study of political attitudes.

Piven, Frances F. and Cloward, Richard A. *Regulating the Poor: The Functions of Public Welfare* (New York: Vintage Books, 1972). This is an important book in the radical tradition. It should end all notions of the "charitability" of the federal and local government toward the have-nots.

Presthus, Robert. *The Organizational Society* (New York: Alfred A Knopf, Inc., 1962). The nuances of the bureaucratic maze are described in some detail by Presthus.

Priestly, J. B. *Thoughts in the Wilderness* (New York: Harper & Row, 1957).

Puri, Shamlal. "Matendo Village: A Model in the Making," *Dar Es Salaam Daily News*, (July 26, 1972).

Quirk, Robert E. *The Mexican Revolution 1914-1915* (Bloomington: Indiana University Press, 1960). A thoughgoing description of the peasant uprisings that shaped the future Mexican politics.

Reich, Wilhelm. *The Function of the Orgasm* (New York: Farrar, Straus, & Giroux, 1961). Reich traces the development of Orgone Therapy and explains his research primarily in terms of a synthesis of sociology, psychology, and biology. Interesting and perhaps just a little weird.

Renshaw, Patrick. *The Wobblies* (Garden City, New York: Doubleday & Company, 1967). An extremely well-documented history of the I. W. W. with a few glimpses at the rest of America in the throes of early industrialization.

Robequain, Charles. *The Economic Development of French Indo-China* (New York: Oxford University Press, 1944). An important book for anyone seeking to understand the imperialist wars in Vietnam.

Robinson, Joan. *The Cultural Revolution in China*, (Baltimore: Pelican Books, 1969). A fine little book by a Marxian but nondogmatic British economist.

Rokeach, Milton. *The Open and Closed Mind* (New York: Basic Books, 1961). Most of the work here revolves around empirical studies done by Rokeach's students on the problem of dogmatism.

Rosenberg, Arthur. *Democracy and Socialism* (Boston; Beacon Press, 1965). The phraseologists and phrase-mongers of "democracy" should start their homework with this one. The beginnings of "social democracy" and bourgeois democracy and the decline of the democratic idea after 1871 are examples of the scale of this work.

Rossi, Adolfo. *L'Agitazione in Sicilia*, E. J. Hobsbawm translator (Milano, 1894).

Rostow, W. Walt. *The Stages of Economic Growth* (Cambridge: Cambridge University Press, 1960). A conservative challenge to the Marxian concept of development written by one of the chief architects of the American "involvement" in Vietnam.

Rubinow, I. M. "Poverty," in R. A. Seligman and Alvin Johnson editors, *Encyclopedia of the Social Sciences* Vol. 12 (New York: The Macmillan Company, 1937). The encyclopedia of the social sciences is worth its weight in gold, and it's heavy, as is this article.

Ruether, Rosemary R. "The Automated Asian Air War," *National Catholic Reporter* (April 21, 1972). An account of the automated genocide in Vietnam.

Rush, Gary B. and Denisoff, R. Serge. *Social and Political Movements* (New York: Appleton-Century-Crofts, 1971). A reader on social movements—has some valuables, others seem to be filler.

Russell, Bertrand. *Freedom Versus Organization: The Pattern of Political Changes in Nineteenth Century European History* (New York: W. W. Norton & Company, 1962). Russell's intellect towers over the rest of us, and we are greatful that he writes in such a readable way. His humanism and sarcasm show through in this valuable book.

Schactman, Max. *The Bureaucratic Revolution: The Rise of the Stalinist State* (New York: The Donald Press, 1962). With insight into both theory and historical action, Schactman comments on Soviet/Stalinist bureaucratic tendencies from the shores of America. Stalin and his biographers get in the way of this ambitious task of dealing with bureaucratic revolution as a world master trend. The debate with dead Marx, Lenin, Trotsky, and Stalin continues.

Scheinitz, Karl de, Jr. *Industrialization and Democracy: Economic Necessities and Political Pos-*

191

sibilities (London: The Free Press of Glencoe, 1964). Faces squarely the relationship between economic "development" and democracy. The nineteenth century Euro-American route to democracy is closed as far as the new twentieth century nation-states are concerned.

Schlesinger, Rudolf. *The Family in the U. S. S. R.* (London: Routledge and Kegan Paul, 1949). A good description of the conservative forces in the U. S. S. R. and their triumph in preserving the family unit.

Schneider, Louis. "Dialectic Sociology," *American Sociological Review,* 36 (August, 1971.) Schneider explicates all the logical possibilities of the dialectical mode in social thought. An important article.

Segal, Ronald. *The Race War* (New York: Bantam Books, 1966). This book, if you take it seriously, is a frightening one. The major conflicts in the world today are not between capitalism and communism, but between the haves of the northern hemisphere and the darker have-nots of the southern hemisphere. Think about it.

Seligman, Ben B., editor. "The Dimensions of Poverty" in *Poverty as a Public Issue* (New York: The Free Press, 1965).

Selznick, Phillip. *T. V. A. and the Grass Roots* (Berkeley: University of California Press, 1956). A good description of how the powerful defuse radical reforms.

Sheldon, Karen. "Eco-Commandos Win Golden Fox," *Clear Creek* (April, 1972).

Shelly, Martha. "Women of Lesbos," *Kaleidescope,* (June, 1970).

Short, Robert S. "The Politics of Surrealism, 1920-36," in Walter Laquer and George L. Mosse, editors, *The Left Wing Intellectuals Between The Wars 1919-1939* (New York: Harper & Row, 1966). This useful article is one of the best in this small volume treating the relationship between radicalism and aesthetics.

Simmel, Georg. "The Poor," *Social Problems,* 13 (Fall, 1965).

Simpson, Eyler N. *The Ejido: Mexico's Way Out* (Chapel Hill: University of North Carolina Press, 1937). A technical analysis of social change in Mexico.

Skolnick, Jerome. *Politics of Protest* (New York: Ballantine Books, 1969). After analyzing the politics of protest for black militants, students, and antiwar demonstrators, Skolnick concludes that the government strategy of force is overcoming massive social and political reform strategies and may yield a society of garrison cities.

Smelser, Neal J. *Theory of Collective Behavior* (New York: The Free Press, 1963). A functionalist "value added" approach to collective behavior. While Smelser has more recently modified his model, it remains the benchmark in studies of collective behavior.

Snyder, Louis L. *The Weimar Republic* (New York: Van Nostrand Rheinhold Company, 1966). Snyder's compact book of readings gives one an excellent "feel" for the tragic times of the Weimar Republic.

Sorokin, Pitirim A. *Social and Cultural Dynamics* (New York: American Book Company, 1937-1941). Elegant and logical application of Integralist philosophy to the whole of Western civilization. The most profound of all old world emigrés to write meaningful sociology in America. Sorokin lives.

Sorokin, Pitirim A. *Social and Cultural Mobility* (New York: The Free Press of Glencoe, 1959). The *necessary* start for anyone interested in social stratification—which means everybody since stratification is what it's all about.

Spender, Stephen. *The Year of the Young Rebels* (New York: Random House, 1968). Spender, one of America's foremost literati, spent a great deal of time watching the student uprisings in France and Eastern Europe. An extremely enlightning little volume.

Spiro, Herbert J. *The Politics of German Codetermination* (Cambridge: Harvard University Press, 1958).

Stein, Lorenz Von. *The History of the Social Movement in France 1789-1850,* Kaethe Mangeberg, translator, (Totawa, New Jersey: Bedminister Press, 1964). "The father of us all."

"The Strange Economics of the Vietnam War," *Ramparts,* (November, 1971).

Studies In the Scope and Method of the Authoritarian Personality, Richard Christie and others (Glencoe, Illinois: The Free Press, 1954). An excellent analysis of the work done by Adorno and others. Christie's work is well balanced in his criticism of the famous F scale studies.

Sturmthal, Adoft, editor. *White Collar Trade Unions* (Urbana: University of Illinois Press, 1966). A reader dealing with eight countries on the implications of the rise of the white-collar worker for the industrial relations system in the advanced industrial nations. The comparative essay by the editors on the successes and failures of unionization of the white-collar asks the right questions.

Sully, Francois. *Age of the Guerrilla* (New York: Avon Books, 1968). A popularized, but dispassionate analysis of the world-wide struggles for "national liberation."

Tannebaum, Edward R. *The Action Francaise* (New York: John Wiley & Sons, 1962). This is a highly readable account of a quasi fascist movement of the French right. Well done.

Thompson, Fred. *The I W W: Its First Fifty Years (1905-1955).* (Chicago: Industrial Workers of the World, 1955). A good account of the anarcho-syndicalist Wobblies, their persecution and eventual demise.

Tilly, Charles. "Collective Violence in European Perspective" in Hugh Davis Graham and Ted Robert Gurr, *The History of Violence in America* (New York: Bantam Books, 1969). Tilly is *the* primary source on European violence.

Toch, Hans. *The Social Psychology of Social Movements* (Indianapolis: Bobbs-Merrill, 1965). Toch's small volume is an extremely readable account of the affiliation-disaffiliation processes of social movement membership. His concept of social movements is so vague as to be nearly beyond use for the sociologist.

Toffler, Alvin. *Future Shock* (New York: Bantam Books, 1970). A popular, yet thoughtful analysis of social change. Remember it's future "shock not schlock."

Torres, Camilo. *Revolutionary Priest: The Complete Writings and Messages of Camilo Torres* (New York: Random House, Inc., 1971). A sometimes moving, sometimes fascinating, always significant chronicle of the growth of a "Christian" from reformist sociologist to revolutionary priest.

Toynbee, Arnold. *The Industrial Revolution* (Boston: The Beacon Press, 1956). Toynebee's analysis is slanted by his humanity and unorthodox Christianity. All in all, not a bad slant.

Tse-Tung, Mao. *On Protracted War* (Peking: Foreign Languages Press, 1967). This has been the Bible for most wars of national liberation for the last two decades.

Turner, Ralph and Killian, Lewis M. *Collective Behavior* (Englewood Cliffs, New Jersey: Prentice-Hall, 1957). This book is a good yet somewhat dated approach to premovement phenomena.

Vajda, Mihaly and Heller, Agnes. "Family Structure and Communism," *Telos* (Spring, 1971).

Vander Zanden, James W. *Race Relations in Transition* (New York: Random House, Inc., 1965). Dated and mediocre. Vander Zanden's Freudian analysis of the civil rights movement is questionable.

Vanek, Jaroslav. *The Participatory Economy* (Ithaca: Cornell University Press, 1971). Another analysis of the workers' councils movement.

Wallace, Anthony F. C. "Revitalization Movements" *American Anthropologist,* 58 (April, 1956). The axial article in the conceptualization of nativistic movements.

Waters, Mary Alice. "Are Feminism and Socialism Related?" In Linda Jenness, editor, *Feminism and Socialism* (New York: Pathfinder Press, 1972). Whither feminism? One possibility is toward an anticapitalistic movement. This little volume argues for women's alignment with other oppressed "classes."

Webb, Marilyn Salzman. "Building the Women's Movement," *Guardian* (November 22, 1969).

Weber, Max. *The Protestant Ethnic and the Spirit of Capitalism* (New York: Charles Scribner, 1958). Weber's answer to Marx.

Weber, Max. *The Theory of Social and Economic Organization*, A. M. Henderson and Talcott Parsons, translators (New York: Oxford University Press, 1947). Weber's analysis of the disenchantment of the western world via bureaucratization.

Weissman, George L., editor. *Revolutionary Students in Poland Speak Out 1964-1968* (New York: Merit Publishers, 1969). A Trotskyist look at the student movements both east and west.

Welch, Robert. *The Blue Book of the John Birch Society*. Belmont, Mass.: John Birch Society, 1961. A good primary source for insights into the rightist conspiratorial mentality. It seems that the civil rights movement was a conspiracy by the eastern establishment which was a conspiracy of communists who in turn represent a front for the "order of Illumanti." Tant pis!

Wells, Lyn. *American Women: Their Use and Abuse,* Southern Students Organizing Committee, Nashville, Tennessee, 1968 (pamphlet).

Wilson, Edmund. *To the Finland Station: A Study in the Writing and Acting of History* (Garden City, New York: Doubleday & Company, Anchor Books, 1953). Social critic and Marxologist at his best when it comes to the intellectual history underlying leftist traditions in the West. Should be read by every potential "radical" be he one in theory or action or both.

Wolf, Eric. "Peasant Rebellion and Revolution" in Norman Miller and Roderick Aya, editors, *National Liberation: Revolution in the Third World* (New York: The Free Press, 1971). This is an excellent article in a truly fine book of readings.

Wolf, Eric. *Peasant Wars of the Twentieth Century* (New York: Harper & Row Publishers, 1969). Wolf is without doubt the most qualified and competent scholar in the area of peasant uprisings.

Wolff, Robert Paul, Moore, Barrington Jr., and Marcuse, Herbert. *A Critique of Pure Tolerance* (Boston: Beacon Press, 1965). These essays criticize the liberal view of the "free marketplace" of ideas. Marcuse has been severely criticized for his article in this book "Repressive Tolerance" and accused of totalitarian tendencies.

"Womens Manifesto" (pamphlet).

Woodward, C. Van. *The Strange Career of Jim Crow* (New York: Oxford University Press, 1955). Woodward describes the tragic collapse of populism into racism in the American South. A historian with sociological talents.

Woolf, S. J. "Italy" in S. J. Woolf, editor, *European Fascism* (New York: Random House, 1969). "Fascism" ranking second perhaps only to "alienation" in terms of frequent misuse and abuse is refreshingly put into accurate perspective in this fine anthology.

Workers Management in Yugoslavia (Geneva: International Labor Office, 1962) (pamphlet).

Worsley, Peter. *The Trumpet Shall Sound: A Study of Cargo Cults in Melanesia* (New York: Schocken

Books, 1968). Ah, that other books on social movements were as well-written or as well-conceived as Worsley's efforts. Worsley's neo-Marxist position is well taken.

Young, Michael. *The Rise of the Meritocracy* (Baltimore: Penguin Books, 1951). A book that proves that good sociology and good satire go together. As it was in the past and present, "inequality" will be scrutinized in the future—even that inequality which results from ranking by merit and effort.

Zald, Mayer N. and Ash, Roberta. "Social Movement Organizations," *Social Forces,* 44 (1966). An ex-tremely useful article in evaluating the reasons for success and failure in movement organizations. Also the reasons for elitism in certain movement organizations are explicated.

Znaniecki, Florian. *Social Role of the Man of Knowledge* (New York: Columbia University Press, 1940). Ranks with Sorokin as an emigre´ making profound contributions to sociology. His book points to some of the social roles people of knowledge have played. It is an appropriate statement and last word for us—hence, this book on movements.

INDEX